PRAISE FOR *UNDERSTANDING A COURSE IN MIRACLES*

"At last there's a balanced, reliable, well-written report on the spiritual teaching that's made a miraculous difference in so many lives, including my own. *Understanding A Course in Miracles* is the 'other' book that every Course student should own."

—JOAN BORYSENKO, PhD, AUTHOR OF *YOUR SOUL'S COMPASS*

"A much-needed, fair-minded, and sensitive assessment of a puzzling, serious, and surprisingly influential element in the spiritual life of the twenty-first century."

—JACOB NEEDLEMAN, PhD, AUTHOR OF *WHY CAN'T WE BE GOOD?*

"Love it or hate it, *A Course in Miracles* is increasingly difficult to ignore. As a grassroots American phenomenon, the Course is deeply spiritual without being religious, and democratic rather than dogmatic. Miller's book is simply a great read, an entertaining and exquisitely accurate rendering of the stranger-than-fiction story of the Course."

—LUCIA CAPACCHIONE, PhD, AUTHOR OF *RECOVERY OF YOUR INNER CHILD*

"When I read D. Patrick Miller's accounts of his own experience with *A Course in Miracles*, I felt for the first time I'd heard an authentic appraisal of the subject and gained an understanding of its power to both attract many people and put off others. This is a superb report on a popular and important spiritual phenomenon."

—DAN WAKEFIELD, AUTHOR OF *RETURNING: A SPIRITUAL JOURNEY*

"Now I have something I can enthusiastically give to my friends and colleagues who ask me about *A Course in Miracles*. This book is a very readable and accurate account of the important and controversial matters surrounding the Course. With careful research and journalistic skill, Patrick Miller weaves together an 'on the edge of your seat' story."

—LEE JAMPOLSKY, PhD, AUTHOR OF *HEALING THE ADDICTIVE PERSONALITY*

Understanding
A Course in Miracles

Understanding
A Course in Miracles

*The History,
Message, and Legacy
of a Spiritual Path
for Today*

D. Patrick Miller
FOREWORD BY IYANLA VANZANT

CELESTIAL ARTS
Berkeley | Toronto

Celestial Arts
an imprint of Ten Speed Press
PO Box 7123
Berkeley, California 94707
www.tenspeed.com

Distributed in Australia by Simon and Schuster Australia, in Canada by Ten Speed Press Canada, in New Zealand by Southern Publishers Group, in South Africa by Real Books, and in the United Kingdom and Europe by Publishers Group UK.

Cover design by Katy Brown
Interior design by Michael Cutter

This book is a revised edition of *The Complete Story of the Course* (Fearless Books, 1997; 978-0-96568-090-5)

Portions from *A Course in Miracles*, "The Song of Prayer," and "Psychotherapy: Purpose, Process, and Practice" copyright © 1978, 1985, 1992, 1996 by the Foundation for Inner Peace, Inc., PO Box 598, Mill Valley, CA 94942.

Portions of *Absence from Felicity, A Course in Miracles and Christianity: A Dialogue*, and the unpublished papers of Helen Schucman are reprinted by the permission of Kenneth Wapnick, PhD, and the Foundation for *A Course in Miracles*.

Transcribed portions of the audiotape "The Universal Course" are published by permission of Miracle Distribution Center and Roger Walsh, PhD.

Portions of *The Guru Papers* are reprinted by permission of Frog Ltd. and North Atlantic Books.

Portions of *Double Vision* are reprinted by permission of Celestial Arts.

The ideas represented herein are the personal interpretation and understanding of the author and are not necessarily endorsed by the publisher of *A Course in Miracles*.

This book is the result of an independent journalistic effort and is in no way financed or sanctioned by the Foundation for Inner Peace, the Foundation for *A Course in Miracles*, or any other Course-related organization.

Brief portions of this book are revised excerpts of articles originally appearing in *Free Spirit* (Brooklyn, NY) and *The Sun: A Magazine of Ideas* (Chapel Hill, NC).

Library of Congress
Cataloging-in-Publication Data

Miller, D. Patrick, 1953–
Understanding A course in miracles : the history, message, and legacy of a spiritual path for today / Patrick Miller.
  p. cm.
Includes index.
ISBN 978-1-58761-312-8
1. Course in miracles. I. Title.
BP605.C68M58 2008
299'.93—dc22
                                    2007051291
First printing this edition, 2008
Printed in the United States of America

1 2 3 4 5 6 7 8 9 10 — 12 11 10 09 08

Contents

Foreword

Most of us have that one friend we consider different, strange, or a bit weird. I had one such person in my life. She was absolutely addicted to the mystical, magical, metaphysical things in life, which she felt compelled to share with me. She was in search of what she called "the keys to a better life." That search took her into many places I dared not go, but I would listen and indulge her because I loved her spunk and energy. I rarely engaged with what she offered until 1986, when she gave me a gift that changed my life forever. The gift was the three-volume set of *A Course in Miracles*: the Text, the Workbook, and the Manual for Teachers. With this gift she gave me three simple directives, which I promptly forgot.

Two years later, I had yet to crack open my friend's gift. Quite frankly, I was not at first impressed by the unattractive blue cover with the dull gold inscription, but I was compelled to pick the book up the day my life fell apart. I was desperate, depressed, and dead broke, packing to move away from the city of my birth and out of a long-term relationship, and crying and begging God for something, anything, to ease my pain. I was afraid to move forward, unable to stay where I was, and totally confused about my current situation. In a miraculous moment, I was drawn into volume I, the Text. The book fell open to chapter 6, "The Lessons of Love." It was in that moment that I remembered my friend's first directive: "It doesn't matter where you start reading, just start." So I did. Several hours later, when I attempted to put the book down, I had a pounding headache. It was then that I remembered her second directive: "Do not try to understand what you read. Take it in and the Holy Spirit will do the rest." The next day, I went back to the beginning of the book. I read the story of how the Course came to be and the list of Principles of Miracles. In the process I remembered my friend's third instruction: "Be willing to give up everything you think you know and have it replaced with the truth. If you can do that, your life will never be the same." It hasn't been.

I have been a serious student of *A Course in Miracles* since 1988. Unlike you, I did not have a book like the one you are holding in your hands. There were no websites that explained or supported the teachings of the Course, and there were few writers like D. Patrick Miller who could explain how to understand or study it. My journey through the Course was sometimes arduous, often challenging, one of pure faith and desire. Each chapter and lesson took me deeper into places within myself that I never knew existed. Each revelation propelled me into a closer connection with the Holy Spirit. Along the way, my thinking shifted; my understanding of myself and God's purpose for my life unfolded and deepened; my heart opened and the fear that once plagued me has dissipated. Today, twenty years later, I can say that my weird friend was absolutely correct: as a student and advocate of the Course, I have seen my life change miraculously and I have never been the same.

Every student of the Course has a favorite chapter or lesson. My favorite lessons are 107, "Truth will correct all errors in my mind," and 131, "No one can fail who seeks to reach the truth." If you are holding this book, it is a safe bet that you are willing to seek and know the truth about yourself, about life, and about the love of God in your life. With the supportive insight of D. Patrick Miller, you will not fail. He will explain to you not only how to understand the Course, but also how to apply its teachings to every experience of your life. That is the goal of the Course; for each student to apply its teachings in a practical way and, in doing so, become a teacher of its message. If you are willing and open to knowing the true meaning and viability of the presence of love in your life, you will not fail. Patrick is a gentle and compassionate teacher, with the ability to explain the mystical and reveal the metaphysical in a clear and concise manner. He has lived and learned the viability of practicality. He shares his knowledge with the guidance of the Holy Spirit, in loving service to the world. He gets the Course because he has been willing to exchange darkness for light and ignorance for knowledge. He understands that life is a curriculum, established to teach us the distinction between what is real and what is not. He is grateful for all that he has experienced and learned. Accepting this knowledge in gratitude will lead you into a deeper understanding by dissolving the errors present in your mind.

In today's world, we often demand quick results. We want to microwave ourselves or our lives so that we will avoid the wait, the work, and the wonder. *A Course in Miracles* is a slow cooker. It moves us methodically through the mental and emotional constructs that have made us intolerant and impatient and made our lives unmanageable. Patrick understands that the Course guides us along the periphery of our consciousness in order to remove the crust of conditioning and false beliefs that obstruct the presence of light and knowledge. He also understands that the process of studying the Course takes time and commitment. His work in this book will make that process a more loving endeavor for you. As a result of his patient commitment to learning and practicing, he offers a bit of understanding to help you ensure that you will create and recognize miracles in your own life. If you are ready to give your patient, willing, committed essence and energy to study the Course, your prayers will rise, your mind will become tender, and your heart will open to the miracle of God's love. My prayer is that you experience the miracle of the Holy Instant in the very first moment you open this book.

Be Blessed!
Iyanla Vanzant

Acknowledgments

This book is in its second life and thus owes its existence to many helpers. For inspiring and supporting the first edition, I'd like to renew my original thanks to Stephanie Gunning and especially Laurie Fox, whose faith in the original manuscript and the Fearless Books edition remained steadfast throughout some early hairpin turns as well as the long haul of publishing independently. I deeply appreciate the vision of Jo Ann Deck and Julie Bennett in acquiring this revision for Celestial Arts/Ten Speed Press, as well as the careful editorial shepherding of Melissa Moore and Sara Golski. In a project of this nature most of the quoted sources provide more information than shows up on the printed page, but I am especially indebted to Judy Skutch, William "Whit" Whitson, and Ken Wapnick for their years-long assistance and willingness to share essential and sometimes sensitive intelligence. Finally, affectionate thanks are due to Nhien Vuong for her insightful recommendations for the improvement of key new material in this edition.

Introduction

VATICAN CITY, 12/20/02 – Mother Teresa appears fast-tracked for sainthood after an announcement Friday that Pope John Paul II has approved a miracle attributed to the late nun's intercession. A Vatican committee approved the miracle earlier this fall, and the Pope formally seconded the finding during a ceremony at the Apostolic Palace Friday. The reported miracle involves a young Indian woman, Monica Besra, who recovered from a stomach tumour after an image of Mother Teresa was placed on the woman's stomach. Doctors consulted by the Vatican judged that the woman's recovery was "without any medical explanation."

—CANADIAN BROADCASTING NEWS ONLINE

The use of miracles as spectacles to induce belief is a misunderstanding of their purpose.

—A COURSE IN MIRACLES

What is a miracle? Is it a sudden and inexplicable healing? Is it an apparition, or the murky outline of a holy symbol appearing on a wall or in the clouds? Or is a miracle just an unusual occurrence met with hopeful expectations?

Whatever the circumstances in which they arise, miracles always symbolize a different kind of reality breaking through the walls of our everyday experience. For the faithful of any religion, the miracle represents proof of divine intervention in earthly affairs. For the skeptical, the miracle is either a hoax, a misinterpretation of mundane phenomena, or an unusual occurrence that science may not yet be able to explain, but eventually will. And for all those who waver between a constant faith and habitual disbelief, the miracle is at least a suggestion that a higher order of reality exists, awaiting some mysterious alignment of outer circumstances and inner preparedness to break through for good and change our lives.

Those who take miracles seriously would likely agree that they occur unexpectedly—even when they have been prayed for—and derive less from human effort or intention than from either supernatural forces or

1

extraordinary capacities of our own subconscious. When someone is called a "miracle worker," it means he or she is regarded as a saint or superhuman with exceptional dedication and nearly magical resources. The idea that any normal person could be trained to produce miracles on a regular basis would probably strike most people as absurd or even sacrilegious. The notion of a textbook that would specifically teach miracle-working would probably be seen as heresy, presumption, or outright fantasy.

Nonetheless, such a textbook exists, and it has become one of the most significant guides to a new kind of spirituality that has been growing rapidly over the last several decades. Published in 1976, *A Course in Miracles* (ACIM) has more than two million copies in print worldwide and has already influenced the thinking of millions. Because it was composed in a secular setting and was not intended as the foundation of a new religion, ACIM does not have a readily identifiable sect of followers. Those who use it regularly commonly refer to themselves as "students" rather than devotees, and many of them are members of a wide variety of religious traditions. Perhaps just as many consider themselves refugees from conventional and authoritarian religions and no longer profess any church affiliation, while still pursuing spiritual experience on their own. Others are agnostic, minimizing the spiritual aspects of the Course while regarding it as a highly effective form of esoteric therapy. There are many thousands of people who have devoted their lives to studying the Course and hundreds who teach it. But there are many more who have sampled it only partially, integrating some of its ideas into their philosophy while shying away from its discipline as a whole. Among its critics from both religious and secular perspectives, ACIM is regarded as everything from a satanic seduction to an artifact of New Age psychobabble.

Having enjoyed a brief surge of celebrity-stoked fame in the 1990s, the Course has largely faded from view in pop culture even as its influence continues to spread. Because the 1,200-page, three-in-one volume is intellectually challenging and requires a minimum of one year of intensive study to complete, ACIM tends to create its own select class of serious students over time. But there are neither qualifying requirements for beginners nor any institutionally approved tests to certify graduates of this course. The book is widely available in trade bookstores in the original English, as well as in eighteen authorized translations around the world.

The Course has spawned a diverse movement that comprises thousands of small study groups, scores of offbeat churches and teaching centers, a few communal experiments, and an untold number of students studying privately, but the teaching of the Course is neither promulgated nor regulated by any central authority. Since the revocation in 2004 of the copyright and trademarks originally held by the two foundations that historically managed the publication of ACIM,[1] it has become the centerpiece of a wholly democratic spiritual movement whose future rests entirely with its far-flung students and self-appointed teachers.

Although there is no particular theological or therapeutic idea in the Course that can be described as completely new, it does represent an unprecedented synthesis of metaphysics, substantially revised Christian theology, and penetrating psychological analysis underpinning a daily meditative discipline. The Course refers to itself as a "mind training" rather than a religious teaching in the usual sense. This unique blend of perspectives and practicum helps explain why the Course appears to be different things to different observers, and also why it is difficult even for veteran teachers to explain exactly what the Course is.

Nonetheless, *A Course in Miracles* is emblematic of a new style of alternative spiritual practice that has become a powerful if underappreciated force in American culture over the last half-century. Although it uses Christian language to convey its message, the Course radically redefines many conventional religious ideas, including the miracle itself. Whereas most religions translate the insights of original prophets into teachings that followers are expected to adopt with little questioning, ACIM offers a direct mystical practice to anyone who volunteers for its unusual discipline. Its intent seems not to be recruiting followers to its creed, but rather inciting authentic transformation of the human psyche.

Significantly, the Course initiates this profound process of change without the intercession of a church, religious hierarchy, or other forms of authority, and also without any threat of punishment or excommunication if its curriculum is not completed. Thus, "enrollment" in the Course, as well as its fulfillment, is left entirely up to the choice and determination of the individual student.

At a time when international politics are laced with religious conflict and U.S. domestic social policies have been significantly influenced by evangelical Christian activists, it is important to understand the contemporary divergence between conventional religion and personal spiritual practice. A good place to start is demographics, by taking a look at how these two phenomena are statistically represented in the general American population. Many readers may be surprised to learn which movement is clearly in the ascendancy and which is at best stagnant or actually declining in popularity.

The Rise of "Personal" Spirituality

Journalists have largely missed or misreported the story of Americans' turning in recent decades toward a deeply felt, personal spirituality that is pursued independently of religious customs and institutions. One of the earliest significant markers of this trend appeared in the January 1988 issue of *Better Homes and Gardens*: a report on "Religion, Spirituality, and American Families," based on a survey it had conducted among its eight million readers a few months before. The survey was returned by eighty thousand people—more than two and a half times the response expected by the editors, and far more people than are usually sampled in public opinion polls—and provided the following information:

> Some results suggest that respondents' spirituality is strongest on a personal level. The largest group (62%) say that in recent years they have begun or intensified personal spiritual study and activities (compared to 23% who say they have become closer to a religious organization). 68% say that when faced with a spiritual dilemma, prayer/meditation guides them most (compared to 14% who say the clergy guides them most during such times). . . .

Although such results were revealing in themselves, it's also worth noting that the title of this mainstream survey of the late 1980s already drew a distinction between *religion* and *spirituality*. The difference would probably have been lost on anyone but theologians just a few decades earlier. A noticeable divergence between the social conventions of religion and the individual pursuit of spirituality most likely took root in the 1960s and has only widened since the late 1980s, as evidenced by more recent data from a variety of sources:

- In January 2002, a *USA Today*/Gallup poll showed that almost half of American adults do not consider themselves religious in the usual sense. In 1999, 54% said they considered themselves religious; that number had shrunk to 50% in 2002. A full third (33%) described themselves as "spiritual but not religious," an increase of 3% over three years. Ten percent said they regarded themselves as neither spiritual nor religious.[2]

- According to an "American Religious Identification Survey" released in 2001 by the Graduate Center of the City University of New York, the most dramatic demographic shift in religious identification is the number of Americans saying they do not follow any organized religion, increasing from 8% (about 14.3 million people) in 1990 to 14.1% (29.4 million) in 2001. During the same period, the number of Americans identifying themselves as Christians shrank from 86.2% to 76.5%, a reduction of nearly 10 percent. If the trend holds, Christians will be outnumbered by non-Christians in America by 2042.[3]

- The Barna Group, an evangelical Christian polling and research organization, noted in a March 2007 report that "one out of every three adults (33%) is classified as unchurched—meaning they have not attended a religious service of any type during the past six months. While that figure is considerably higher than the one out of five who qualified as unchurched in the early Nineties, it is statistically unchanged since 36% were recorded as having avoided religious services in the company's 1994 study." The Barna Group also notes that although 38% of the American population (84 million people in 2006) identified themselves as "evangelicals," only 8% (18 million) met the Barna Group's nine-point "evangelical filter," an increase of just 1% over the previous decade.[4]

The fact that evangelical Christians (by any count) are significantly out-numbered by Americans who do not consider themselves religious may be surprising to many, considering the prominence of evangelical activists in the press and their recent influence on society. For instance, after the national election of 2004, some analysts attributed the winning edge of President Bush's victory to the mobilization of evangelical voters in the so-called "red states." (Bush's final popular vote margin over John Kerry was 2.5 percent.)

The evangelicals' social perspectives and political agenda also receive substantial and continuing coverage in the media, particularly in regard to such hot-button issues as abortion, gay rights, stem-cell research, and the teaching of creationism versus evolution in the public schools. Yet as the just-cited data suggest, the overall number of Christians is steadily declining, and a substantial and growing proportion of the population prefers to be identified as "spiritual but not religious."

There are at least three major factors contributing to this dramatic disparity between popular perceptions of America's spiritual evolution and its real nature. First is the media's failure to pay attention to the actual shifts of belief that are occurring quietly alongside the more easily reported controversies that involve religion. Second, evangelicals simply have a mission to spread their creed. Over the last two decades they have done an increasingly effective job of enhancing their media profile and their political clout, even if the effect on the number of people espousing their cause is negligible.

Third, the "mission" of people who are turning away from organized religion toward a more individual style of spiritual practice could well be described as the polar opposite of evangelism. Rather than trying to convert others to their beliefs, the new spiritualists are questioning their own beliefs, and privately experimenting with alternative perspectives. And rather than feeling the evangelicals' need to persuade others to adhere to a traditional vision of absolute truth, the new spiritualists are bent on experiencing mystical truths by their own direct experience, and then basing their moral decisions on what they have learned.

It is also through direct, unmediated mystical experience that many of the new spiritualists are gravitating to a perception of reality that is not only at odds with traditional Western religion, but contrary to the popular assumptions of our culture as well. It is in this context that the peculiar nature and history of ACIM become keenly relevant.

What Is the Course?

A Course in Miracles is a self-study curriculum that guides students toward a spiritual way of life by restoring their contact with what it calls the Holy Spirit or "internal teacher." The Course uses both an intellectual and an experiential approach within its 650-page Text (providing the philosophical foundation of the teaching), 500-page Workbook of 365 meditations (prescribing a daily transformative discipline), and 90-page Manual for Teachers (adding a variety of insights useful to advanced practitioners). Published by the nonprofit Foundation for Inner Peace in 1976, the Course was written down in shorthand from 1965 to 1972 by Dr. Helen Schucman, a research psychologist at Columbia University, and dictated to her supervisor Dr. William Thetford, director of Columbia-Presbyterian Medical Center's Department of Psychology, who typed the manuscript.

Schucman said she was writing down an "inner dictation" given to her by a mysterious "Voice," and she never claimed authorship of the material, remaining personally ambivalent about its message until her death in 1981. There is no central organized religion or membership institution built around the Course, and no "guru" widely accepted as an embodiment of the teaching.

As a psychological discipline, the Course encourages the transformation of the self through the constant practice of forgiveness. As a spiritual training, it insists on a complete reversal of ordinary perception, urging acceptance of spirit as the only reality and of the physical world as a mass illusion (similar to the Buddhist and Hindu notions of *samsara* and *maya*, two terms designating the everyday world we see as a kind of dream).

Thus, although the Course uses some Christian terminology, its metaphysics is more aligned with Eastern mysticism than traditional Western religion. In fact, ACIM directly challenges significant elements of contemporary Christianity, particularly the doctrines of sin and crucifixion. For instance, it argues that the significance of the Resurrection is not that Jesus Christ died to atone for the sins of humankind but rather that, as an advanced being who was fully cognizant of the illusory nature of the physical world, Jesus neither suffered nor died on the cross. The Course further maintains that everyone shares the potential to achieve such an enlightened consciousness.

The theological challenge of the Course is intensified by the fact that the authorial "Voice" clearly identifies itself as Jesus Christ, bringing a correction of traditional Christianity to the world in modern psychological language. Its corrective tone is clear in such passages as the following:

> If the Apostles had not felt guilty, they never could have quoted me as saying, "I come not to bring peace but a sword." This is clearly the opposite of everything I taught. Nor could they have described my reactions to Judas as they did, if they had really understood me. I could not have said, "Betrayest thou the Son of Man with a kiss?" unless I believed in betrayal. The whole message of the crucifixion was simply that I did not. . . . As you read the teachings of the Apostles, remember that I told them myself that there was much they would understand later, because they were not wholly ready to follow me at the time. (CH6, I, 15)

Although the Course does not identify itself as philosophically superior to any other teaching—stating that it is only one version of a "universal curriculum"—it does suggest that serious students may progress faster by its use than by any other spiritual method. The Course's alleged authorship and its challenge to Western religious tradition have served to make it simultaneously popular with people seeking alternative spiritual guidance and troubling to its critics, especially in conservative Christian circles.

The Purpose of This Book

This volume is a substantially revised edition of my 1997 title *The Complete Story of the Course: The History, the People, and the Controversies Behind "A Course in Miracles"* published under my own imprint of Fearless Books. Although at the time I began research for that book I had been a Course student for twelve years, I was largely an outsider to the Course movement. The book was intended to provide a journalistic overview of the ACIM phenomenon without taking on the task of explaining central themes of the teaching.

Ten years later, I can no longer lay claim to a reporter's outsider status, as I have been much more involved with Course organizations through my business as a publisher. In addition to marketing *The Complete Story* through a number of Course groups, in 2003 I published *The Disappearance of the Universe* by Gary Renard, a popular overview of ACIM principles. (That book was subsequently sold to Hay House, but my foreword still appears in the current edition and I retain a financial interest.) I have also spoken at many Course conferences and editorialized on the politics of the spiritual movement through a section of my website titled "The Continuing Story of the Course."

Thus this book is much more the work of an insider to the Course phenomenon than *The Complete Story* was. In the central four chapters comprising part II, this edition offers a new overview of basic principles of the Course teaching—a feature not included in the original book. Unlike most books written about the Course, this one features a journalistic perspective through its reliance on a variety of voices besides my own, including students and prominent teachers. Like my first book on the subject, this volume also presents critical voices across a broad spectrum, from the evangelical to the secular. As an independent journalist and a spiritual seeker, I have long been convinced of the necessity of presenting a balanced view of a teaching I use and admire.

It's my intent that this book will serve as the standard popular reference on *A Course in Miracles* for years to come, and I feel that my twenty-three years of intensive work as a student and researcher of ACIM constitute a necessary minimum of experience for attempting such a presentation. I'm grateful to my longtime friend and colleague Richard Smoley, also a veteran ACIM student, for contributing an appendix to this book, "A Comparison of Miracles," analyzing the differences between early drafts of ACIM and the standard published version.

For all its influence, *A Course in Miracles* remains a fringe element of American spirituality, widely viewed as a superficial New Age teaching and mostly ignored by academic theologians for that reason. Yet ACIM continues to spread by the enthusiastic word of mouth of its students, and it's safe to say that this unusual "mind training" will reach millions more people in the near future. This widespread and ever-growing recognition would have likely stunned the reticent scribes of the material—if not so much as they were once stunned to find themselves writing down the spectacularly strange and compelling teaching now known to so many simply as "the Course."

✎ ENDNOTES ✎

When sources are not clearly identified within the text itself, they will be briefly denoted at the end of each chapter, as provided here for this introduction. Quotations from *A Course in Miracles* are sourced clearly either by a text reference (such as a Workbook lesson number) or by a simple notation of the Text chapter, section number, and paragraph number. For instance, CH6, I, 15 denotes chapter 6, section I, paragraph 15 of the standard, numbered edition of the ACIM Text published by the Foundation for Inner Peace. Quotations taken from the Manual for Teachers, the "Psychotherapy" pamphlet, and "The Song of Prayer" pamphlet are likewise denoted by title, part, and paragraph numbers.

1. For a history of the Course copyright controversy and details on its resolution, see chapter 3 under the section "Copyrights and Coffee Mugs."
2. Sourced in Cathy Lynn Grossman, "Charting the Unchurched in America," *USA Today*, March 7, 2002.
3. "American Religious Identification Survey 2001," published by The Graduate Center of the City University of New York, 365 Fifth Avenue, New York, NY, www.gc.cuny.edu/faculty/research_briefs/aris/aris_index.htm.
4. Source: www.barnagroup.com: "'Born again Christians' are defined as people who said they have made a personal commitment to Jesus Christ that is still important in their life today and who also indicated they believe that when they die they will go to Heaven because they had confessed their sins and had accepted Jesus Christ as their savior. . . . 'Evangelicals' are people who meet the born again criteria described above plus seven other conditions. Those include saying their faith is very important in their life today; believing they have a personal responsibility to share their religious beliefs about Christ with non-Christians; believing that Satan exists; believing that eternal salvation is possible only through grace, not works; believing that Jesus Christ lived a sinless life on earth; asserting that the Bible is accurate in all that it teaches; and describing God as the all-knowing, all-powerful, perfect deity who created the universe and still rules it today. Being classified as an evangelical is not dependent upon church attendance or the denominational affiliation of the church attended."

PART I

ORIGINS AND HISTORY

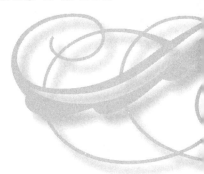

CHAPTER 1

How the Course Came to Be

Columbia University in 1965 was perhaps not the sort of place one would have expected to find the stirrings of spiritual renewal. In the College of Physicians and Surgeons, the psychology professors' struggle to affirm their discipline as a respectable branch of medical science went forward, attended by the usual amount of professional jealousy, fierce competition, and outright backbiting.

In the midst of this chaotic march of scientific progress, Dr. William N. Thetford, the reticent and scholarly director of the psychology department of the Columbia-Presbyterian Medical Center, one day decided that he'd had enough of the academic sparring. "There must be another way, and I'm determined to find it," he announced in an uncharacteristically forceful speech to his chief colleague, a sharp-tongued research psychologist fourteen years his senior, Dr. Helen Schucman. Moved by Thetford's commitment to a change in style, Schucman vowed to help him usher in a new era of cooperation with their peers, with a noticeable degree of success.

Over time the new outlook would prove largely ineffective in Thetford and Schucman's own severely conflicted relationship. But the momentary alignment of these two professors' sympathies seemed to catalyze an eruption of decidedly mystical energy on Schucman's part that left the rational scientist in her groping for explanations. Unexpectedly, Schucman began to experience a recurrence of the symbolic visions she had witnessed in her youth—visions that had largely ceased in young adulthood when she bitterly ended her search for God.

But now, at the age of fifty-six, Schucman found herself involved in a dramatic progression of waking dreams and visions in which she was gravitating toward a mysterious duty she felt she had "somehow, somewhere, agreed to complete." In these reveries she was sometimes spoken to by an inner "soundless voice" who clarified the meaning of various events for her. Over time this voice became an authoritative presence whom she referred to as the "Voice" (or jokingly as the "Top Sergeant"). She was not unaware of the Top Sergeant's self-professed identity, but evaded acknowledging it.

In the late summer of 1965, Schucman experienced a vision in which she entered a cave by a windswept seashore and found a large, very old parchment scroll. Unrolling the aged parchment with some difficulty, she found a center panel bearing the simple words "GOD IS." As she unrolled the scroll further, more writing was revealed to the left and right of the center panel. The familiar Voice told her that if she wanted, she could read the past on the left panel, and the future on the right—an apparent offering of clairvoyant capacities. But Schucman pointed to the words in the center of the scroll and said, "This is all I want."

"You made it that time," replied the Voice. "Thank you."

After this vision Schucman's anxiety lessened somewhat, and she thought with relief that her inner turbulence might be receding for good. At Thetford's suggestion, she had begun recording her inner experiences, and she was about to make an entry on October 21 when the Voice spoke clearly in her mind. "This is a course in miracles," it said with authority. "Please take notes."

Schucman was soon on the phone to Thetford, her precarious emotional equilibrium once again threatened. She told Thetford what the Voice was suggesting to her and asked in panic, "What am I going to do?"

Thetford was calm and curious. "Why don't you take down the notes? We'll look them over in the morning and see if they make any sense, and throw them out otherwise. No one has to know."

Thus began seven years of difficult extracurricular labor for Helen Schucman, in which she would faithfully, though often unwillingly, scribe the material that became *A Course in Miracles* and read aloud her shorthand notes to Thetford, who volunteered to type them. The prolonged and profound inner conflict that Schucman felt about her peculiar task is clear in this excerpt from Schucman's unpublished autobiography:

> As for me, I could neither account for nor reconcile my obviously inconsistent attitudes. On the one hand I still regarded myself as officially an agnostic, resented the material I was taking down, and was strongly impelled to attack it and prove it wrong. On the other hand I spent considerable time in taking it down and later dictating it to Bill, so that it was apparent that I also took it quite seriously. I actually came to refer to it as my life's work, even though I remained unconvinced about its authenticity and very jittery about it. As Bill pointed out, I must believe in it if only because I argued with it so much. While this was true, it did not help me. I was in the impossible position of not believing in my own life's work. The situation was clearly ridiculous as well as painful.[1]

In fact, early in her work Schucman argued with the Voice about the purpose of the undertaking and her role in it:

> I soon found I did not have much option in the matter. I was given a sort of mental "explanation," though, in the form of a series of related thoughts that crossed my mind in rapid succession and made a reasonably coherent whole. According to this "information" the world situation was worsening to an alarming degree. People all over the world were being called on to help, and were making their individual contributions as part of an overall, prearranged plan. I had apparently agreed to take down a course in miracles as it would be given me. The Voice was fulfilling its part in the agreement, as I would fulfill mine. I would be using abilities I had developed very long ago, and which I was not really ready to use again. Because of the acute emergency, however, the usual slow, evolutionary process was being bypassed in what might be described as a "celestial speed-up." I

could sense the urgency that lay behind this "explanation," whatever I might think about its content. The feeling was conveyed to me that time was running out.

I was not satisfied. Even in the unlikely event that the "explanation" was true, I did not regard myself as a good candidate for a "scribal" role. I stated my opposition silently but strongly.

"Why me?" I asked. "I'm not even religious. I don't understand the things that have been happening to me and I don't even like them. Besides, they make me nervous. I'm just about as poor a choice as you could make."

"On the contrary," I was assured. "You are an excellent choice, and for a very simple reason. You will do it."

I had no answer to this, and retired in defeat. The Voice was right. I knew I would do it. And so the writing of the "course" began.

It should be remembered that Schucman already had a full-time job as a professor at Columbia-Presbyterian when she decided to take on the persistent challenge of writing down dictation from a most unconventional superior.

I would feel the writing coming on almost daily, and sometimes several times a day. The timing never conflicted with work or social activities, starting at some time when I was reasonably free to write without interference. I wrote in a shorthand notebook that I soon began to carry with me, just in case. I could and very often did refuse to cooperate, at least initially. But I soon learned I would have no peace until I did. Even so, I maintained my "right to refuse" throughout. Sometimes I refused to write for over a month, during which I merely became increasingly depressed. It always required my full conscious cooperation.

Evenings turned out to be a favored time for "dictation," especially for additional "assignments." I objected bitterly to this and often went to bed defiantly without writing anything, but I could not sleep. Eventually, I got up in some disgust and wrote as directed. . . .

The writing was highly interruptable. At the office I could lay the notebook down to answer the telephone, talk to a patient, supervise a junior staff member, or attend to one of our numerous emergencies, and return to the writing without even checking back to see where I left off. At home I could talk to my husband, chat with a friend, or take a nap, going back to the notebook afterwards without disturbing the flow of words in the slightest. . . . It was as if the Voice merely waited until I came back and then started in again. I wrote with equal ease at home, in the office, on a park bench, or in a taxi, bus, or subway. The presence of other people did not interfere at all. When the time for writing came external circumstances appeared to be irrelevant.

Among those who knew her there is a general agreement that Schucman exhibited a dramatic dissociation of personality around the issue of the Course. Bill Thetford always felt, in fact, that this split was essential to her work in recording it.

"She was usually in some degree of conflict," Thetford told me in a brief meeting about a year before his death in 1988. "In order to do this work Helen had to be in a rather dissociated mental state. She had to shift to the appropriate focus for taking down the Course material, and she was very precise and accurate about it, very much as if she were tuning into an FM channel. She frequently said to me, 'I don't want to know what it says. I'm only concerned with its grammar and syntax. If it starts making errors in syntax, then I refuse to continue with it.' She could get the material down without much difficulty, because it came to her quite clearly. But when she stopped, she would shift back to her ordinary state of ego awareness. Those states didn't necessarily connect. She was quite aware that what the Course had to say was not how she experienced the world.

"This was obviously a very unusual situation," Thetford added, "but perhaps it's the only way it could have happened given Helen's personality. She really stayed out of the way and certainly didn't try to become a high priestess. She didn't want that role."

When I asked Thetford if some of that reluctance had to do with the professional identities that both of them had to protect during the years of transcription, he laughed emphatically. "Yes, the Course was our guilty secret!" he admitted. "Professors at Columbia didn't do this kind of thing, particularly in the department of psychiatry. Can you imagine? Hearing voices, taking down material of this kind . . ."

In fact, as Thetford recalled, Schucman's anxiety about the Course material was such that he often had to keep one calming hand on her and the other on the typewriter as she read aloud her notes. Occasionally her resistance to the meaning of the material would break down, as Schucman admitted:

> The writing continued over years, and although the acute terror I felt at the beginning gradually lessened over time I never really got used to it. Yet despite periods of open rebellion, it never seriously occurred to me to give it up even though the whole thing struck me as a major and often insulting interference. There were, however, a few rare times when I felt curiously transported as I wrote. On these occasions the words seemed almost to sing, and I felt a deep sense of trust and even privilege. I noticed afterwards that these sections turned out to be the more poetic ones. But these were brief periods of respite. For the most part I was bleakly unbelieving, suspicious, and afraid. Yet distressing as the writing generally was, reading the material to Bill afterwards was infinitely more so. We had agreed that I would read my notes to him at the end of the day, and he would type them. I hated to hear what I had written. I was sure it would be incoherent, foolish and meaningless. On the other hand I was likely to be unexpectedly and deeply moved and suddenly burst into tears.

Although Schucman's personal notes were vague about the identity behind the Voice, the overt historical references made in the material itself were unmistakable. In a discussion of the meaning of the crucifixion, the Voice said:

> *I elected, for your sake and mine, to demonstrate that the most outrageous assault, as judged by the ego, does not matter. As the world judges these things, but not as God knows them, I was betrayed, abandoned, beaten, torn, and finally killed. It was clear that this was only because of the projection of others onto me, since I had not harmed anyone and had healed many.* (CH6, I, 9)

. . . My one lesson, which I must teach as I learned it, is that no perception that is out of accord with the Holy Spirit can be justified. I undertook to show this was true in an extreme case, merely because it would serve as a good teaching aid to those whose temptation to give in to anger and assault would not be so extreme. I will with God that none of His Sons should suffer. (Ch6, I, 11)

At the close of her autobiography, Schucman disclosed a telling assessment of this mystical authority who had so dramatically intervened in her conflicted life.

Where did the writing come from? It made obvious use of my educational background, interests and experience, but that was in matters of style rather than content. Certainly the subject matter itself was the last thing I would have expected to write about. . . .

I have subsequently found out that many of the concepts and even some of the actual terms in the writing are found in both Eastern and Western mystical thought, but I knew nothing of them at the time. Nor did I understand the calm but impressive authority with which the Voice dictated. It is largely because of the strangely compelling nature of this authority that I have referred to the Voice with a capital "V." I do not understand the real authorship of the writing, but the particular combination of certainty, wisdom, gentleness, clarity and patience that characterized the Voice made that form of reference seem perfectly appropriate.

At several points in the writing the Voice itself speaks in no uncertain terms about the Author. My own reactions to these references, which literally stunned me at the time, have decreased in intensity and are now at the level of mere indecision. I do not understand the events that led up to the writing. I do not understand the process and I certainly do not understand the authorship. It would be pointless for me to attempt an explanation.

Kenneth Wapnick, PhD, author of a detailed history of the Course scribing titled *Absence from Felicity* (FACIM, 1991), issues a disclaimer about this statement of Schucman's. Noting that she began her autobiography at Bill Thetford's suggestion—he thought it could serve as an introduction to be published with the Course—Wapnick feels that Schucman was writing to shore up her facade as "a hard-nosed scientist who suddenly woke up one day and started writing down words from a mysterious voice." In fact, Wapnick says, Schucman had been hearing the Voice for some time before October 21, 1965, and knew exactly to whom she was listening.

"I challenged Helen about this image of herself she wanted to put out there," recalls Wapnick. "I told her, 'This is what people are going to have as a legacy, and you know it's not true. Why don't you write it the way it really happened?' She agreed and started over, but it brought up such anxiety that she ended up making what she had written even worse! So I said I'd never mention it again. That's how the autobiography ended up the way it is." (In the version of her autobiography in my possession, Schucman never clearly identifies the author of ACIM.)

Lessons in Relationship

As Helen Schucman and Bill Thetford labored at their secret task, revealing it to only a few intimates over the seven years of transcription, they were not sure of its ultimate purpose beyond a private and prolific lecture on the betterment of their relationships to each other and their professional colleagues—an unexpected answer to Thetford's commitment to "another way." And no one who knew them would have denied that their particular relationship, which had begun seven years before the Course's inception, sorely needed help.

As Wapnick relates, a "tremendous animosity" existed between the assertive, abrasive Schucman and her passive-aggressive boss. "They would argue throughout the day, and then in the evening would often spend another hour or so on the phone going over their mutual grievances, each of them desperately convinced of the correctness of his [or] her position. Constantly critical of each other, their discussions were seemingly endless."[2]

In a two-hour film documentary about the Course released by the Foundation for Inner Peace in 1987, Bill Thetford alluded to the fact that Helen Schucman "wanted more from our relationship than I felt I was able to give"[3]—likely an oblique reference to Schucman's early romantic attraction to Thetford, who was homosexual. But the relationship between Schucman and Thetford seemed a good deal more complicated than unrequited affection could explain, particularly in light of the fact that the one thing they reportedly never argued about was the Course.

Wapnick, who met the two of them while they were working jointly on a chapter to be published in the *Comprehensive Textbook of Psychiatry*, says Thetford and Schucman were at "total war" over that professional project, but suffered no bitterness or competition when the subject matter turned to the Course. "The difference was astonishing," he recalls.

According to Wapnick's book *Absence from Felicity*, the first five chapters of the Text of ACIM were edited in order to remove earlier personal instructions to Schucman, many of them giving specific advice about her relationship to Thetford and clarifying their mutually supportive roles. (See appendix II for more information on early drafts of the Course.) But Schucman's resistance to guidance was intense and she did not hesitate to challenge the inner authority she heard. Wapnick's book reveals the following internal dialogue recorded in Schucman's notes but not included in the Course:

[Jesus]: Everyone experiences fear, and nobody enjoys it. Yet, it would take very little right-thinking to know why it occurs. Neither you nor Bill have [*sic*] thought about it very much, either.

[Helen]: I object to the use of a plural verb with a properly singular subject, and remember that last time in a very similar sentence, He said it correctly and I noted it with real pleasure. This real grammatical error makes me suspicious of the genuineness of these notes.

[Jesus]: What it really shows is that *you* are not very receptive. The reason it came out that way, is because you are projecting . . . your own anger, which has nothing to do with these notes. You made the error, because you are not feeling loving, so you want me to sound silly, so you won't have to pay attention. . . .

You and Bill have been afraid of God, of Me, of yourselves, and of practically everyone you know at one time or another.

Although such personal directives were excised from the Course itself, their existence helps explain some of the odd passages remaining wherein the author seems to be personally chiding the reader: "You may insist that the Holy Spirit does not answer you, but it might be wiser to consider the kind of questioner you are." (CH9, I, 7)

Regardless of how much personal instruction Schucman was to receive internally, her resistance to applying the message of the Course appeared substantial to the end of her life. In his later years Bill Thetford seemed better able to integrate the teaching into his attitudes and behavior. Although Schucman could explain the Course intellectually and would leap to its defense if she felt it was being challenged or distorted, neither she nor Thetford could fulfill its lessons in the very relationship to which it seemed, at first, to be solely directed.

As Wapnick writes, "By the time I met them in the late fall of 1972, right after the Course was completed, their relationship was at an all-time low, and it only seemed to worsen from there. It was almost as if Helen were determined to prove that the Course was ineffective at least, and deleterious at worst, enabling her to feel more justifiably bitter about her life."[4]

Nonetheless, this unlikely team did complete its task. The massive Text was fully recorded by October 1968, almost exactly three years since it had begun. The Voice had earlier told Schucman that the material would be complete when she heard the word "Amen." The last paragraph of the Text reads:

> *And now we say "Amen." For Christ has come to dwell in the abode you set for Him before time was, in calm eternity. The journey closes, ending at the place where it began. No trace of it remains. Not one illusion is accorded faith, and not one spot of darkness still remains to hide the face of Christ from anyone. Thy will is done, complete and perfectly, and all creation recognizes You, and knows You as the only Source it has. Clear in Your likeness does the Light shine forth from everything that lives and moves in You. For we have reached where all of us are one, and we are home, where You would have us be.* (CH31, VIII, 12)

For all her resistance and skepticism, Schucman's devotion to the original Text manuscript was remarkable. She retyped it twice on her own, then worked with Thetford to enter chapter and section headings into what had been one long, unbroken discourse. Tempted often to change the wording to suit her own predilections, Schucman always thought better of it. "Any changes I made were always wrong in the long run, and had to be put back," she admitted. The material "had a way of knowing what it was doing, and was much better left exactly as it was." (According to Ken Wapnick, Schucman's and Thetford's later editing of the early chapters of the Text was done with the explicit direction of the Voice. The nature and extent of that editing has caused some controversy in Course circles, as noted in appendix II.)

For about a week after the initial editing and typing of the Text had been completed, Schucman felt relaxed and released from her task. But soon she began to experience a sense of purposelessness. "There was lots of work to do, but somehow it did not fill the void in my life that became increasingly large and oppressive." At the end of six months, Schucman was both emotionally depressed and physically ill, and the thought crossed her mind that there might be more dictation work ahead of her. She mentioned the idea to Thetford, but it was her husband, Louis—who had generally paid little attention to the Course project—who seconded her notion that the writing might not be finished. Schucman reacted with predictable exasperation, but six weeks later she began to record the Workbook.

> It was not so hard as the text had been. In the first place, I liked the general format even though I found the first few "lessons" rather trivial. Nevertheless, I thought it swung rather quickly into good style and very acceptable blank verse, a realization which helped me a good deal. Also, the process of writing itself was no longer particularly strange to me. And finally, I approved of the precision of the arrangement of the workbook. It said at the outset exactly what it was going to do, and then proceeded to do it. Even its end was predetermined. It stated at the outset that there would be one lesson a day for a period of one year, and that was exactly the way it turned out.

Schucman's reference to blank verse denotes the fact that large portions of the Course are written in unrhymed iambic pentameter. According to

Ken Wapnick, this is true for the two last chapters of the Text in their entirety, as well as everything following Lesson 99 in the Workbook.

Clive Matson, a well-known writing teacher in northern California who earned his MFA in poetry from Columbia University, scanned some pages from the last chapter of the Course Text at my request and reports that the prose he examined showed a consistent iambic rhythm but was not technically pentameter because the form is in prose paragraphs, not ten-beat lines of verse. However, he made a startling discovery when he picked the following paragraph at random and converted it to ten-beat lines:

> *Only the self-accused condemn. As you prepare to make a choice that will result in different outcomes, there is first one thing that must be overlearned. It must become a habit of response so typical of everything you do that it becomes your first response to all temptation, and to every situation that occurs. Learn this, and learn it well, for it is here delay of happiness is shortened by a span of time you cannot realize. You never hate your brother for his sins, but only for your own. Whatever form his sins appear to take, it but obscures the fact that you believe them to be yours, and therefore meriting a "just" attack.* (CH31, III, 1)

Matson found that the paragraph broke precisely into sixteen lines of iambic pentameter—"with not one syllable too few or too many," he reports. "I was astonished." Another paragraph he selected fit the form exactly as well.

In a rare public appearance at a 1976 panel discussion, Helen Schucman confirmed that the literary style of the Course was one thing that helped make the experience of scribing it tolerable to her: ". . . it is quite a literary thing and it does require a certain background . . . I happen to like this stuff from a literary viewpoint. I'm kind of a snob, but there are many of us. You know, salvation really shouldn't cut us out simply because we're snobs."[5]

With little upset or delay on Schucman's part, the scribing of the Workbook took place from May 1969 to February of 1971, followed by the Manual for Teachers beginning in April 1972 and ending about five months later. From that time until 1978, Schucman would receive dictation from the same Voice for a number of religious poems and two pamphlets, "Psychotherapy: Purpose, Process, and Practice" and "The Song of Prayer."

How the Course Went Public

In the first few months following the Course's completion, Bill Thetford showed the material to four people: two close friends, a Catholic priest, and Hugh Lynn Cayce, son of the famed psychic and channel Edgar Cayce who founded the Association for Research and Enlightenment (ARE) in Virginia Beach, Virginia. According to Robert Skutch's brief Course history *Journey Without Distance* (Celestial Arts, 1984, 2001), Hugh Cayce felt the work to be "tremendously important" with the potential for changing "millions of lives." Thetford had begun reading the work of Edgar Cayce long before, during the eruption of visions Helen Schucman had experienced just prior to the initial scribing of the Course. When Thetford prevailed upon Schucman at that time to examine the Cayce legacy, she initially dismissed most of it as "spooky." Over time she would positively revise her opinion. In fact, Hugh Cayce became close enough to both Thetford and Schucman that one of the earliest copies of the manuscript would be dubbed "the Hugh Lynn version" or "HLC version" and stored in the ARE library. (Cayce was not involved in the editing of the Course.)

That was the same version of the manuscript first read by Kenneth Wapnick, who would eschew his chosen life as a monk to work closely with Schucman on further rounds of editing until the end of January 1975. At that point the Course recorders and Wapnick no doubt felt a sense of satisfaction that their extraordinary project was completed. But had it been left up to Schucman, Thetford, and Wapnick—all introverts—the Course might never have progressed beyond a bulky, photocopied manuscript shared gingerly with their confidants. If the Course was to reach a wider audience—and none of the principals felt certain that it should—a different kind of personality would have to enter their small circle.

With Judith Skutch that different personality arrived, as well as what might be called the "third force" of the Course phenomenon. The first force, that of academic psychology and psychotherapy, was originally conveyed by the mind-set and professional background of Helen Schucman and Bill Thetford, and it is still evidenced today by the strong presence of professional therapists and counselors in the Course constituency. The second force of mystical spirituality was primarily conveyed by the voice of the Course itself, augmented by the influence of Ken Wapnick and echoed in the contemporary popularity of ACIM with many ministers and teachers of various faiths. Skutch would facilitate the joining of these forces with the ill-defined, much-maligned social current of the last several decades called the New Age.

Although these three forces overlap in a number of ways—within both the Course community and the culture at large—they are sufficiently dissimilar to have spawned a great deal of confusion about the true nature of *A Course in Miracles*. Their confluence in one phenomenon has made the Course appear to be different things to different people: a modern restatement of Gnosticism, a psychospiritual study of human nature, or a New Age treatise on metaphysics.

Skutch's connection to New Age culture lay in her longstanding involvement in parapsychology. The Brooklyn-born daughter of Samuel Rothstein, a lay leader of world Jewry, Skutch was raised in a busy household full of people having meetings, discussing intriguing ideas, and founding organizations—a social condition that she apparently replicated throughout her adult life. Prior to encountering ACIM, Judy and her second husband, Bob Skutch, ran a sort of ongoing "consciousness salon" in their spacious apartment on Central Park West, as well as an organization called the Foundation for Parasensory Investigation. Judy taught continuing education courses at New York University, and the Skutch household hosted the likes of psychic showman Uri Geller, guru Baba Muktananda, alternative oncologist Dr. Carl Simonton, and a host of other prominent personalities interested in the esoteric.

A few weeks before she would encounter the Course, Skutch felt herself painfully trapped in a paradox of opposite emotions. "It looked like I had a perfect, exciting life," she recalls. "We had a house in Connecticut and a large apartment in New York with plenty of rooms for all sorts of meetings to go on at once. It was a fulfilling and electric time to be alive. But deep down inside I could feel myself sinking into a real pit of despair. Somehow I knew I wasn't really fulfilled, and I didn't even know what that meant. I was talking about healing all the time and didn't feel the least bit healed myself. One night I locked myself in the bathroom and started pounding my head against the wall, asking in tears, 'Won't somebody up there please help me?' I know now that what I was experiencing was spiritual deprivation. But I didn't know that at the time."

Soon Skutch consulted with a numerologist who told her that she would shortly meet a much older woman who would be the most important teacher of her life, and also that she would become involved in publishing a highly significant spiritual document. With only a little publishing experience in her background, Skutch was skeptical of the prediction. Nine days later she met Bill Thetford and Helen Schucman at the Columbia-Presbyterian Medical Center's cafeteria, introduced by a mutual friend who thought the two psychologists might be interested in Skutch's explorations of holistic healing. As Skutch has described the meeting:

> After the usual small talk, I brought up the subject I had wanted to discuss, but neither of them showed any interest in holistic health. Bill and Helen kept talking about research in general, and the more they talked the more I wondered what I was doing there. Then I began to feel there was something on Helen's mind that she was not revealing, though for the life of me I couldn't imagine what it might be. All I knew was that it didn't have anything to do with the research designs she was discussing. And then, as we were eating our desserts, I heard myself saying something I couldn't believe. I turned to Helen, and out of my mouth came "You hear an inner voice, don't you?"
>
> Helen blanched, and there was a strained look on her face as she said, very faintly, "What did you say?"
>
> Bill pushed his chair back from the table, saying, "Why don't we all go back to our office? I think we'd be a lot more comfortable there."[6]

In the office, Skutch was introduced to Ken Wapnick and told, over the ensuing two hours, the story of the scribing of *A Course in Miracles*. She left their office awkwardly hefting the entire manuscript in a shopping bag, already intuiting that the Course might well become her life's work. She began reading the manuscript that night, never stopping to sleep.

That was how Judy Skutch entered the small circle of Course intimates for whom the material was the focus of their lives. Meeting with Schucman, Thetford, and Wapnick three or four times weekly in her apartment, Skutch asked them to do the Workbook exercises with her for a year. (That would make the third time through for Thetford and Schucman, and the second for Wapnick.)

If Schucman, Thetford, and Wapnick lacked public-relations savvy, it's obvious that Judy Skutch made up for all of them and then some. Thetford once joked that Skutch was taking their little group to a New Age gathering in order to meet five thousand of her closest friends. In fact, Skutch's enthusiasm for spreading the word about the Course induced Schucman, Thetford, and Wapnick to engage in a brief period of traveling and speaking about the Course, from California to London. This phase would not last long, however, as Schucman did not enjoy the limelight, and both she and Thetford did not wish to shoulder the burden of ACIM's "public life."

That was clearly the work of Judith Skutch. In August 1975 she began to distribute photo-reduced versions of the Course under the auspices of the Foundation for Parasensory Investigation, having become aware that interest in the Course was growing "exponentially." This version became known as the "Criswell edition" because Skutch made the copies on the advice of a friend and consultant, Eleanor Criswell. Schucman approved the distribution while cautioning Skutch to procure a copyright. In later years the distribution and copyright status of this edition would prove to be a critical issue in the ACIM copyright controversy (summarized in chapter 3).

As the photo-reduced copies circulated, several offers to publish the material professionally in abridged forms surfaced but were refused. As Skutch has written, "As [the Course] had not been edited for simplification, it seemed it should not be edited for profit-making, and we knew we had not yet come across the appropriate method for printing and distributing it."[7]

Finally, on Valentine's Day 1976 the ACIM inner circle met to discuss the need to publish the Course in a professionally bound volume. Deciding to consult the Voice of the Course as a group, Skutch, Wapnick, Thetford, and Schucman silently asked for guidance, and as Skutch relates, each received a different directive:

Helen had heard that those who will devote their lives to this alone should do the job. I had heard that it should be a nonprofit organization, so those who could not afford the price could receive scholarship copies as a "gift of love." Bill added that the Course should not be changed in any way from the original, and Ken's directive was that somehow or other we must all be involved.[8]

In short order they realized that they constituted the only group who fit all these criteria, and that must mean that they were destined to publish it. When they further asked where the money was to come from, neither Thetford nor Wapnick heard an answer. Schucman reported that she felt "Judy will be told what to do," and indeed Skutch received the unspecific message: "Make the commitment first." Realizing that this could mean the commitment of all her assets to the publication of the Course, Skutch nonetheless assented.

But the next morning Skutch received a phone call from Reed Erickson, a wealthy industrialist in Mazatlán, Mexico, who was studying a photo-

From left to right: Kenneth Wapnick, Helen Schucman, Bill Thetford, and Judith Skutch in 1975.

copied manuscript of the Course. He urged Skutch to print a hardcover edition of the Course as soon as possible, and she informed him that the decision to do so had been made without knowing where the money would come from. Erickson then revealed that he had called to offer the proceeds of a real estate sale to cover the printing of five thousand hardcover copies of ACIM. Erickson subsequently sent a check for $20,000 (the first third of the total expense) directly to Long Island printer Saul Steinberg, who shepherded the production of the Course through typesetting, printing, and binding. The entire project was completed by June 22, 1976, the official publication date of the first bound volumes of *A Course in Miracles*.

By that time the name of Bob and Judy Skutch's nonprofit organization—the Foundation for Parasensory Investigation—had been changed to the Foundation for Inner Peace, according to guidance received by Helen Schucman. On this point at least, Schucman apparently felt no resistance to the instruction she received. After all, as Ken Wapnick recalls, she regarded psychics and channelers and the like as "funny people."

∽ ENDNOTES ∽

1. Ken Wapnick has said that Helen Schucman made at least "eight and a half" starts on her autobiography. Unless noted otherwise, the quotations in this book come from a seventy-page typewritten version provided to me by Judy Skutch. In that manuscript Schucman refers to Bill Thetford as "John" to protect his identity; I have restored the correct name in all instances.
2. Kenneth Wapnick, *Absence from Felicity: The Story of Helen Schucman and Her Scribing of* A Course in Miracles (Roscoe, NY: Foundation for *A Course in Miracles*, 1991).
3. Bridget Winter, *The Story of* A Course in Miracles (Tiburon, CA: Foundation for Inner Peace, 1987) film documentary.
4. From Wapnick, *Absence from Felicity*.
5. Helen Schucman quoted in "The Experience of Scribing the Course," *Miracles Magazine*, No. 3, Summer 1992.
6. Judith Skutch and Tamara Cohen, *Double Vision* (Berkeley, CA: Celestial Arts, 1985).
7. Ibid.
8. Ibid.

CHAPTER 2

Who Were
Schucman and Thetford?

At least 15 percent of the general population sooner or later "hears" an inner voice offering information or guidance, according to psychologist Arthur Hastings, author of a study of channeling titled *With the Tongues of Men and Angels* (Harcourt, 1991). "Regardless of the validity of the claims of supernatural agency, the fact remains that mentally healthy individuals experience these phenomena," he writes. "Moreover, a large number of these messages contain meaningful information and exhibit knowledge and talents of which the channeler is completely unaware."

The whole notion of channeling is inherently controversial: either you find it credible or you don't. Although virtually every prominent channel has claimed to be surprised by the initiation of his or her exotic talent, Helen Schucman appears to be unique in her long-term resistance to and resentment of an extraordinary channeling task that she nonetheless completed—not to mention her unwillingness to become a spokesperson for the message she recorded.

If one finds it credible that Jesus Christ would choose anyone to record a lengthy lecture to the modern world, it's worth examining the characters of Helen Schucman and Bill Thetford to investigate the question Schucman herself posed: Why them? If one finds it credible only that these two sophisticated psychologists worked for seven years in service to Schucman's conscious design or subconscious ideation, the source of the Course certainly appears less supernatural—but all the more enigmatic.

Helen Schucman, the Reluctant Mystic

The first major critical examination of ACIM appeared in *Psychology Today* in September 1980, in an article by former *TIME* magazine writer John Koffend titled "The Gospel According to Helen." Characterizing the Course as the latest item in a "veritable supermarket of cults, religions, and psycho-mystical movements" arising in America, the article cast doubt on the veracity of the Course's genesis story and questioned the reluctance of Schucman and Thetford to take personal credit for their labor. At the time, Schucman was still alive but declined to be interviewed. "If Christ was so willing to identify himself to a mere mortal named Helen," the article charged, "why are she and Bill Thetford so reluctant to admit their complicity in the Lord's work?"

Written before the rise to celebrity of such publicity-conscious channelers as J. Z. Knight (Ramtha) and Kevin Ryerson, this dated criticism could now almost be taken as praise for the humility of the Course scribes. But it certainly attests to the paradoxes in the character of Helen Schucman, which have contributed to the spread of misinformation about her personality and religious background. In a skeptical examination of channeling appearing in *The Fringes of Reason*, a 1989 special edition of the Whole Earth Catalog, editor Ted Schultz raised the possibility that the Course is a massive artifact of "cryptomnesia" or hidden memory. Using quotations first published in Jon Klimo's book *Channeling* (Tarcher, 1987), Schultz cited two well-known sources from the counterculture of psychology:

. . . Esalen co-founder Michael Murphy points out: "[Schucman] was raised on that kind of [spiritualist] literature. Her father owned a metaphysical bookshop." And transpersonal psychologist Ken Wilber says, "There's much more of Helen in the Course than I first thought. She was brought up mystically inclined. At four she used to stand out on the balcony and say that God would give her a sign of miracles to let her know he was there. Many ideas from the Course came from the new thought or metaphysical schools she had been influenced by . . .."

Both Murphy and Wilber were incorrect. According to Schucman's unpublished autobiography, her father, Sigmund Cohn, a successful career chemist and metallurgist whose parents had been Jewish and Lutheran, evinced no spiritual inclinations himself. In the longest talk she could remember having with him as a child, he answered her innocent questions about God with a studied neutrality. Although Schucman's mother dabbled in both Theosophy and Christian Science at different periods, the young Helen was emotionally estranged from both parents; the chief religious influences on her early life were a Roman Catholic governess and a black Baptist maid. Helen was actually baptized in the maid's church in early adolescence, but was disappointed to feel nothing change within her afterward. In adulthood Schucman developed a fascination with the rituals of the Catholic church, but never considered conversion to the faith.

It was Helen's husband, Louis Schucman, who owned a bookshop featuring rare books and Americana. According to Helen, he "riffled through some material on mysticism on and off, finding the subject of some interest though hardly worthy of scientific investigation." Thus there is little evidence of "new thought" or metaphysical schools exerting significant influence on Schucman before the transcription of the Course, as noted in her own writing in chapter 1.

However, in response to the mystical experiences that Schucman had begun sharing with him, Bill Thetford was developing an interest in esoterica in the months before transcription of the Course. He convinced Schucman to accompany him to the Virginia Beach headquarters of the Edgar Cayce Foundation, the Association for Research and Enlightenment, in the late summer of 1965, shortly before the first words of the Course were taken down. As noted earlier, the Cayce connection made Schucman uneasy at first, and she resisted examining that material then. Thetford continued an exhaustive study of comparative religion and mysticism after the Course transcription had begun, but Schucman read only sparingly in the field, usually at Thetford's insistence.

Once, on a family trip to Lourdes at age twelve, Schucman actually did stand on a balcony one evening and ask God for the miracle sign of a shooting star—which, to her amazement, she received. But an inner conflict between religious faith and scientific rationality that would characterize Schucman's later life was apparent even then, for the adolescent girl promptly debunked her own mystical experience. As Schucman recalled in her autobiography:

> I stood quite still until the stars had faded away and the sky was dark again. And then I remembered. Our guide had told us that this was the time for meteor showers in this part of the world, and they would be coming pretty often soon. It was not really a miracle at all . . . Perhaps, I said to myself, the water and the healings and the crutches were all like the meteor shower. People just thought they were miracles. It all could happen that way. You can get fooled so easily.

By the time Schucman reached college, her adolescent religiosity was waning as she became "happily involved in systems of thought, the laws of reasoning, and logic in particular." She also experienced a secret ambition that she found herself unable to fulfill. Although pleasing her mother with the announced plan to become, like her, an English teacher, Schucman actually "had no doubt that some day I would be a great writer, probably an internationally famous novelist. I would live by myself and write. I would be different from other people, but distinctly better. In view of my secret goal, the intense difficulty I had in writing anything was particularly trying to me."

Also trying for Schucman was a life-threatening illness not long after her college graduation that initiated an anger with God that would never entirely abate. Overweight, insecure, and very lonely as a child—her brother was fourteen years older—Schucman developed a severe eating disorder in her teens that resulted in a serious gall bladder condition by her early twenties. Having put off surgery for months while living in increasing pain, Schucman decided to give God a try on the night before her operation:

There was a chance, I supposed, that he existed after all. Certainly the fact that I did not believe in him had nothing to do with his existence one way or another. In any case, there could be no harm in attempting a reasonable compromise. I would put the operation in God's hands in case he existed, and if things turned out all right I might even be able to believe in him again. There was nothing to lose by trying. I said the Lord's prayer, put my operation in the hands of God, and went to the hospital the next day with my medal of the Blessed Virgin around my neck.

But Schucman nearly died, and she was not able to leave the hospital for four months. Unconscious for a long time after the surgery, she awoke to find herself in the care of a deeply religious nurse who said that it was a "miracle" Schucman had pulled through—a miracle for which the nurse had already offered a mass of thanksgiving.

"I did not see it that way myself," recalled Schucman. "If this was God's idea of making things turn out all right, I thought, he certainly had a nasty sense of humor . . . I told the nurse I could not stop her from praying, of course, but added that I would appreciate her not asking God for another miracle until I was at least strong enough to cope with this one."

In later years, as Schucman took up postgraduate work in psychology, she "shifted from agnosticism to angry atheism," arming herself with "scientific weapons, prepared and even eager to do battle with ideas even remotely religiously toned. . . . I firmly believed I had overcome superstition at last, and was finally looking at things realistically." By Schucman's account, this was her antireligious and decidedly bitter state of mind by the time she became a colleague of Bill Thetford.

But Ken Wapnick, a near-constant companion of Schucman in her later years, was never convinced that she so thoroughly divorced herself from God. "Helen's atheism makes a good story," he suggests, "but it's not really true. You can't be that militant against something unless you believe in it at some level. There were periods of Helen's life when she went to Mass every day; she was attracted to it without believing in it. She had two purses full of Catholic rosaries and medals, accumulated prior to the Course. She had a deep knowledge of the Bible. Helen really adopted a pose, because she was a psychologist who had to be an atheist."

She was also a natural-born visionary periodically entranced by mystical experiences that left her breathless. Having married the bookish Louis Schucman in 1933 at the age of twenty-three, Helen found a reassuring stability in their dependable if dispassionate relationship. That did not mean she was above resenting him fiercely. When he once insisted that they take a subway instead of a cab to a social engagement on a wintry evening, she sulked angrily in her seat as Louis sat calmly reading the paper:

> I grew increasingly sure I would come down with a pneumonia, probably in both lungs. As an additional hazard, people were coughing and sneezing all around us, and I could almost see the germs attacking. I became convinced that my husband's thoughtlessness would probably have a fatal outcome. His contented absorption in his newspaper did not help matters, either. Besides being dangerous, the whole situation struck me as thoroughly revolting. The train smelled of garlic and peanuts, and the people looked shabby and dirty. Across the aisle a child with hands streaked with chocolate patted his mother's face and left smudgy fingerprints on her cheek. Next to her, another mother was wiping off her coat where her baby had thrown up. A child a few seats down picked up some chewing gum from the floor and put it in his mouth. At the far end of the train a group of old men were arguing heatedly and perspiring freely. I closed my eyes in disgust, feeling sick to my stomach.
>
> And then a stunning thing happened. It was as though a blinding light blazed up behind my eyes and filled my mind entirely. Without opening my eyes, I seemed to see a figure of myself walking directly into the light. She seemed to know exactly what she was doing. It was, in fact, as if the situation was completely familiar to her. For a moment she paused and knelt down, touching the ground with elbows, wrists and forehead in what looked like an Eastern expression of deep reverence. Then she got up, walked to the side, and knelt again, this time resting her head as if leaning against a giant knee.

The outline of a huge arm seemed to reach around her and she disappeared. The light grew even brighter, and I felt the most indescribably intense love streaming from it to me. It was so powerful that I literally gasped and opened my eyes.

I saw the light an instant longer, during which I loved everyone on the train with that same incredible intensity. Then the light faded and the old picture of dirt and ugliness returned. The contrast was truly shocking. It took me several minutes to regain a semblance of composure. Then I reached uncertainly for my husband's hand.

At that point Helen tried to explain her stunning experience of light and all-encompassing love to Louis. Patting her hand and assuring Helen that it sounded like "a very common mystical experience," Louis then told her not to give it another thought—a response that would remain characteristic of Louis's attitude toward all spiritual matters, including the Course, in the years to come.

Meeting "The One I'm Supposed to Help"

Schucman was undecided about a profession all the way through her thirties. She tried more than once to partner Louis at his bookstore, but they tended to quarrel. Even after she decided to pursue graduate work in psychology, she expressed doubt about the choice and hesitated to enact it. Finally she did return to New York University in 1952, where she had done her undergraduate studies, and earned a PhD in clinical psychology by 1957. The fact that she finished near the top of her class was remarkable considering that she was phobic about both reading and writing; Ken Wapnick would later tease her about being nearly a "functional illiterate."

Nonetheless her term papers earned high compliments from her professors, and soon after graduation she wrote a successful grant proposal based on her doctoral study about the learning abilities of children with severe mental retardation. With the offer of a teaching position at NYU, Schucman's long-delayed vocation seemed to be shifting into gear. Envisioning herself at the head of a large research department, Schucman submitted several additional grant proposals that she hoped would definitively launch her career.

Finding herself highly anxious on the day the grants were being considered, she wandered into a Catholic church, lit a candle, and presented God with a "nonnegotiable demand" that her proposals be approved. But she walked angrily out of the church knowing somehow that her plans would not play out as she wished. Indeed, the grants were rejected that evening, and Schucman spent the next several weeks feeling bitter and depressed, refusing to exploit any number of professional connections that could have easily landed her a job.

When she finally roused herself to call a colleague, he immediately provided her with a list of promising leads. But that same colleague then took a call from William Thetford, a recent arrival at Columbia-Presbyterian Medical Center, asking if he knew of a good research psychologist for a project Thetford had to staff. Schucman subsequently received an urgent call from her contact, who told her to forget the list he'd just given her and call Thetford immediately. Schucman recalled their meeting:

As I walked into his office a few days later I made the first of a series of silent remarks that I did not understand myself, and to which I paid little attention at the time.

"And there he is," I said to myself. "He's the one I'm supposed to help."

I was to make a somewhat similar remark a few days later, after Bill and I got to know each other better. It was another of those odd, unrelated things that somehow began to break into my consciousness without any connection with my ongoing life. For a brief interval I seemed to be somewhere else, saying, as if in answer to a silent but urgent call, "Of course I'll go, Father. He's stuck and needs help. Besides, it will be only for such a little while!" The situation had something of the quality of a half-forgotten memory, and I was aware only of being in a very happy place. I had no idea to whom I was speaking, but I somehow knew I was making a definite commitment that I would not break.

Like herself, Schucman's new boss had ended up working at Columbia-Presbyterian by an unexpected route. Previously employed at the Cornell University Medical Center, Thetford had been urged by a friend to apply for the position of head of the psychology department at Presbyterian Hospital. Ambivalent about the opportunity, Thetford attempted a characteristically indirect maneuver. He requested that he also be appointed an associate professor, thinking that his presumption would make him an undesirable candidate. But his request was eventually granted, and Thetford joined Columbia-Presbyterian in February 1958.

When Helen Schucman met Thetford a few months later, she thought he looked haggard and in need of supportive company. But she found her new position "ghastly," and they were both extremely uncomfortable working in a highly competitive academic and medical environment. Over the next seven years Schucman felt that things got worse instead of better. She described their professional predicament this way:

> Bill was apt to withdraw when he perceived a situation as demanding or coercive, which he frequently did. . . . He rarely attacked openly when he was angry or irritated, which he frequently was, but was much more likely to become increasingly aloof and unresponsive, and then openly angry. I, on the other hand, tended to become over-involved and then to feel hopelessly trapped and resentful. . . . Bill and I seemed to be trapped in a relationship which, although we hated it in many ways, could not be escaped.

In retrospect, these unlikely partners would conclude that their relationship could not be escaped because it was there to serve a purpose other than their worldly profession. When Thetford finally made his "There must be another way" speech to Schucman in June 1965—admitting later that every word of it felt trite and sentimental—Schucman unexpectedly found herself filled with the conviction that he was right, and that she would join him wholeheartedly in the attempt to look at their personal and professional difficulties in a new light and to pursue cooperation over competition.

Ultimately the better way to which these two committed themselves reaped greater benefits between them and their colleagues than between the two of them. But almost immediately Schucman began to experience frequent episodes of what Thetford later described as "heightened visual imagery."[1] Since childhood Schucman had always seen clear mental pictures, like black-and-white snapshots, whenever she closed her eyes: "The pictures could be of anything; a woman with a dog, trees in the rain, a shoestore window, a birthday cake with lighted candles, a flight of stairs down the side of a cliff."[2]

Between June and September 1965, however, these mental pictures took on new qualities of color, motion, and sometimes plot. They were essentially dreams, except that Schucman did not have to be asleep to see them. Some occurred during Schucman's early attempts to meditate, a discipline that Thetford was reading about at the time. Irritated by his enthusiasm, Schucman "did not feel that our agreement to try a new approach to problems justified entering into 'crackpot' areas." Nonetheless, she consented to meditating with Thetford for a short period each day, and to doing it on her own in the morning and just before bed.

The waking dreams that Schucman experienced during these and other periods of repose constituted a progressive recognition of an inner metaphorical and spiritual life—a life in which she often appeared to be some kind of priestess from ancient times, as well as other figures in a variety of historical periods. Thetford sometimes appeared in them as well.

In a significant series of dreamlike images, Schucman found herself floating down a stream in a small boat, deciding to use a grappling hook to recover what she knew must be "buried treasure" on the stream bed. She pulled up a large chest, which to her disappointment contained neither jewels nor coins, but only a large black manuscript binder with the word "Aesculapius" (the Greek god of healing) on the spine. Only much later, well after transcription of the Course had begun, did Schucman and Thetford realize that the dream book resembled the binders in which they secured the transcription of Schucman's dictation from the Voice.

Along with the dreams also came a number of psychic experiences. Schucman once found herself certain that a distant friend of Bill Thetford was considering suicide, and tried to mentally send him the message that "the answer is life, not death." That evening Thetford called the man and learned that he had indeed been so severely depressed that afternoon that he had picked up a gun and considered shooting himself. But some feeling he couldn't describe had changed his mind.

At another time Schucman became convinced that she and Thetford would see a church—whose details she could precisely describe from an inner vision—when they went to visit the Mayo Clinic in Rochester, Minnesota. But the church was not in the area near the clinic where she had expected it. Finding it became so "outrageously important" to Schucman that she and Thetford hunted down twenty-four churches in the town before giving up. On their way out of town, Thetford picked up a historical guidebook at the airport that showed a picture of Schucman's church; it had been torn down years before to accommodate the Mayo Clinic.

What Schucman later called this "magic phase" of waking dreams and psychic intuitions essentially ended with the vision in which she saw the words "GOD IS" on an ancient scroll and accepted that message as "all I want." Shortly thereafter, the dictation of *A Course in Miracles* would begin.

A Forceful Helper

The plentiful stories of Helen Schucman's phobias, mystical experiences, and religious ambivalence could suggest a portrait of a dotty, anxiety-plagued woman who achieved little of substance in her life besides the scribing of an esoteric spiritual manuscript. In fact, she was an accomplished academic who held down a demanding position in a high-pressure atmosphere for most of twenty years, progressing from the rank of assistant to associate professor and impressing many with her intellect and her direct, sometimes forceful advice to friends and associates. Never desiring children of her own, she nonetheless developed a special fondness for the severely retarded children with whom she worked for years at a New York clinic. And she was unarguably devoted, sometimes to the point of possessiveness, to the new "family" of spiritual intimates delivered to her by ACIM.

Judy Skutch was one recipient of Schucman's focused attention. "I have to preface everything about Helen by saying that she was the greatest teacher I have ever known," declares Skutch. "And I was forty-four when I met her, and had a lot of life experience as well as a good bit of schooling and graduate work." Still, Skutch admits, Schucman "was not an easy teacher. She didn't mince words. She went right to the heart of things, sometimes so fast that it took your breath away. You felt as if someone had thrown a basketball hard in your stomach, because the wind had been knocked out of you by something she said, and she was right.

"This didn't make her the easiest person in the world to be with. But that forcefulness was tempered with loving advice, discussions about family members, shopping trips together, that kind of thing. I was clearly a junior, and she was an elder; I called her Mama and she called me Kitten."

Skutch recalls that Schucman did not try to influence her personal decisions except as they pertained to the Course. Although clearly relieved and appreciative that Skutch was assuming the public-relations duties associated with publication of the Course, Schucman was nonetheless "a little apprehensive about the Course being brought into a community interested in psychism, because Helen did not feel that was what the Course was about. I think my having taught at NYU gave me the right credentials, in Helen's mind, for bringing the Course to public awareness.

"She was very concerned about my appearance as a Course representative," Skutch continues. "There was still some hippie stuff going on in the seventies, and although I was really too old for it, I still liked it. But this was not a style Helen liked on me, and she asked me not to wear it when I spoke about the Course. She also didn't like high heels; she thought they were unsafe and too suggestive in a sexual way. One day she said we were going shopping for new shoes, and she made me buy a pair of shoes exactly like hers: totally flat with round toes and crêpe soles, the Mary Jane style. Personally I wouldn't have been caught dead in shoes like that, but she insisted this was a better style for me."

Like the other Course principals, Skutch saw two Helen Schucmans: "There was the Helen who was fearful, contracted, controlling, suspicious, judgmental, and at times irrational. That was the Helen I felt uncomfortable with, because I never knew where I was at with her. And then there was the Helen who handed me *A Course in Miracles*, who took it down in as pure a form as possible, and gave it to me to give to the world. That was the Helen whom I revered, and my real teacher.

"The fact that there were those two Helens reminded me that I am equally split," Skutch reflects. "There's the personality that I consider myself to be—the ego—and there's the higher consciousness that I consider my Self. Helen allowed me to see which one was taking charge at different times."

It should also be noted that many people outside Helen Schucman's intimate circle saw only her helping aspect, whether they were Course students or not. Course teacher Jon Mundy, who met Schucman about a month before Judy Skutch, received "a lot of personal counseling from Helen, and I always found her very helpful, very intuitive. I don't think I was close enough to experience her difficult side."

In telephone conversations and a few face-to-face encounters, Schucman counseled Mundy on subjects ranging from whether he should break up with a girlfriend—"she said, 'I think you'd better let her go,' which was something I didn't want to hear at the time but it soon proved to be right on target"—to whether he should break with the Methodist church, where he served as a minister for fourteen years. "Every time I was ready to chuck the whole thing, Helen thought it was important that I stay." (Mundy did eventually break with the Methodists to start his own eclectic ministry, and he became a popular speaker at spiritual conferences.)

Finally, there were many people—relatives, parents of developmentally disabled children, academic colleagues—who turned to Helen Schucman for advice and never heard of ACIM. In fact, it appears that the majority of people who directly encountered her in her professional and daily life in New York City did not know of the monumental task that she ambivalently referred to as her true "life's work." As Ken Wapnick has observed:

> To practically all who knew her, then, Helen was a brilliant research psychologist, witty conversationalist, a friend eager to be of professional help to those in distress, a woman immaculate in appearance and prone to excessive shopping (with a weakness for jewelry and shoes), and a somewhat neurotic person preoccupied with sickness and the threat of inclement weather; but hardly one whose internal life centered on religious concerns that directly involved Jesus: a well-kept secret indeed.[3]

Bill Thetford, the Shy Professor

Born in 1923, William Thetford was the last of three children in a middle-class Chicago family traumatized by tragic losses. A brother died in infancy, and when Thetford was nine, his eleven-year-old sister contracted streptococcus. Although his parents were Christian Scientists, they consulted both medical doctors and church practitioners for their daughter, to no avail. After her death Thetford's parents renounced their religion and became socially withdrawn, curtailing their son's religious experience in childhood. His parents were still grieving their daughter's death when Thetford himself contracted a severe case of scarlet fever, soon compounded with rheumatic fever. In recovery he suffered a cardiac infarction, and his survival looked doubtful.

Several months of intensive care preserved the young boy's life, but for the next two years he was not able to rise from bed. Missing three years of schooling altogether, he was tutored by his mother in arithmetic and spent most of his time reading voraciously. Although he returned to school as a fourth-grader, he was moved ahead and graduated from the eighth grade within two years, and he later finished high school with honors. He majored uncertainly in psychology at DePauw University in Indiana, also enrolling in premed in case that proved to be a more definitive career opportunity. Deferred from military service because of the effects of his childhood illness, Thetford graduated from DePauw in 1944 with an acceptance of his application to the University of Chicago Medical School in hand, although he was still uncertain about his future vocation.

At that point a pattern of accelerated opportunities began to take shape in Thetford's life. Because World War II had created a shortage of talented manpower in many professional areas, Thetford's first college job carried considerable responsibility. He was placed on the University of Chicago's faculty payroll as an administrative officer overseeing buildings that served as testing areas for top-secret atomic research. At one point Thetford was in charge of a decontamination team that tried to "clean" radioactive areas, and he wore a Geiger counter at work from morning until night. Excited by the strategic urgency of this work and still ambivalent about his prospective career, he decided not to pursue medical school in the fall of 1944, remaining in his position with the atomic research project.

But with the dropping of the first atomic bomb on Hiroshima in August 1945, Thetford's sympathies reversed abruptly. "I think all of us were aghast at the extent of the devastation," he wrote, "and I felt clearly that my participation on the project had come to an end. Since I no longer felt a moral commitment to continue, I resigned that same month."[4]

A few weeks later Thetford took the suggestion of some friends in graduate school to sign up for a course on "Client-Centered Psychotherapy" being offered by a new professor on campus, Dr. Carl Rogers. "For reasons which are as obscure to me now as they were then,"[5] as Thetford later wrote, Rogers quickly appointed Thetford as an instructor in the course and also asked him to become a research assistant at a new counseling center. Thetford protested that he was unqualified, but Rogers insisted that he accept these roles in the study and development of a new psychotherapy founded on the premise of "unconditional positive regard." As Thetford recalled, "[F]or me to have gone directly from being involved with total annihilation to a professional practice based on perfect love seemed, to say the least, ironic."[6]

At any rate, after receiving his PhD in psychology in 1949, still feeling "thoroughly unqualified for practically anything," Thetford took a position with the Michael Reese Hospital in Chicago, working on a project under the direction of Dr. Samuel J. Beck, the leading authority on Rorschach testing. It was during his two and a half years there that Thetford developed the conviction that he should never be a university professor, despite several academic job offers, because "I felt I had nothing to profess, and was unwilling to put myself in a position where this might become apparent to others."[7]

Thetford later enrolled at a school of psychiatry in Washington, D.C., that emphasized the importance of interpersonal relations in therapy. This was followed in 1954 by a directorship at a psychiatric institute in Hartford, Connecticut, and then an appointment as chief psychologist under Harold G. Wolff, a leading specialist in psychosomatic medicine, at Cornell University. Thetford's antipathy to the academic life had eased by this time, and "before I knew it I became an instructor and a year later I was promoted to assistant professor."[8] About a year later, in 1957, Thetford would ambivalently but successfully pursue the position at Columbia University that would lead to the intersection of his life with Helen Schucman's.

The CIA Connection

Thetford's early experience with top-secret government security may have facilitated connections with the intelligence community that would persist throughout his academic career. One professional vita lists him as a "Government Psychologist" from 1951 to 1954, including one year (1953) serving as a consultant to the Foreign Service Institute in Beirut, Lebanon.[9] According to William Whitson of the Foundation for Inner Peace, Thetford was actually in the employ of the Central Intelligence Agency during this period, working as a researcher in the field of personality assessment. Thetford apparently also did a short stint as a CIA field agent; Whitson says that his single mission involved the debriefing of a Christian missionary's daughter who had been held captive by the Chinese government.

Years later, during and after the scribing of the Course, Thetford and Schucman would jointly write several papers covertly subsidized by CIA-funded research groups (which used a variety of cover names, including the "Human Ecology Fund"). These groups all related in some way to the CIA's interest at the time in assessing human behavior. Many other university psychologists in the fifties and sixties were likewise funded for research, including Carl Rogers. As Rogers told investigative reporter John Marks in his 1979 exposé *The Search for the Manchurian Candidate: The CIA and Mind Control* (Norton), "We really did regard Russia as the enemy, and we were trying to do various things to make sure the Russians did not get the upper hand."

Some of this academic research may have been later exploited by the CIA for operational purposes, especially the development of mind control technologies. At any rate, the interests of Schucman and Thetford were research-oriented, and there is no evidence to suggest that they had any direct involvement in the CIA's failed attempts to exploit mind control or so-called "brainwashing."

Nonetheless, the public record of Thetford's intelligence connections has contributed to conspiracy theories on the Internet, including such claims as "professional publication data and other material links show the channeling of *A Course in Miracles* to be covered with the fingerprints of the CIA's mind control program, MKULTRA."[10] Although Whitson—who has extensively researched Thetford's intelligence connections—calls these charges spurious, he does recall Thetford joking that the typewriter used to convert Helen Schucman's shorthand notes for the Course into manuscript was paid for by the CIA. Apart from that ironic and unverifiable detail, it is difficult to see the strategic value of the content of the Course to government security interests.

Thetford's Role in Recording ACIM

Whether one views it as happenstance or predestined preparation, several major elements of Thetford's character made him suitable to become Schucman's helper in the recording of the Course. Perhaps most significant was his reluctance to "profess" a distinct philosophy of his own. It's safe to assume that few other academics of his status could have resisted the temptation to revise, add to, or even co-opt a major project on which they were assisting a junior colleague, regardless of the project's nature or origin.

Second, Thetford's intellectual curiosity and flexibility would counterbalance Schucman's judgmental tendency and help both of them deal with a system of psychospiritual thought that substantially challenged their psychoanalytic training. Thetford's brush with humanistic psychology may have also prepared him for the transpersonal dimensions of the Course material.

Finally, the younger professor's passivity is probably what made it possible for him to tolerate Helen Schucman's contrariness, albeit not happily. It remains a sad irony that the tenuous balance of the relationship between the two Course recorders never matured into a healthy reciprocity. In 1977, the year following publication of ACIM, Schucman was forced to retire from Columbia-Presbyterian at age sixty-eight, having managed to remain on staff two years past retirement age. In 1978 Thetford took an early retirement and moved to California along with Bob and Judy Skutch and the Foundation for Inner Peace. Although they spoke often by phone and occasionally saw each other, Thetford and Schucman essentially parted ways without directly resolving the many difficult issues of their professional relationship of almost twenty years.

In California, where he often said he was practicing forgiveness full time, Thetford became a dedicated student of the Course in various venues while steadfastly refusing to become identified as a teacher or spokesman.

Schucman progressively withdrew from both Course-related activities and society in general until the terminal illness that struck her in 1980, leading to her almost complete isolation before she died the following year.

Frances Vaughan, a leading figure in transpersonal psychology (see chapter 8), got to know Bill Thetford well after he moved to Tiburon, a peaceful and affluent bayside town in Marin County that was then home to the Foundation for Inner Peace. Meeting with Thetford in a small Course study group every day for two years, and then twice a week for several years thereafter, Vaughan was always impressed with his sincerity, self-effacing quality, and serious commitment to personal change through the application of Course principles.

"Bill felt that the Course was a sacred trust that he and Helen had been charged with," Vaughan recalls. "He really did commit himself to using it, whereas Helen always maintained a certain resistance. Bill was able to transform all the other relationships he'd had at Columbia that had been so problematic, and by the time he retired he felt that he had made peace with those people."

Vaughan credits Thetford with teaching her "to take my judgments more lightly, because I was prone to get upset when I thought somebody was distorting or misinterpreting the Course. He accepted that everybody has a different perception of the Course, and that's okay because we can't know how the teaching will affect people working with it in different ways."

Indeed, during the last two years of his life spent in La Jolla near San Diego in Southern California, Thetford became affiliated with a social set of Course students whom his New York academic colleagues doubtlessly would have perceived as New Age and "touchy-feely." Although Ken Wapnick has written that the Bill Thetford of northern California was always "a slight shock" for him to see—"Bill in sneakers and blue jeans, he who while in New York was almost never without a jacket and tie"[11]—the Bill Thetford of Southern California loosened up even further. In a lengthy interview published in *Miracles Magazine* (no longer published), La Jolla Course teachers Jack and Eulalia Luckett recalled how Thetford learned to accept group hugs, try hands-on healing, enjoy singing in a group, and even wear a silly party hat at a birthday party he had initially refused to allow for himself.

"Nobody in Tiburon had ever seen this face of Billy . . ." Jack Luckett remarked. "Jerry [Jampolsky] would call every now and then, or he would come down, and would see the growth in Bill. And he would thank everybody, for he could see the opening up, the blossoming . . . the comfort Bill had with himself." Luckett also recalled that Thetford allowed he was getting "too old not to be flexible," and in a demonstration of his lifelong love of puns, thereafter referred to himself often as "flexi-Bill."

"I always appreciated Bill's sense of humor," Frances Vaughan recalls, "and his lack of pretension about being forgiving or even particularly good. He was shy, a very private person and contemplative by nature. He could live a very monklike existence and be at peace with that."

Although Thetford was reportedly often depressed and there are indications that his intimate life was quite troubled at times, his private nature seems to have limited how much was known by others about his personal struggles. It is known that he lived with a male lover in New York for ten years, and with a woman in northern California for four; one close observer opines that Thetford was "mentally straight but biologically gay." What seems most likely is that his almost overwhelming tendency toward ambivalence permeated every aspect of his life. Frances Vaughan says, for instance, that despite her long friendship with Thetford she couldn't hazard a guess about his politics—"there were aspects of life on which Bill just didn't make a statement," she recalls.

"Getting Out of Its Way"

A final contrast between the characters of Helen Schucman and Bill Thetford can be observed in the different ways they experienced their final days. Struck by pancreatic cancer in 1980, Schucman progressively withdrew from the world and became increasingly despondent and dependent on her husband, Louis; Ken Wapnick; and a devoted housekeeper. Some acquaintances were so disturbed by Schucman's deterioration that they curtailed their own visits; as Wapnick observed, "the discrepancy between the Helen they knew—impeccably groomed and socially appropriate, wise and helpful . . . and the Helen they now were experiencing—physically disheveled, preoccupied with her own disturbing thoughts, and totally unresponsive to anyone beside herself—was so glaring as to be disturbing, painful, and even frightening."[12]

In his book *A Still, Small Voice* (Ignatius Press, 1993), Father Benedict J. Groeschel, who studied under Schucman and Thetford at Columbia and first saw the Course while it was being recorded and transcribed, wrote of the

> incredible darkness that descended upon Helen Schucman in the last years of her life. This woman who had written so eloquently that suffering really did not exist spent the last two years of her life in the blackest psychotic depression I have ever witnessed. Her husband cared for her with an incredible devotion, and her friends did the best they could. But it was almost frightening to be with her. I clearly observed that the denial of the reality of suffering could have catastrophic consequences.

(Groeschel's book concludes that the Course itself is a "false revelation" and a "spiritual menace to many.")

Judy Skutch remembers a poignant encounter with Schucman in her last months that suggests her dying constituted a process of spiritual surrender she had steadfastly resisted all of her life. "I was sitting with Helen one day when she seemed completely removed from the world. She was making repetitive motions and drumming her fingers on the couch, not interacting with me at all even though I was holding her hand. I was beginning to feel useless, wondering if I should leave, when she suddenly turned to me and said, 'Do you know why I'm dying?' I said, 'No, Mama, I don't.' Then she looked me straight in the eye as if to say, *stupid girl*, but instead she said, very forcefully, 'To get out of its way,' and then she retreated inside herself again. That was one of the last things she ever said to me."

Schucman was probably referring to a conversation with Ken Wapnick from a few days earlier, when he remembers suggesting to Schucman that in the process of dying her ego-self would finally get out of the way of the Course's message. On her last night, Wapnick and Louis Schucman left the hospital when Helen's condition, now obviously terminal, seemed to be stabilizing; three hours later they received a call that she had died. As Wapnick writes in *Absence from Felicity,*

We returned to the hospital, and Helen was still in her bed. Her face had a remarkably quiet expression of peace, so different from the tortured disquiet we had grown so accustomed to seeing those many months. I suddenly recalled what Helen had shared with me on several occasions, a thought that always brought her great comfort. Jesus had told her that when she died, he would come for her personally. Who can really know what was in her mind in those closing instants? Yet, her peaceful face was unmistakable, and spoke convincingly for an experience of knowing, at the very end, that her beloved Jesus had indeed kept his promise, as she had kept hers. The priestess had returned home.

Seven years later, in the summer of 1988, Bill Thetford was staying at the Tiburon home of Judy Skutch and Bill Whitson while visiting northern California. The playfulness of his La Jolla lifestyle was in evidence on the day before a July Fourth party that Judy Skutch was planning for thirty people; she was startled to see Thetford dance a little jig in the living room, exclaiming, "I'm free, I'm finally free. I'm flexible!"

Worried that he might be having some kind of manic episode, Skutch asked him what he meant. "He looked me in the eyes," Skutch recalls, "put his hands on my shoulders and said, 'I am not holding any grievances.' I said, 'Oh, come on,' and then I asked him about several problematic people from his past. He had a specific answer for every one, that he'd written to so-and-so, and gone to meet someone else, and extended his love and forgiveness to everyone.

"Then I said, 'And what about Helen?' He laughed and said, 'How could I not forgive Helen? She was the opportunity for me to learn forgiveness.' Although Bill had a great sense of humor, I don't think he was trying to be funny. I thought he said this with real joy."

The next morning Skutch asked Thetford if he still felt so ebullient. "He said, 'Sure, it's freedom day. It's my freedom day.' And I said, 'Well, I'm glad it's still working,' because I was a little suspicious of all this." When she asked him if he wanted to come along with her to the grocery store, Thetford said he would walk and catch up with her.

"I must have made a face," Skutch recalls. "I guess he could see I was worried about having to wait for him, because he said, 'Don't worry, dear, if

I'm not there in time you go home without me.' Well, a chill went through me and I put my arms around him and said, 'I'll *never* go home without you.' He just patted me on the head and smiled, and off he went." Skutch then gathered her shopping list, purse, and keys, and went to her car. She had driven a short distance down the driveway when she saw Thetford collapsed there, dead from a heart attack.

The dramatic difference in how Helen Schucman and Bill Thetford each was able to make use of the spiritual teaching they brought into the world emphasizes yet another of that teaching's paradoxes. Although it consistently urges a surrender of ego-driven perception and motivations upon its students—promising that the ego's voice will be replaced by the beneficent guidance of a mystical agency called the Holy Spirit—*A Course in Miracles* also stresses that surrender cannot be forced upon anyone. "The power of decision is my own," the Course suggests in Workbook Lesson 152—a principle that could not be more clearly demonstrated than by the example of Helen Schucman.

Bill Thetford and Helen Schucman in 1976.

In his foreword to *Journey Without Distance*, the late Willis Harman, who served as the first president of the Institute of Noetic Sciences, told yet another story of Schucman's deliberate resistance to the spiritual teaching she gave the world.

Helen hardly seemed to embody the inner peace that the Course puts forth as its goal. She found much to complain about, and her life seemed to contain more than the usual amount of pain. I once asked her how it happened that this remarkable document she had been responsible for had brought wisdom and peace to so many, and yet it was seemingly ineffective for her. I will never forget her reply. "I know the Course is true, Bill," she said—and then after a pause, "but I don't believe it."

✍ ENDNOTES ✍

1. From Bridget Winter, *The Story of* A Course in Miracles (Tiburon, CA: Foundation for Inner Peace, 1987) film documentary.
2. Helen Schucman, from an unpublished autobiography.
3. Kenneth Wapnick, *Absence from Felicity: The Story of Helen Schucman and Her Scribing of* A Course in Miracles (Roscoe, NY: Foundation for *A Course in Miracles*, 1991).
4. From a written record excerpted in Robert Skutch's *Journey Without Distance* (Berkeley, CA: Celestial Arts, 1984).
5. Ibid.
6. Ibid.
7. Ibid.
8. Ibid.
9. See www.miraclestudies.net/BillVita.html.
10. See www.urantiagate.com/conspiracy/fleas.html.
11. From Wapnick, *Absence from Felicity*.
12. Ibid.

CHAPTER 3

How the Course Teaching Has Spread

Of all the distinctions that set *A Course in Miracles* apart from other spiritual teachings, one of the most noteworthy is its *timing*. Most teachings of similar depth and complexity, whether mainstream or esoteric, originated hundreds if not several thousand years in the past. Major teachings such as Christianity, Buddhism, and Islam originated with sole prophets whose messages were later written down, revised, and translated. Virtually every spiritual tradition was initially shepherded by a small band of followers, taking many decades or even centuries to evolve into forms that would earn the devotion of large numbers of people.

But the Course sprang into being, complete and self-contained, in the middle of the latter half of the twentieth century—just as mass worldwide communications were increasingly achieving the speed of light. Even before the Course was published as a book, many people gained access to its message through photocopies, a modern complement to the "word of mouth" by which ancient traditions were first disseminated. In the twenty-first century, the Course is disseminated and discussed over the worldwide electronic network known as the Internet—for which there is no historical analogue unless one gives a lot of credence to long-distance telepathy.

Another significant factor in the rapid spread of the Course is its *accessibility*. Unlike most religious teachings, the Course has no central orthodoxy controlling who can become its students, requiring any sort of initiation or church attendance, collecting dues or requesting tithes, keeping an eye on the faith of followers, or issuing rules for their comportment. Anyone can buy the book and study it, in whole or in part, alone or with company, as one wishes. Students can also drop it or speak ill of it without fear of excommunication or retaliation by any religious authority.

On the other hand, anyone can decide to start teaching the Course without certified training or official approval. As the Manual for Teachers asserts,

> *A teacher of God is anyone who chooses to be one. His qualifications consist solely in this; somehow, somewhere he has made a deliberate choice in which he did not see his interests as apart from someone else's. Once he has done that, his road is established and his direction is sure. A light has entered the darkness. It may be a single light, but that is enough. He has entered an agreement with God even if he does not yet believe in Him. He has become a bringer of salvation. He has become a teacher of God.* (MANUAL, 1, 1)

However, the Manual also specifies that teachers of the Course curriculum must have finished the Workbook exercises (MANUAL, 16, 3). Because the dictation of these lessons to Helen Schucman was preceded chronologically by the Text, completion of the entire Course would seem to be an implied and reasonable requirement for its instructors. But there is no one anointed or appointed to verify anyone's qualifications.

The net result is a free-for-all in the style and quality of teachers, study groups, schools, and service organizations inspired by the Course. A friend of mine was surprised to learn I was writing a book on ACIM because he had once encountered a study group that convinced him all Course students were "total flakes." I've encountered a wide disparity in the quality of Course groups myself. The first one I attended, for a period of about six weeks early in my personal study, was both intellectually challenging and emotionally supportive. Later I dropped in on a group monopolized

by an organizer who seemed content merely to read the Course in a dron-
ing voice, without comment or questioning from anyone else, for at least
forty-five minutes at a stretch. (I did not return for a second experience.)
While researching the revision of this book in 2007, I participated in a Text
reading and discussion group in northern California that operated very
democratically and occasionally verged on group therapy.

Established teaching programs range from the collegiate environment of
the Foundation for *A Course in Miracles* (FACIM) in Temecula, California,
to the church and ministerial school called the Community Miracles Center in San Francisco, to the controversial residential institute in Wisconsin
called Endeavor Academy. (See appendix I for a directory of the oldest and
largest Course groups and teaching centers.) A number of Course teachers
support themselves in whole or in part by lecturing and leading groups on
their own. In fact, one of the surprising aspects of the Course story is how
many careers (scores, if not hundreds) have been spawned and supported
by a spiritual teaching still too young to be called a tradition.

At this writing (mid-2007) there are nearly two thousand Course study
groups in fifty-seven countries worldwide, according to information provided online by Miracle Distribution Center, an ACIM teaching center and
information clearinghouse based in Anaheim, California. In the United
States, groups can be found in all fifty states plus Puerto Rico and the Virgin
Islands. There are ninety-three groups in the Netherlands, sixty-five in England, fifty-one in Argentina, forty-six in Australia, thirteen in South Africa,
and one each in such countries as Japan, Croatia, Pakistan, and the West In-
dies. Most are English-speaking, but the number of foreign-language groups
is growing with the spread of the various Course translations.

In the United States, Course students seem to come from all classes,
races, lifestyles, and prior religious backgrounds, although I've long observed that there seems to be a predominance of middle-class Caucasians.
In my attendance of Course conferences held in the United States in recent
years, I've also noted that most Course students tend to be in their mid-
forties or older. During my research I've encountered students who are or
have been Jewish, Catholic, Episcopalian, Mormon, Christian Scientist,
mainline Protestant, Christian fundamentalist, American Buddhist, Islamic, agnostic, and atheist. Because of the autonomy of ACIM study groups

and the unknown number of students following the Course privately, reliable statistics on age, race, religious affiliations, and other demographic factors are impossible to come by.

A Perennial Best Seller

After photocopied versions of the Course were supplanted by a quality hardcover edition in 1976, the first-year sales were modest, about five thousand copies. In 1977 *Psychic* magazine editor James Bolen changed his publication's name to *New Realities*, partly to overcome Helen Schucman's resistance to a story about the Course appearing therein. The first issue featured an interview with Judy Skutch, and helped boost second-year sales of the Course to 7,500.

In 1980 a largely hostile story on the Course appeared in *Psychology Today* (see chapter 2), but helped sales nonetheless. Publisher Judy Skutch says that's when she realized that "it didn't matter what anybody said about the Course as long as they spelled the name right. People were just drawn to it." By 1984 sales of the Course were approaching 30,000 copies annually; with the release of the softcover edition in 1985 that figure rose to 60,000 and the Course was on its way to becoming a perennial best seller. During the mid-to late 1980s the Course and its study groups began to receive press coverage from major regional newspapers, including the *Oregonian, San Francisco Examiner, Dallas Times Herald, Anchorage Daily News, Philadelphia Inquirer, Atlanta Journal, New York Times, Guardian of London,* and *Record* of Perth, Australia.

The largest single leap in Course sales occurred after the 1992 publication of Marianne Williamson's *A Return to Love,* when sales rose from 70,000 to 105,000—an increase of 50 percent. Thereafter the numbers leveled off to about 85,000 copies annually, prior to release of the new Viking edition of the Course in the spring of 1996. Viking announced a release of 100,000 copies supported by a $75,000 publicity campaign, the first time the Course has ever been advertised directly by its publisher (Helen Schucman received guidance that the Foundation for Inner Peace was not to advertise the Course itself). But initial sales of the Viking edition were less than expected; original publisher Judy Skutch told me that the heavily advertised edition performed no better in its first year than the Foundation edition had done in years before. Over the five-year licensing period, sales of 220,000 copies were sufficient for Viking to express interest in keeping the property, but the Foundation decided to take it back and has since turned down at least one other major publisher interested in licensing ACIM. Sales of the Course rose about 5 percent soon after the 2003 publication of Gary Renard's *The Disappearance of the Universe*, which brought many new and lapsed students to ACIM. As of 2007, the Course was selling about 40,000 English copies annually. Since publication of the first edition in 1976, nearly 1.6 million copies have been distributed worldwide, with foreign editions bringing the total number of ACIM books in distribution to more than two million.

Copyrights and Coffee Mugs

For more than ten years copyright protection of ACIM was one of the hotter intramural controversies of the Course community, after the Foundation for Inner Peace (FIP) and its sister foundation the Foundation for *A Course in Miracles* (FACIM) strengthened a previously laissez-faire policy regarding excerpting of the Course and the use of its trademarked name in other publications or commercial endeavors. The tighter policy was a reaction to an increasing trend toward reprinting parts of the Course in books and other media without FIP permission or conventional citations of the source. This first became a significant issue with the publication of Marianne Williamson's best seller *A Return to Love*, in which a number of Course excerpts were quoted without citation. (FIP requested quote citations in subsequent paperback editions of *A Return to Love*, and the author and her publisher, HarperCollins, cooperated.)

The new restrictions were not well received by major Course groups, teachers, and writers, most of whom felt it amounted to an attempt by the Foundations to control how the Course was disseminated and taught. For their part, both FACIM and FIP maintained that they acted only to maintain the identity and integrity of the Course in the face of increasing usage of its ideas, name, and text without proper acknowledgment. They also asserted that copyright protection of the Course was always part of Helen

Schucman's guidance about how the teaching was to be presented to the world—although it is clear that their sense of how to apply that guidance changed over the years.

For instance, in 1989 FIP president and Course publisher Judy Skutch told me that "we were guided to give the copyright freely without questioning or judgment. If people want to make Miracles coffee mugs, they can." While I was researching the first edition of this book in 1995, FACIM president Ken Wapnick explained to me that a new, stricter copyright policy included trademarking of the title *A Course in Miracles* and the acronym ACIM because both were increasingly being used to promote commercial ventures neither affiliated with nor approved by FIP. "We don't want people making Miracles coffee mugs," remarked Wapnick.

With the assumption of Course publishing duties by Viking Penguin, the issue of copyright protection intensified. In 1996 Penguin Books USA filed an infringement suit against the New Christian Church of Full Endeavor (commonly called Endeavor Academy) in Baraboo, Wisconsin, for their publication and distribution of a number of booklets that reprinted portions of ACIM without permission or acknowledgment of the copyright, which by then was assigned to Penguin by its licensing arrangement with the Foundation for Inner Peace. Endeavor answered with a motion to dismiss the suit based on a thirteen-point challenge to the original 1975 copyright in the name of Helen Schucman and FIP. While this case slowly wound to a conclusion, the Foundations were involved in other litigation involving Course groups, including the Circle of Atonement in Sedona, Arizona, and individual students and teachers who were attempting to make the Course freely available online or making other uses of the material without approval.

Finally, in 2004, the copyright controversy effectively ended when federal district judge Robert W. Sweet of the Southern District of New York ruled that the copyright should be voided on the basis of one of the challenges raised by Endeavor Academy: that distribution of photocopies of an early draft of the Course (the so-called Criswell edition), which may not have all borne a copyright, had essentially placed it in the public domain. In 2005 the trademarks were lifted as well, and the Course became freely available online.[1] New editions of ACIM began to appear in print, including one published by Endeavor Academy, and the so-called "Original Edition" published by the Course in Miracles Society of Omaha, Nebraska. This edition comprises an earlier draft of the standard Course, in which there are some noticeable differences in the first five chapters of the Text. (For a comparison of early drafts to the standard edition published by the Foundation for Inner Peace, see Richard Smoley's analysis "A Comparison of Miracles" in appendix II.)

Jerry Jampolsky and Attitudinal Healing

Public awareness of the Course has spiked dramatically at several points in its history after the publication of books that presented its basic message in simpler and shorter forms. The first of these was *Love Is Letting Go of Fear* (Celestial Arts) by psychiatrist Jerry Jampolsky, which sold several million copies after its 1979 release, followed by two other successful titles, *Goodbye to Guilt* (Bantam) and *Teach Only Love* (Bantam). Jampolsky had encountered the Course in 1975 when a manuscript copy was handed to him by Judy Skutch. At the time he considered himself an atheist and was struggling to maintain his psychiatric practice in the midst of his own deep depressions.

"In a very snobbish way I said I'd look at one page, but that was it," Jampolsky told me. "So I read one page, and for the first time in my life I heard an inner voice saying, 'Physician, heal thyself. This is your way home.' I've never been able to articulate this exactly, but I had a feeling of oneness with all the world, and oneness with God. I knew my whole life was going to be different."

Several months after beginning his study of ACIM, Jampolsky met Helen Schucman and Bill Thetford and was "convinced of their integrity and ordinariness," solidifying his faith in the Course teaching. Soon afterward, Jampolsky was consulting at the University of California Medical Center in San Francisco when he observed a young child with terminal cancer asking a doctor what it was like to die. Instead of answering, the physician changed the subject. Jampolsky soon "received guidance to start a center that would be based on the healing principles of *A Course in Miracles*, but in such a way as not to use any religious language. We would start with children who were dying. My guidance was that these children were very wise spirits who could help each other and everyone who volunteered to help them."

Thus was born the first Center for Attitudinal Healing in Tiburon, California, which would spawn a worldwide network of more than 130 centers providing support to people facing a wide array of physical, social, and cultural crises. For instance, the Attitudinal Healing Center of Oakland, California, caters its services to the needs and challenges of inner-city youth, including an "ArtEsteem" program that "uses the arts for expression, self-esteem, community building, and academic and emotional literacy."[2]

In a sense, the Centers could be regarded as the first and most widespread "missionary work" inspired by *A Course in Miracles*, contradicting a common criticism that its philosophy encourages students to withdraw from worldly concerns or deny the most unpleasant facts of life. The twelve principles of Attitudinal Healing, providing the framework and philosophy by which Center groups operate, are expressed more simply than the Course itself but are unmistakably rooted in its teaching:

Attitudinal Healing Principles

1. The essence of our being is love.
2. Health is inner peace. Healing is letting go of fear.
3. Giving and receiving are the same.
4. We can let go of the past and the future.
5. Now is the only time there is and each instant is for giving.
6. We can learn to love ourselves and others by forgiving rather than judging.
7. We can become love finders rather than fault finders.
8. We can choose and direct ourselves to be peaceful inside regardless of what is happening outside.
9. We are students and teachers to each other.
10. We can focus on the whole of life rather than the fragments.
11. Since love is eternal, death need not be viewed as fearful.
12. We can always perceive ourselves and others as either extending love or giving a call for help.

In another important sense, however, Attitudinal Healing is not a missionary extension of the Course, because ACIM is neither promoted nor offered to people who attend AH workshops and programs. People who wish to found centers in their own locales are not expected to be familiar with the Course, although adherence to the principles of Attitudinal Healing is required and training for facilitators is offered.

Now in his eighties, Jerry Jampolsky continues to travel and lecture on Attitudinal Healing along with his wife, Diane Cirincione, PhD. In 1995 he was the recipient of the prestigious Pride in Profession Award granted by the American Medical Association for promoting the art and science of medicine.

Marianne Williamson: A Provocative Prophet

The popularity and public recognition of *A Course in Miracles* peaked in the mid-1990s following the release of *A Return to Love* (St. Martin's Press, 1992), a mixture of autobiography and personal reflections on the Course by a former cabaret singer and self-styled New Age minister named Marianne Williamson. The daughter of liberal, middle-class Jewish parents in Houston, Texas, Williamson has said that she was "raised to raise hell whenever hell needed to be raised."[3] After leaving Pomona College in 1972, Williamson wandered the country following romances, temporary jobs, and doomed plans for the future. "There are a lot of things from those years I can't remember," she confessed in *Return*. "Like a lot of people at that time—late sixties, early seventies—I was pretty wild."

By 1977 Williamson was living in New York City for the second time, working temp jobs to finance her fledgling career as a cabaret singer. Some listeners thought she wasn't bad, others thought she should hold on to her day job, and still others enjoyed her patter between numbers more than the songs themselves. Williamson first saw the Course that year, but was initially put off by its Christian language. Her serious study began in 1978 when she was feeling depressed because of trouble with bronchitis, which was making it difficult to sing. Soon she volunteered her services at the Foundation for Inner Peace when it was still in New York, working there for three months and later helping out for a few weeks at FIP's new home in Tiburon, California. Following a pattern not uncommon among serious students of the Course, Williamson's life became much more difficult as her study intensified, leading her into a "dark night of the soul" spanning several years after she moved back to Houston in 1979.

After the failures of a brief marriage and an attempt to run a bookstore/coffeehouse with an ambitious cultural arts program, Williamson approached a spiritual surrender, a "grandiose, dramatic moment where I invited God into my life . . ." As she reported in *Return*:

> After that, nothing felt the way I expected it to. I had thought that things would improve. It's as though my life was a house, and I thought God would give it a wonderful paint job—new shutters, perhaps, a pretty portico, a new roof. Instead, it felt as though, as soon as I gave the house to God, He hit it with a giant wrecking ball. "Sorry, honey," He seemed to say, "There were cracks in the foundation, not to mention all the rats in the bedroom. I thought we better just start all over."

By 1983 Williamson was indeed starting over, driving her mother's Oldsmobile to Los Angeles to take a secretarial job with the Philosophical Research Society. She soon became the group's weekly lecturer on ACIM. Although her fast-paced, funny, sometimes strident presentations quickly outgrew the limitations of the Society, it would be a couple of years before she was making a living from public speaking. By 1986 she was speaking to full houses in both Los Angeles and New York. Her Course-inspired but multifaceted philosophy seemed to hit a particular chord with gay men facing the specter of the AIDS epidemic, leading to the inspiration for the Center for Living—a combination hospice and cultural center for people facing catastrophic illness—that she helped found in Los Angeles and later in New York.

Williamson's enthusiastic public speaking and ambitious social activism built the foundation for the seemingly instant fame that followed the publication of *A Return to Love* in 1992. America's most popular daytime talk-show host, Oprah Winfrey, invited Williamson on to her show and announced that she had bought copies of the book for everyone in the studio audience. This endorsement sparked a bookselling frenzy, moving 750,000 copies of the HarperCollins title in just a few weeks. Soon Williamson seemed to be showing up everywhere, from *Larry King Live* on CNN to the tabloid press. In early 1995 there was a flurry of press attention about the invitation extended to Williamson and several other human potential speakers to confer with President Bill Clinton at Camp David; it was also revealed that Williamson had lunched a number of times with First Lady Hillary Clinton. One rumor had it that Williamson tried her hand at presidential speechwriting, prompting disclaimers from the White House.

In general Williamson's fame eclipsed that of the Course itself, sometimes creating a chicken-and-egg confusion about her relationship to it. Soon after appearing on a Larry King television special devoted to the subject of miracles—in which she hastened to correct King's offhand reference to "her course in miracles"—Williamson told me, "I could just imagine all those Course students out there screaming 'What?!' or thinking that I told him to say that. There are ideas out there that I wrote the Course or have some sort of monopoly on it. I don't even consider myself a representative of the Course, nor an advanced student. I think I'm a good intermediate student. But I talk about a lot of things that are not from the Course at all. I'm a popularizer of spiritual themes, and I certainly don't think the Course has a monopoly on spiritual truth."

Not surprisingly, Williamson has been subject to the ups and downs of fame in American pop culture. Although *TIME* magazine once identified her as a "Mother Teresa for the '90s," administrative controversies at the Centers for Living resulted in public charges of hypocrisy, self-promotion, an overcontrolling managerial style, and a quick temper. The Centers eventually closed, but a related service organization in Southern California called Project Angel Food continues today, delivering free meals to people afflicted with HIV/AIDS and other serious illnesses. Although Williamson would continue to write popular books during the nineties, including *A Woman's Worth* and *Illuminata*, she reduced her public appearances for a while and made herself less available to the press.

In 1998 Williamson accepted an invitation from the Church of Today in Warren, Michigan (now called Renaissance Unity), to become its pastor. She served there for five years before resigning in the midst of a controversy over the direction of the church, particularly Williamson's attempt to take it out of the national Association of Unity Churches. After leaving the church, Williamson continued to write and lecture and founded the Peace Alliance, a national effort to establish a U.S. Department of Peace. At this writing she is the author of nine books, four of which have been *New York Times* best sellers, and she has a show on the XM satellite radio network that is part of the "Oprah and Friends" feature block.

In December 2006, *Newsweek* magazine named Marianne Williamson as one of the fifty most influential baby boomers in America. As the most prominent popularizer of the Course, she is a paradoxical prophet of a teaching often perceived to be apolitical, as it explicitly advises its students to "seek not to change the world, but choose to change your mind about the world." But Williamson has never shied away from being outspoken or from taking controversial, left-leaning positions on social issues.

In a 1993 interview with Course writer Paul Ferrini following some of the negative press attention she had received, Williamson admitted that "I'm a girl who does have an edge. . . . [but] the press wasn't angry because I'm a bad girl; the press was angry because I'm a good girl."[4] When I asked Williamson to expound on this remark, she explained that "people would say to me back then that the press just couldn't stand that I had weaknesses like everyone else. But I don't think my weaknesses angered them; what angered them were my strengths."

"None of us claim to be role models," comments Beverly Hutchinson, founder of Miracle Distribution Center, who has worked with Williamson in many workshops and benefits. "I think the first sign of a real Course teacher is someone who says she's still a student and always will be." Or as the Course itself says of "teachers of God": "They are not perfect, or they would not be here." (MANUAL, INTRO, 5)

Other Course-Inspired Writers

Ideas and principles from *A Course in Miracles* have provided inspiration to other popular writers and teachers, including Wayne Dyer, author of such best-selling books as *The Power of Intention* and *There's a Spiritual Solution to*

Every Problem; Iyanla Vanzant, author of *One Day My Soul Just Opened Up* and *Yesterday, I Cried*, and founder of the Inner Visions Institute for Spiritual Development; and Hugh Prather, author of *Spiritual Notes to Myself* and *A Little Book of Letting Go*. Although these writers have not directly promoted the Course, they have mentioned or quoted the teaching in their work.

In 2003, I published Gary Renard's first book *The Disappearance of the Universe: Straight Talk About Illusions, Past Lives, Religion, Sex, Politics, and the Miracles of Forgiveness* under the Fearless Books imprint. This unusual work, claiming to be the record of nine years of Renard's in-the-flesh conversations with two "ascended masters," focuses on the teachings of ACIM in a humorous and often irreverent style. The book proved immediately popular with Course students while also sparking some controversy over its veracity and verifiability. Acquired by the major New Age publisher Hay House and released in a new edition in the autumn of 2004, *Disappearance* has over two hundred thousand copies in distribution worldwide. It was followed by Renard's second book, *Your Immortal Reality*. At this writing, Gary Renard travels worldwide to promote his books and has become a popular fixture on the ACIM speaking circuit.

In the wake of Marianne Williamson's fame, the Course briefly became trendy in the entertainment industry, leading to offhand mentions of it in the popular media. For instance, the second season (2000) of the eight-year sitcom *Will & Grace* included an episode in which the lead male character, Will, made this apology to his comic foil, Grace: "I'm sorry I always make you eat breakfast at my house. I'm sorry I got you involved with *A Course in Miracles*. I'm sorry I took the batteries out of Mr. Good Vibrations and put them in my alarm clock."[5]

The Course in Unity and Recovery

Although the metaphysical bent of *A Course in Miracles* does not harmonize well with the philosophies of conventional Christian churches (see chapter 9), the teaching has found a friendly reception in the neo-Christian movement known as Unity. Sometimes called "New Age Christianity," Unity was founded in 1889 by an American couple, Charles and Myrtle Fillmore, who "sought health by changing their ideas about God and themselves."[6] The movement has since grown to over two million followers in more than nine hundred ministries worldwide. Generally identified as a major branch of the New Thought movement—which promotes the idea of the divinity of humankind—Unity distinguishes itself by an explicit endorsement of the teachings of Jesus Christ. In practice, Unity organizations generally embrace a wide range of spiritual beliefs and perspectives, and they interpret the Bible metaphysically rather than literally. Although never officially endorsed by Unity, the Course seems to have become one of its frequent companions.

Paul Hasselbeck, dean of Spiritual Education and Enrichment at Unity Village in Missouri where Unity ministers are trained, says that "it's fair to characterize Unity's attitude toward the Course as going back and forth over the years. Even though the official stand at Unity Village or the Association of Unity Churches may have been adverse at times, individual churches still had the authority to welcome ACIM." Hasselbeck, who taught the Course for a decade in Puerto Rico, feels that there is relatively little difference between the Course and Unity philosophies. "One area that is frequently seen as a difference," he notes, "is that it is commonly believed that Charles Fillmore taught that the physical universe was created by God, whereas the Course clearly states that the physical universe was not created by God. I have researched and found many situations in Charles' works and others that support the Course's position."

The Course is also popular with recovery groups of every description. That connection has become sufficiently well known that in 1995 one of the leading publishers of recovery materials, Hazelden, released a book by recovery and meditation writer Karen Casey titled *Daily Meditations for Practicing the Course*. Not intended as a substitute for the Course's own yearbook of meditations, Casey's book offers 365 daily thoughts and essays that echo the general Course philosophy, including "Change the mind and the behavior follows," "Joining with others is how healing occurs," and "God knows no wrath."

At a 2007 Course conference in San Francisco, I was handed a 160-page booklet titled *Applying AA Experience to ACIM—A Proposal*, credited to an anonymous author who claims "over 24 years of AA experience" and suggests that "the AA meetings, steps, traditions, and concepts can readily be adapted to ACIM." It is not uncommon to hear the description of *A Course in Miracles* as "graduate work" for followers of the Alcoholics Anonymous tradition.

The Course in Prisons

The central Course themes of forgiveness and personal responsibility are increasingly reaching into the growing national subculture of the incarcerated. In 1982, an attorney named Bob Plath started a Course study program inside San Quentin Prison in Marin County, California. At its peak the program encompassed four different weekly ACIM group meetings of inmates at all security levels, and it continued for five years. One San Quentin Course student was David Magris, who served sixteen years on charges of murder, kidnapping, armed robbery, and burglary, and who sat on death row before California temporarily repealed the death penalty in 1972.

Encountering the Course about seven years into his term, Magris was already involved in rehabilitative programs and says that he "had already decided I had the power to change. But I needed more avenues for growth. I had resolved the basic motivations for my crimes, but I was still carrying a considerable amount of guilt. To talk about the past always left me strained, drained, and sad. The Course was essential to me in gaining a better understanding of self-forgiveness."

Magris also observed the effects of regular Course meetings on his fellow inmates: "I think everybody in the group was substantially moved and changed. They all became more comfortable in expressing themselves, and the Course lessons helped them learn to take criticism from their peers. This definitely changed their decisions and behavior on the yard and improved their relationships to the staff."

Off parole since 1985, Magris serves on the board of directors of Centerforce, a northern California nonprofit organization whose mission is "to strengthen individuals and families affected by incarceration through a comprehensive system of education and support."[7] He has long been active in the movement to abolish the death penalty, and in public appearances for that cause he has sometimes been accompanied by Dennis Tapp, whom Magris shot and nearly killed during the youthful crime spree that landed him in San Quentin. They were reconciled after Magris left prison.

In Boston, Course student Robin Casarjian has undertaken an ambitious prisoner education project under the auspices of her National Emotional Literacy Project for Prisons. Author of a successful trade book titled *Forgiveness: A Bold Choice for a Peaceful Heart* (Bantam, 1992), Casarjian found an unexpected receptivity to her message when she first visited a prison in 1988, and she began working with the incarcerated on a regular basis. In 1995 she self-published a book titled *Houses of Healing: A Prisoner's Guide to Inner Power and Freedom*, which is distributed free to prisons nationwide, with eighty-five thousand copies now in circulation. This work is supported entirely by donations to Casarjian's nonprofit organization; its board of directors includes popular health writer Joan Borysenko, PhD, whose work has also been influenced by the Course.

The first self-help book devoted entirely to prisoners, *Houses of Healing* couches some of the fundamentals of the field—including relaxation, self-observation, anger and grief work, and meditation—in simple, accessible terms. Scattered throughout the book are adaptations or direct quotations of Course Workbook lessons: "There is another way of looking at the world," "I could see peace instead of this," "The power of decision is my own."

A rape victim and an opponent of the death penalty who advocates a complete reversal in prison objectives—from the present emphasis on punishment to a focus on rehabilitation and reeducation—Casarjian feels that the psychospiritual solution to the prison problem is also the most practical one. Of the two million Americans now behind bars, says Casarjian, "ninety percent of them are coming back into society no matter how many prisons we build. The kind of experience people have in prison is going to determine their success or failure when they return to society.

"People change," she adds, "and people in prison change. They are either going to change for the better in terms of emotional healing, maturity, and personal responsibility, or they are going to become more wounded, more despairing, and more likely to strike out against others in the future."

Another Course-related prison project is Visions for Prisons in Costa Mesa, California, founded by Dan Millstein, an abandoned child of teenage parents who grew up to become a self-identified "criminal who never got caught." An adherent of Transcendental Meditation who encountered the Course in 1987, Millstein later met Jerry Jampolsky and asked him how to start an Attitudinal Healing group. Jampolsky told him simply, "Go do it. You're it!" Millstein soon began taking the principles of yoga, meditation, and Attitudinal Healing into prisons and schools. In 1995, Millstein and Visions for Prisons won one of three International Jampolsky Awards given to honor exceptionally successful and innovative applications of the Attitudinal Healing principles.[8]

Where Will the Course Go?

Within the first ten to fifteen years following publication of ACIM, it might have been reasonably accurate to typify ACIM students by their psychotherapeutic or New Age connections. Those constituencies remain significant elements of the Course audience today. But these correlations have more to do with where the Course originated and how it was first publicized than with any particular appeals of its message. The demographics of Course students have since become impossible to characterize, increasingly crossing all borders of class, race, nationality, and preexisting spiritual orientations. Robert Perry of the Circle of Atonement in Sedona, Arizona, says that he feels "the only thing that all Course students have in common today is owning a blue book."

That observation captures something of the unique nature of the ACIM phenomenon, which might best be described as a subtle cultural influence rather than a full-fledged movement. Without a central orthodoxy and with no standards for membership in an identifiable church, the Course remains in the background of the American spiritual landscape. Although it is no longer in the public eye as it was in the 1990s, it continues to find new students. Prominent Course philosopher Ken Wapnick has always maintained that *A Course in Miracles* is likely to be truly understood by relatively few people for many years to come. Its uneven yet continuing growth in popularity over more than thirty years suggests that the teaching is more than a fad, but it could well be decades before ACIM is recognized as a major cultural influence. That development is likely to go hand in hand with the slow yielding of traditional, organized religion to more metaphysical perspectives and practices.

In 1999, at the height of the copyright controversy then involving a number of Course organizations, Hugh Prather wrote a bracing essay titled "What is the Course? Will it exist in the 21st century?" Widely reprinted and commented on in the ACIM community, Prather's essay predicted a dim future for ACIM if its followers and teachers continued to battle among themselves over the rights to the teaching:

> So what will happen to the book in the 21st century? My guess is that it will continue to decline in popularity and eventually become so associated with the organizations and personalities that war over it that they will become its meaning in the eyes of the public. The words "A Course in Miracles" will end up symbolizing something quite unlike their true meaning, just as has happened on a much larger scale with the words "Christian," "Jesus," and "the Bible."[9]

As it happened, the revocation of the copyright effectively ended the battling among Course organizations and increased the democratization of an already free-wheeling spiritual culture. It now seems less likely that the meaning of ACIM will be supplanted by the personalities and organizations representing it. On the other hand, there is a possibility of its message being distorted or diluted by a variety of versions that are likely to arise and compete with the historical standard edition.

But Prather cogently warned of a more insidious threat to the spread of the authentic Course: the tendency of its students and teachers to *identify* with the teaching rather than simply live by its principles, and by so doing to create the very aura of ego-driven "specialness" that ACIM consistently urges its students to unlearn. Thus Prather argued that the best living examples of *A Course in Miracles* might not be those who are identified as famous or influential teachers:

> Those individuals we know intimately who we believe are close to being awake, seem to have no interest in contrasting themselves with other people. Generally speaking, they live simple, ordinary lives. They are comfortable if not restful to be around. Their time is usually devoted to unimportant things and their hearts to "unimportant" people. They have no inflexible concepts or rigid patterns and there is nothing particularly unusual about the subjects they choose to talk about or anything outstanding in the personal mannerisms they exhibit. They are easily pleased, and often they are happy for no apparent reason. Because their own egos are no longer destructive, they find other people's egos amusing and endearing. Above all, they are equal and familiar. They would not be good subjects for a magazine profile. And yet, into the mundane, everyday circumstances of their lives, they quietly pour their comfort and their peace . . .
>
> *A Course in Miracles* can survive in the 21st century, in fact it can transform the 21st century, if those who see the Reality it points to choose to extend themselves beyond their ego boundaries and make the interests of another their own. . . . Every day we have hundreds of little encounters with other people in our activities and in our minds. In each of these contacts we leave something behind, and that something determines whether the Course continues to exist. Only by giving the tiny miracles of understanding, support, forbearance, and happiness can we assure that this precious teaching does not fall on deaf ears and dead hearts.

Prather's reference to the everyday encounters we experience echoes ACIM's assertion that everyone is always teaching and learning: "To teach is to demonstrate. There are only two thought systems, and you demonstrate that you believe one or the other is true all the time. From your demonstration others learn, and so do you. The question is not whether you will teach, for in that there is no choice. The purpose of the course might be said to provide you with a means of choosing what you want to teach on the basis of what you want to learn." (MANUAL, INTRO, 2) According to ACIM, the two thought systems we choose between are love and fear—and everyone who chooses love is essentially a teacher of the Course. While that may sound like an obvious choice to most people, it's a choice that most of us find difficult to keep making on a consistent basis. That's because, from the Course point of view, consistently choosing love entails a profound surrender of the world as we know it.

✤ ENDNOTES ✤

1. The court's ruling on the ACIM copyright excluded some brief portions of the book, most notably the Clarification of Terms and Text Preface, that did not appear in the so-called Criswell edition, as well as other material channeled or directly authored by Helen Schucman. As a statement from the Foundation for Inner Peace clarifies, ". . . the Second Edition, the Urtext, and the Hugh Lynn Cayce versions of *A Course in Miracles* (to the extent they differ from the Criswell edition); 'The Gifts of God' (which contains Helen's poetry and a fourteen-page scribing which bears the same name as the book); the supplemental pamphlets entitled 'The Song of Prayer' and 'Psychotherapy: Purpose, Process and Practice'; all of Helen Schucman's unpublished writings; and the current and future foreign translations of *A Course in Miracles* are not in the public domain as a result of this court decision. Because we have, for many years now, published the version of *A Course in Miracles* that contains the Clarification of Terms and the Text Preface, we want to make sure that people understand that this version of the Course has not been placed into the public domain as a result of the lawsuit—and, particularly, that certain portions of that version of the work remain protected by copyright. . . . *A Course in Miracles* as published by the Foundation for Inner Peace represents the form of publication approved by both Helen Schucman and William Thetford, both of whom lived for many years after the initial publication of the Course, and both of whom, we believe, would have approved of the improvements represented by the Second Edition."
2. See www.ahc-oakland.org.
3. Quoted from Elena Oumano, *Marianne Williamson: Her Life, Her Message, Her Miracles* (New York: St. Martin's Press, 1992).

4. Quoted from Marianne Williamson, interview by Paul Ferrini, *Miracles Magazine* No. 3, May 1993.

5. Quoted from "There But for the Grace of Grace," Episode 2.21 of *Will & Grace*. Original airdate 5/9/2000. Written by Michelle Bochner Spitz.

6. From an online statement published by the Unity Movement Advisory Council. See www.unity.org.

7. See www.centerforce.org.

8. See www.visionsforprisons.org.

9. All excerpts reprinted with the permission of Hugh Prather and Miracle Distribution Center.

PART II

THE MESSAGE OF
THE COURSE

 CHAPTER 4

A New Curriculum of Love

To understand the aim of *A Course in Miracles*, it's necessary to grasp that it is not primarily attempting to change its students' religious beliefs, morals, or behavior in the manner of most religious teachings. Rather, the Course, which describes itself as a "mind training," is focused on changing the way that human consciousness typically works.

In the simplest terms, the aim is to help students learn to let their minds be consistently inspired by love, rather than compulsively driven by fear. In Course lingo, this means learning to attune to—and accept—the everyday guidance of the "Holy Spirit" in place of the habitual drives of the ego. (In Course terms, the Holy Spirit is essentially an ambassador of God in our own minds, because the original creative intelligence known as God is actually unaware of the illusory world we have created through our false, fear-driven perceptions.) One learns to hear and follow a different internal voice primarily through the constant application of forgiveness—to oneself, to all other people, and to the world at large. As Workbook Lesson 332 suggests, "Fear binds the world. Forgiveness sets it free." Forgiveness is thus the means for working miracles, as the Course defines them—and it defines them unconventionally.

Chapter 1 of the Course Text opens with a list of fifty "principles of miracles" that shed some light on the differences between "Course miracles" and the kind we are accustomed to hearing about in the news or religious literature. Following are a few of the principles that help distinguish this new kind of miracle:

Miracles occur naturally as expressions of love. The real miracle is the love that inspires them. In this sense everything that comes from love is a miracle.

Miracles are thoughts. Thoughts can represent the lower or bodily level of experience, or the higher or spiritual level of experience. One makes the physical, and the other creates the spiritual.

A miracle is a service. It is the maximal service you can render to another. It is a way of loving your neighbor as yourself. You recognize your own and your neighbor's worth simultaneously.

Miracles are natural signs of forgiveness. Through miracles you accept God's forgiveness by extending it to others.

Miracles are expressions of love, but they may not always have observable effects.

A major contribution of miracles is their strength in releasing you from your false sense of isolation, deprivation, and lack.

A miracle is never lost. It may touch many people you have not even met, and produce undreamed of changes in situations of which you are not even aware.

One of the first conclusions that can be drawn from these principles is that ACIM does not generally treat the miracle as a rare, spectacular event that proves the existence of God or the correctness of faith. The Course does not deny the possibility of spectacular miracles, or the capacity of human beings to produce them. In fact, it asserts that "few appreciate the real power of the mind, and no one remains fully aware of it all the time. . . . It is hard to recognize that thought and belief combine into a power surge that can literally move mountains." (CH2, VI, 9) But the Course is primarily interested in miracles as *the optimal vehicle of relationship*: miracles are "expressions of love" and "natural signs of forgiveness" that heal the human condition of "isolation, deprivation and lack."

In this sense, ACIM is a manifesto proclaiming the *democratization* of miracles. They are no longer the exceptional or supernatural handiwork of saints and angels, but rather the natural if often forgotten calling of human beings. "Forgiveness is my function as the light of the world," Workbook Lesson 62 reminds the reader. Further, it is not dramatic demonstrations of miracle-working that matter, for miracles may not always have "observable effects" while nonetheless producing "undreamed of changes in situations of which you are not aware."

Yet miracles are also thoughts of a particular kind, the kind that reminds Course students to view reality in spiritual rather than material terms. It is this choice of awareness, reinforced by the everyday work of forgiveness, that "reverses the physical laws" and enables the "sudden shifts into invisibility" that enable authentic healing. Just how much our ordinary consciousness differs from a consistent spiritual awareness is hinted at in another miracle principle: *"Miracles are natural. When they do not occur something has gone wrong."*

Miracles in Practice

So how do Course students experience miracles as they progress on their chosen spiritual path? Greg Mackie, a writer and teacher associated with the Circle of Atonement teaching center in Sedona, Arizona, wrote to me about how a severely wounded friendship was healed through his application of ACIM principles:

> I once had an exchange with a friend of mine that led to the severing of the friendship. She was extremely offended by something I said, so offended that she compared me to an Islamic terrorist. This really upset me. I felt angry and hurt, because I believed that she had profoundly misunderstood what I had said. I felt unfairly treated, and was holding some pretty major grievances against her as a result of this incident.

So I began a long process of applying the Course to this relation-ship. . . . In particular, I got a lot of mileage out of the practices in the Workbook in which you select a specific person to forgive. These practices had a powerful effect over time. I certainly can't claim that I forgave her completely, but I know I made real progress. The anger and hurt slowly dissipated, and I found myself experiencing feelings of genuine goodwill toward her.

Eventually, after a number of months had passed, I came into contact with her again, and something amazing happened. Com-pletely out of the blue, she apologized for the harsh things she had said to me months before, and said she wanted to bury the hatchet. I immediately accepted her apology, and just like that, the two of us were friends again. . . .

This whole experience truly felt like a miracle to me. I really thought we would never be friends again in this lifetime, and yet the ugly, seemingly irreparable rift between us was somehow healed. I feel immensely grateful for this. In my mind, it feels like a beautiful illustration of one of my favorite lines from the Course: "The holiest of all spots on earth is where an ancient hatred has become a present love."

Kathi J. Kemper, MD, is the author of *The Holistic Pediatrician* (Harper, 2002) and chairs a program for holistic and integrative medicine at Wake Forest University School of Medicine. She told me about a frightening en-counter during which concentrating on Course principles seemed to pro-vide her with a miraculous rescue from danger:

I was attending a convention in Philadelphia. After the evening speaker I returned to my hotel room to freshen up before another round of discussions. As I stood in the bathroom combing my hair, I noticed a large man dressed in army fatigues standing in the bathtub. As I whirled around, he grabbed my arm and started to close the door. My mind seemed to split in two and everything seemed to hap-pen very slowly. I could hear myself screaming and knew the terror of imminent attack. But another part of my mind clicked onto the

Course: "You are my brother. This is a mistake. You can't attack me. There can be nothing but love between us."

These thoughts were repeated over and over in my mind very clearly, even though I could hear my own screaming as if from a distance. We were looking in each other's eyes during this time. Before the door was shut all the way, he stopped and said, "There must be some mistake. I think I have the wrong room." He let go of my arm and fled the building.

For me this experience is a powerful affirmation of the truth of love and how we are all connected to that truth even when we seem to be thinking, saying, doing, or even screaming very different things. The stranger seemed to be attacking me; I seemed to be screaming; yet on some deeper level, we were acknowledging our oneness, and recognizing that everything else we think, do, or say is a mistake.

I often think of this experience when I am confronted with the question, "What would you do if faced with a gunman threatening you or a loved one? Obviously this is where people think the rubber meets the road and that we'd either shoot the person, defend ourselves, or let someone be shot. I don't know what the right behavior is for anyone; nor do I know what I will "do" if I'm ever faced with that situation again. I only pray that some part of my mind will remain sane enough to remember the truth of our oneness.

Robert Capozzi of Alexandria, Virginia, wrote to me that he experiences miracles as inner shifts in consciousness:

The miracle is the ability to cease ego chatter. It's the ability to undo unloving imaginings. This can be accomplished by appealing to one's Higher Self, to God, the Holy Spirit, or Jesus; the symbolism doesn't matter. I liken it to a spiritual or psychological sponge, clearing one's consciousness. . . . This state of mindfulness seems to be a reasonably peaceful place. By practicing the Course on a moment-by-moment basis, long periods of fear are obliterated. That relief itself is a miracle.

However, occasionally one can experience another level of peace. While this is not what I would call an "out-of-body" experience, that begins to capture the feeling. It feels as if for up to a half hour of time, a deep sense of peace pervades one's consciousness, without any ego chatter or even a thought. I call these "high" miracles. Another way to put this is that the Higher Self remains firmly in charge, rather than "battling" with the ego for control of one's consciousness.

Many Course students credit the teaching with not just a shift in attitude or scattered miraculous events, but also a positive reshaping of their life as a whole. Charlie Cowan was one of the directors of the Northwest Foundation for *A Course in Miracles*. He has recently retired and moved to Federal Way, Washington. As Cowan told me:

I've been an ardent student of the Course since 1986; my loving and loved wife Shirley shares my devotion. I can't speak for anyone else, but as for me, I have invested everything I ever thought I owned in the Course and its principles. One of those principles is: Giving and receiving are, in fact, the same thing; you cannot but receive what you give. Since I am a terrifically selfish individual, I had to give *all* to the principles I teach in order to learn.

As for what I received in return:

1. Recovery from alcoholism
2. Loving and loved wife, Shirley
3. Friends with whom I can share a laugh and a tear at any time, for any reason
4. Happiness
5. Peace of mind
6. Personal receipt of miracles in my life and those around me
7. Restoration of my relationship with God
8. Realization of a loving relationship with my family of birth
9. Forgiveness of my temporal father
10. Forgiveness of myself
11. Reunion with my daughter and son

And what did all this cost me?
1. My guilt
2. My fear
3. My pain
4. My loneliness
   Not bad for an old drunk, don't you think? Fair trade in my book.

A Path of Exceptional Personal Responsibility

Despite such reports of beneficial or even miraculous effects of the Course discipline on its students, it's important to understand that the teaching is not focused on improving the conditions of one's life in the everyday world. That's because the Course holds that the tangible world of time and space that we live in is fundamentally illusory—and so are the bodies and personalities we are so intimately identified with. Thus, unlike conventional psychotherapy or "self-help" perspectives, ACIM does not provide techniques for improving one's egocentric strategies in order to find more love, more self-esteem, or more success. If such benefits do accrue, they are essentially side effects of gaining spiritual vision, which looks beyond the everyday world to a higher reality.

In fact, things can get worse in the short term for new Course students, because they are led rapidly toward the surrender of egocentric values and perceptions that they have long held dear. As the text following Lesson 128, "The world I see holds nothing that I want," explains:

> *The world you see holds nothing that you need to offer you; nothing that you can use in any way, nor anything at all that serves to give you joy. Believe this thought, and you are saved from years of misery, from countless disappointments, and from hopes that turn to bitter ashes of despair. No one but must accept this thought as true, if he would leave the world behind and soar beyond its petty scope and little ways.*
>
> *Each thing you value here is but a chain that binds you to the world, and it will serve no other end but this. For everything must serve the purpose you have given it, until you see a different purpose there. The*

only purpose worthy of your mind this world contains is that you pass it by, without delaying to perceive some hope where there is none. Be you deceived no more. The world you see holds nothing that you want.

But if one is to give up all investment in the ordinary world in order to follow the Course discipline, where's the payoff? The text for the next lesson (129), "Beyond this world there is a world I want," suggests the rewards of gaining spiritual vision:

You cannot stop with the idea the world is worthless, for unless you see that there is something else to hope for, you will only be depressed. Our emphasis is not on giving up the world, but on exchanging it for what is far more satisfying, filled with joy, and capable of offering you peace. Think you this world can offer that to you?

It might be worth a little time to think once more about the value of this world. Perhaps you will concede there is no loss in letting go all thought of value here. The world you see is merciless indeed, unstable, cruel, unconcerned with you, quick to avenge and pitiless with hate. It gives but to rescind, and takes away all things that you have cherished for a while. No lasting love is found, for none is here. This is the world of time, where all things end.

Is it a loss to find a world instead where losing is impossible; where love endures forever, hate cannot exist and vengeance has no meaning? Is it loss to find all things you really want, and know they have no ending and they will remain exactly as you want them throughout time? Yet even they will be exchanged at last for what we cannot speak of, for you go from there to where words fail entirely, into a silence where the language is unspoken and yet surely understood.

Although some popularizers of the Course, like Jerry Jampolsky and Marianne Williamson, have emphasized the benefits of prayer and positive intention in improving one's life in the world, a considerable contingent of ACIM students follow a more self-confrontational line. These students view the Course as a relatively difficult and lifelong discipline that focuses on the dissolving of ego, or what the Course calls "removing the blocks to the awareness of love's presence" (from the Text Introduction). According to the Course, developing a profound and consistent attitude of forgiveness removes those blocks, and forgiveness also opens one to the guidance of the Holy Spirit, an inner voice of wisdom that far surpasses the fear-driven counsel of the ego.

Foremost among the teachers of this traditional perspective are Kenneth and Gloria Wapnick, the husband-and-wife founders of the Foundation for *A Course in Miracles* (FACIM), whose board of directors overlaps with that of the ACIM publisher, the Foundation for Inner Peace. (Traditionally, FIP has tended to the publication and translation duties associated with the Course whereas FACIM has functioned as its educational counterpart.) For nearly twelve years FACIM occupied a spacious residential teaching center in upstate New York before moving to its current headquarters in Temecula, California, which still offers classes and an electronic curriculum but no residential facilities. Ken Wapnick was a close friend and confidant of Course scribe Helen Schucman (see chapters 1 and 2) and is arguably the leading philosopher of the freewheeling spiritual movement inspired by ACIM. He has authored over twenty books on the teaching and consistently strives to stay true to what he views as a very challenging yet profoundly transformational teaching.

"We spend a lot of time helping people realize what the Course is not," Ken asserts. "It's not biblical; it's neither Judaism nor Christianity; it's not Christian Science; it's not New Age, Joel Goldsmith, or Edgar Cayce. The most common mistake that people make is to superimpose upon the Course their prior spiritual path. That's a natural mistake, but as long as you make it, you won't understand what the Course is saying."

And what does ACIM say that distinguishes it from other paths?

"Fundamentally the Course says that only spirit is real and there's nothing else. It also says that God is not involved in the world of matter. Where it really goes beyond other traditions is in saying that we made up the world—as well as time and space—in an attempt to attack God."

In the words of the Course itself:

The world was made as an attack on God. It symbolizes fear. And what is fear except love's absence? Thus the world was meant to be a place where God could enter not, and where His Son could be apart from him. (WORKBOOK PART II, 3, 2)

This message is so disturbing to some Course students, says Ken, that "they alter the message, deciding that the Course means God didn't create the *horrors* in the world. But the Course is quite clear that the entire physical universe is not of God's making, but our own."

Adds Gloria, "This is the one concept to which people have always had tremendous resistance. People find it very difficult to deal with because the direct implication of God not being responsible for this world is that we are. This means that you have to take responsibility for your existence and everything about it—and who wants to do that?"

Still, the key to working Course-style miracles is in learning to take on that exceptional degree of personal responsibility. "Because Course students learn that they must accept responsibility for everything they think and do, eventually they become much less prone to rationalize their ego and their sense of victimization," suggests Ken. "This doesn't mean that their egos disappear. But students do begin to understand that their egos are to blame for their problems. They find hope in the realization that they don't have to change the whole world, or other people, in order to find peace."

"Before the Course I was prone to blame everyone else for everything that happened to me," admits Gloria. "We all tend to do that. After the Course, I realized that you have to take responsibility for your own life. You're not just a cork bobbing around on the ocean of life, being hurled around by the waves and the stormy weather."

Although it's clear that some students find a softer message in the Course than that which the Wapnicks convey—or follow only the parts that offer reassurance—there are countless stories of students responding to its teaching with a notable resistance, sometimes to the point of committing violence against the book itself. I have heard accounts of the Course being thrown across rooms, tossed into rivers, even soaked with lighter fluid and set afire. The record for destruction of ACIM is perhaps held by one student who complained that he was "probably making the Foundation for Inner Peace rich" by having destroyed at least seven copies of the Course in his ongoing study. Yet many of these same students buy new copies and return to their study, raising the question of what keeps them going. What is it that feels good about studying ACIM?

"What feels good is the sense of hope that the Course provides," Ken suggests. "Not a naive hope that God or the Holy Spirit will descend and take away your problems, but real hope that the possibility of happiness rests within yourself. Even if you haven't fully chosen that, you know that you can eventually change your mind by asking for help."

"The Course works if you apply it," Gloria asserts, "and if you ask for help and correction. The Course reminds you that the Holy Spirit is always available within your mind. Many Course students have realized that nothing works in this world—no economic system, no political system, no religious system. These people realize that they want to awaken from the dream, and they recognize that the Course is what's going to help them awaken."

Ken believes the difficulty of the Course results from a conscious design evidenced not only by the psychological challenge it presents, but also by its very language. "I think it's no accident that the sentence structure is difficult. If you like Shakespeare, you'll love the style, but it doesn't make it any easier to comprehend. Concepts aren't explained in a linear way, with definitions clearly given and principles built upon principles logically. Rather, the Course's logic is circular, or what I would call *symphonic*. The way it's written you have to spend a long time unraveling it, struggling with it, even resisting it. The purpose of that process is to help you undo the ego's way of thinking and begin to listen to the Holy Spirit. Some have reacted by saying all that struggle is really not necessary, but I believe that's the way the Course is meant to be experienced."

For new students struggling to follow the Workbook's path to contacting a reliable source of inner guidance, perhaps the most difficult challenge the Course presents is distinguishing between the voice of one's own ego and the voice of the Holy Spirit. Is there a way to tell for sure what kind of guidance one is listening to?

"The Course offers some means of distinguishing," Ken suggests, "one of them being that when you are following the Holy Spirit's guidance, you are 'wholly without fear.' But really the question is misplaced. The focus should not be on how you can tell which voice you're hearing, but on clearing out the obstacles to the voice of the Holy Spirit—namely, guilt and the ego's sense of specialness. The more you get rid of these interferences, the more you will hear the true voice of the Holy Spirit. The question of 'who's who?' will then arise less and less."

Gloria adds that Course students shouldn't expect the Holy Spirit to be a clearly discernible "voice" inside their heads, à la Helen Schucman. "The Holy Spirit can reach you in a dream, a phone call, something you overhear that 'clicks' for you. Because the Course does refer to a voice, sometimes people get confused and think they have to hear one in a literal sense."

Although the Course doesn't claim to be superior to other spiritual paths, it does claim to function as a kind of spiritual accelerator. There are cryptic suggestions that Course students will save "thousands of years" by steadfastly practicing its lessons, as well as inferences that adherence to its method will work much faster than a lifetime of meditation practice or conventional religious approaches to "fighting sin." But that's not to say that spiritual acceleration necessarily feels good in the short term.

"One of the ways people report such acceleration is that things get worse for them much more quickly," Ken asserts. "People either encounter the Course during crisis or go into crisis soon after taking it up. The Course speeds up one's process by getting to the root of the problem: the mind's decision to keep separate from God. That's the fundamental problem of humanity. The Course focuses so directly on that problem that you don't have to spend time on meditation, rituals, or other religious disciplines. Even though the process takes many, many years, within the greater scheme of things you're speeding along because you're getting to the root of the real problem."

A Path to the "Happy Dream"

Despite the fact that *A Course in Miracles* is not focused on self-help and may even induce a spiritual crisis for some students, it asserts nonetheless that the faithful student will be drawn into increasing happiness through following the discipline. The ultimate aim of the curriculum is to prepare students for what the Course calls *knowledge,* a state of timeless awareness that surpasses all perception and is completely suffused with love. The Course implies that knowledge is not a state that can be attained in the world as we know it, because our world is a perceptual illusion, or an ongoing serial dream. Yet through the discipline of forgiveness, we can learn to have happier dreams than we have ever known—the kind of dreams that show the way to full recognition of one's ultimate reality as spirit:

> *You will first dream of peace, and then awaken to it. Your first exchange of what you made for what you want is the exchange of nightmares for the happy dreams of love. In these lie your true perceptions, for the Holy Spirit corrects the world of dreams, where all perception is. Knowledge needs no correction. Yet the dreams of love lead unto knowledge. In them you see nothing fearful, and because of this they are the welcome that you offer knowledge. Love waits on welcome, not on time, and the real world is but your welcome of what always was. Therefore the call of joy is in it, and your glad response is your awakening to what you have not lost.* (CH13, VII, 9)

 CHAPTER 5

Forgiving What Did Not Occur

In Gary Renard's popular book *The Disappearance of the Universe*, the practice of forgiveness is described as "where the rubber meets the road" for serious students of *A Course in Miracles*. Although the idea of pardoning the trespasses of others and ourselves is prominent in many religious traditions, in none does forgiveness take on the primacy and urgency with which the Course treats it—especially in such Workbook Lessons as "Forgiveness is the key to happiness" (121), "Forgiveness offers everything I want" (122), and "Forgiveness ends all suffering and loss" (249).

At times, the Course displays an almost sardonic view of human nature as it leads students into specific forgiveness exercises, such as this excerpt from the commentary following Workbook Lesson 46, "God is the Love in which I forgive":

Begin the longer practice periods by repeating today's idea to yourself, as usual. Close your eyes as you do so, and spend a minute or two in searching your mind for those whom you have not forgiven. It does not matter "how much" you have not forgiven them. You have forgiven them entirely or not at all.

If you are doing the exercises well you should have no difficulty in finding a number of people you have not forgiven. It is a safe rule that anyone you do not like is a suitable subject. Mention each one by name, and say:

God is the Love in which I forgive you, [name].

The purpose of the first phase of today's practice periods is to put you in a position to forgive yourself. After you have applied the idea to all those who have come to mind, tell yourself:

God is the Love in which I forgive myself.

The equation of God with love as a healing and enlightening force is common in the Course, further distinguishing it from traditional religions that posit God as a life-giving but also judgmental being whose nature is superior to ours. Quite to the contrary, ACIM suggests that both God and humanity exist in the realm of ideas:

You do not find it difficult to believe that when another calls on God for love, your call remains as strong. Nor do you think that when God answers him, your hope of answer is diminished. On the contrary, you are more inclined to regard his success as witness to the possibility of yours. That is because you recognize, however dimly, that God is an idea, and so your faith in Him is strengthened by sharing. What you find difficult to accept is the fact that, like your Father, you are an idea. And like Him, you can give yourself completely, wholly without loss and only with gain. Herein lies peace, for here there is no conflict. (Chi 5, VI, 4)

In this sense, the Course approach to forgiveness can be seen as a discipline of learning to release our grip on all the ego-driven ideas we entertain about reality—a huge and often contradictory collection of ideas that ultimately lead to suffering—in exchange for one idea that heals: "God is but Love, and therefore so am I." (That particular meditation is repeated no fewer than thirty times in the Course Workbook, as a recurring motif during a review of Lessons 151–170.)

Elsewhere the Course suggests that there are only two emotions—love and fear—and that fear is a delusion, meaning that only love is real. Thus, all the forgiveness exercises of ACIM focus on the release of fear-based grievances in order to purify one's awareness of everything but "God as Love."

As radical as this prescription may sound already, ACIM goes considerably beyond all traditional descriptions of forgiveness when it insists that the student must progress from an ordinary style of forgiving—that is, pardoning others and oneself for real or perceived crimes, sins, or personal offenses—to releasing everyone from the idea that anything evil, sinful, or hurtful has ever actually occurred: "Be willing to forgive the Son of God for what he did not do." (CH17, III, 1) The justification for this stance relies on the Course definition of spiritual reality as the only reality, all else that we experience being delusory:

> *The betrayal of the Son of God lies only in illusions, and all his "sins" are but his own imagining. His reality is forever sinless. He need not be forgiven but awakened. In his dreams he has betrayed himself, his brothers and his God. Yet what is done in dreams has not really been done. It is impossible to convince the dreamer that this is so, for dreams are what they are because of their illusion of reality. Only in waking is the full release from them, for only then does it become perfectly apparent that they had no effect upon reality at all, and did not change it. Fantasies change reality. That is their purpose. They cannot do so in reality, but they* can *do so in the mind that would have reality be different.* (CH17, I, 1)

"Saved by the SOBs"

"What the Course has to say about the unreality of the world is difficult to grasp," admits veteran Course teacher Carole Howe, whose experience with ACIM dates back to 1977. "But that idea is where you eventually come to, not where you start. You start with people being in pain, driven by their feelings of unworthiness. The Course leads you by the hand through that sort of self-discovery, and it does this primarily through relationships. The idea is that the SOBs out there will save you, because you learn to notice what comes up for you in their presence. Instead of running away, you realize that difficult people are *triggering*, not *causing*, your own feelings of guilt, fear, and unforgiveness. Then you have a chance to deal with what has come up in a responsible way."

An example of dealing with "what comes up" can be found in the words of a Los Angeles police detective (name withheld by request) who acknowledges that his profession tempts him to "see the world in the light of hate, anger, greed and fear." As he wrote to me describing the demands and dilemmas of working every day in a high crime district:

> I was beginning to feel that I was no different from the people I was trying to put in prison. I nearly quit. . . . Then I began reading the Course in a bookstore. As I was thumbing through it, an amazing realization hit me: I *am* no different than the people I was trying to put in prison. Perhaps becoming a police officer was my way of dealing with what was inside of me . . . what *is* inside of me. I can't lie and say that all of a sudden I see the people I prosecute as holy, loving children of God. I would have to see myself that way first. But I do see that it is my perception of people and the world that creates the pain, the anger, fear, greed and hate I have been living in for such a long time.
>
> As a detective I have worked on the worst crimes you could imagine. I know it will be very difficult to forgive child molesters, and to think of them as holy and loving. However, I do see that the Course seems to say that the evil I see in these crimes and people is merely my own view of the world. I truly believe this. The world I see is of my own creation.

Most of us who have not been convicted of a crime would balk at the notion of seeing ourselves as no different from those who have been. And even those who value forgiveness in general would probably object to the notion of forgiving those who have perpetrated the most heinous crimes against humanity. Michael Berkes, PhD, a former banker and financial consultant living in northern California, faced this challenge after becoming a Course student and looking back on the tragedy of his family's experience in the Holocaust. Born in Palestine, he spent his earliest years on a kibbutz but was brought to his parents' native Transylvania just as the Nazis were coming to power in the mid-1930s. Berkes was shocked to see the sacking of a synagogue and the burning of Jewish businesses, and could not understand why his schoolmates did not resist beatings from Fascist hoodlums. But what was to come would prove far worse, as he told me in a lengthy interview:

> When the Nazi persecution began in earnest my parents found a kindly priest who was willing to give us papers certifying that we were "cradle-born Catholics," providing that we took instruction and asked to be converted. This added a layer of guilt and confusion to my troubled soul while I lived through slave labor and the Allied bombings. After the war I found out what had happened to almost all of my extended family beyond my parents and myself: they were slaughtered in the death camps. . . .
>
> When we were liberated and learned all this, I found that I was unable to deal with the pain, unable to grieve, and unwilling to return to Israel. All I could [do] was swear that the curse of being a Jew would not be passed on to my children. For the next thirty years I lived the lie of being a Gentile. I tried to repay the kind priest and lessen my guilt by becoming a practicing Catholic, but that only served to increase my inner confusion and deep guilt.
>
> When I came across the Course and learned that "forgiveness is the key to happiness," I balked, argued, and resisted for a long time. How could I forgive the murder of my grandmother and many other relatives by the lowlife who seemed to have crawled out of the viscera of abomination? Even closer to home, how could I forgive my father for tearing me out of my free and happy surroundings in the kibbutz, and subjecting me to vicious racism? Finally, how could I forgive myself for turning my back on my native land and the religion of my forefathers, pretending for thirty years that I was something I was not?
>
> It took me untold hours of working with the Course to admit a slight chance of forgiving myself. I had to repeat the struggle to forgive my father. Oddly it was easier to look upon the perpetrators of the Holocaust once I had worked through forgiveness of myself, my parents, relatives, and friends. I started by forgiving the "little Nazis" and then the bigger ones, until I finally got all the way to Hitler.

I remember a propaganda film showing him at his Eagle's Nest in Bavaria, playing with the two German shepherd dogs he obviously loved very much. This led me to the thought that he must have been terribly abused as a child to have become an adult who could only trust dogs with his love. Then I thought of the Course, asking me to see the face of Christ in front of the one I need to forgive, in order to overcome my grievances. I did that, and it worked.

I cannot say that forgiveness on that scale is finished and done with for me. I have to return to basics every time I find myself blaming an evil "them" for the problems of the world. But with the realization that I have "unforgiven" again, the work of "reforgiving" becomes easier and quicker.

Berkes's experience with forgiving deep wounds of victimization points to the essence of ACIM-style forgiveness, as a transformation of consciousness that heals the pain of separation and inequality that inevitably arises between perpetrators and their victims. For in the Course point of view, forgiveness that does anything less than restore a loving, equalizing unity between people is not only incomplete, but actually destructive.

Understanding "Forgiveness-to-Destroy"

In "The Song of Prayer," one of two short documents that Helen Schucman channeled from the Voice of the Course in addition to ACIM itself, there is a substantial commentary on the nature and effects of incomplete or manipulative forgiveness, which is labeled "forgiveness-to-destroy":

Forgiveness-to-destroy has many forms, being a weapon of the world of form. Not all of them are obvious, and some are carefully concealed beneath what seems like charity. Yet all the forms that it may seem to take have but this single goal; their purpose is to separate and make what God created equal, different. The difference is clear in several forms where the designed comparison cannot be missed, nor is it really meant to be.

In this group, first, there are the forms in which a "better" person deigns to stoop to save a "baser" one from what he truly is. Forgive-

ness here rests on an attitude of gracious lordliness so far from love that arrogance could never be dislodged. Who can forgive and yet despise? And who can tell another he is steeped in sin, and yet perceive him as the Son of God? Who makes a slave to teach what freedom is? There is no union here, but only grief. This is not really mercy. This is death. (SOP 2, II, 1–2)

But if real forgiveness cannot flow from an attitude of moral superiority, argues "The Song of Prayer," neither can it originate from a conviction of shared sinfulness—a conviction that forms the basis for much of traditional Christian practice. The attitude that "we are all sinners" is, from the Course point of view, simply another means of using forgiveness for destructive ends.

Another form, still very like the first if it is understood, does not appear in quite such blatant arrogance. The one who would forgive the other does not claim to be the better. Now he says instead that here is one whose sinfulness he shares, since both have been unworthy and deserve the retribution of the wrath of God. This can appear to be a humble thought, and may indeed induce a rivalry in sinfulness and guilt. It is not love for God's creation and the holiness that is His gift forever. Can His Son condemn himself and still remember Him?

Here the goal is to separate from God the Son He loves, and keep him from his Source. This goal is also sought by those who seek the role of martyr at another's hand. Here must the aim be clearly seen, for this may pass as meekness and as charity instead of cruelty. Is it not kind to be accepting of another's spite, and not respond except with silence and a gentle smile? Behold, how good are you who bear with patience and with saintliness the anger and the hurt another gives, and do not show the bitter pain you feel.

Forgiveness-to-destroy will often hide behind a cloak like this. It shows the face of suffering and pain, in silent proof of guilt and of the ravages of sin. Such is the witness that it offers one who could be savior, not an enemy. But having been made enemy, he must accept the guilt and heavy-laid reproach that thus is put upon him. Is this love? Or is it rather treachery to one who needs salvation from the pain of guilt? What could the purpose be, except to keep the witnesses of guilt away from love? (SOP 2, II, 3–5)

All forms forgiveness takes that do not lead away from anger, condemnation and comparisons of every kind are death. For that is what their purposes have set. Be not deceived by them, but lay them by as worthless in their tragic offerings. You do not want to stay in slavery. You do not want to be afraid of God. You want to see the sunlight and the glow of Heaven shining on the face of earth, redeemed from sin and in the Love of God. From here is prayer released, along with you. Your wings are free, and prayer will lift you up and bring you home where God would have you be. (SOP 2, II, 8)

While "The Song of Prayer" suggests that a certain purity of forgiveness is necessary to attain the ultimate spiritual freedom, the fact is that most people have to start where they are—facing what is unforgiven in their lives with whatever degree of surrender and open-heartedness they can muster. Yet a less-than-perfect form of forgiveness may still have far-reaching effects, as I discovered when the need to forgive became a powerful imperative in my own life.

Watching Reality Change

I encountered *A Course in Miracles* more than twenty years ago, when I was in the early stages of a serious illness involving a collapse of my immune system diagnosed as chronic fatigue syndrome. (See chapter 11 for more about my experience with ACIM.) Reading the Text and using the Workbook simultaneously brought me to the realization that my illness stemmed largely from unrecognized and unresolved anger about many things, but centered on my parents.

I had hardly thought about forgiveness before this stage of my life, and what little experience I had with it probably did not proceed far beyond the confines of forgiveness-to-destroy. To me, pardon was something to be meted out in accordance with the severity of someone's else's mistakes or crimes, depending on how generous I might be feeling on a particular day.

But I can't remember thinking about or practicing forgiveness much at all before my encounter with ACIM.

Thus the radically egalitarian Course approach to forgiveness struck me as both mysterious and challenging to my view of reality. Yet the suffering of my illness was a sufficiently strong impetus for change that I decided to give it a try. I had come to realize that my chief complaint against my parents was that together they had seemingly done little to reduce the negative effects of my mother's emotional problems on our family. Diagnosed with manic-depressive disorder (now called bipolar disorder) by a psychiatrist in the 1960s, my mother experienced wild swings of behavior, from hyperactive busyness to a withdrawn hostility, deteriorating every few years into near-psychotic episodes that occasioned week-long hospital stays, electroshock treatments, and powerful psychiatric drug regimens. I felt that my father's passivity contributed to my mother's problems, and so I had grown to see them as collaborators in a pact of pain that my two sisters and I had been forced to endure while growing up.

The Course approach to forgiveness had nothing to do with analyzing this history or coming to terms with my own tendencies as an "adult child" of a dysfunctional family. I was directed simply to hold the image of my parents in my mind and think, "God is the Love in which I forgive you." I used this lesson and similar ones many times with my parents, all in the privacy of my mind, while mentioning nothing about this meditative work to them. They lived across the continent, so I felt insulated from having to talk about forgiveness openly—and as a result I expected the work to have no effect on our actual relationship. I hoped only that my own long-held grievances might ease, thus allowing my body to recover from the tension and anger it had long held.

But there was a big surprise in store for me. When my parents decided to come to the West Coast to talk to my physician about my illness, I decided to tell them about my new spiritual discipline and particularly my work with forgiveness. I began the conversation tentatively, saying only that I had begun to look at the effects of chronic anger in my life without saying where that anger was sourced. Thus I was stunned when my father took my mother's hand and said, "Yes, I've never been able to understand why your mother has been so angry all her life. And I have to admit that

I've never known what to do about it." In an unusually quiet tone, my mother said, "I've never understood why I'm so angry myself."

In an instant, my long-held grudge against my parents fractured. Suddenly they had jointly admitted what I had never heard them admit before. In the days following their visit, I experienced not only a powerful emotional release and some improvement of my physical symptoms, but I also began to wonder about why there had been such a dramatic shift in the relationship between the three of us. At first I thought that my private forgiveness meditations had somehow enabled my parents to become more honest and open. Then I began to wonder if in fact they had been honest and open before, but I had simply never heard them because my resentment had been in the way. Who had changed after all this time? Myself, my parents, or all of us?

This questioning began to soften the hard picture of the past within myself, helping me realize that I could no longer be sure of exactly what had transpired in my early life. As the text of Lesson 182 of the Course suggests, "The childhood of your body, and its place of shelter, are a memory now so distorted that you merely hold a picture of a past that never happened." At the very least I recognized that my parents had not deliberately perpetrated punishment on me and my sisters, but instead had struggled to do the best job they could as parents while struggling with nearly overwhelming problems rooted in their own past. As I released my parents from the long-held idea that they had intentionally harmed me, I realized that I was in an early stage of "forgiving what did not occur."

That episode did not end my forgiveness work with my parents. I would later write a volume of meditations titled *A Little Book of Forgiveness* that was dedicated to my mother and roughly chronicled the seven years of illness and healing that set me on a spiritual path. Today I still sometimes find unproductive ideas or patterns of behavior in myself that seem rooted in the history of my family of origin. But I am usually quick to realize that these "hauntings" have less to do with what occurred in the past than my attachment to ego-driven discomfort in the here and now—an attachment that may drive me to find convenient excuses to maintain my pain.

When the Course suggests, in Lesson 284, that "I can elect to change all thoughts that hurt," it is implying an in-the-moment forgiveness of oneself by reminding the student that both resentment and release are voluntary states of consciousness. How long we choose to remain in psychological suffering depends in large part on how long we continue to believe that it serves us in some way. As ACIM suggests in chapter 2,

> *Tolerance for pain may be high, but it is not without limit. Eventually everyone begins to recognize, however dimly, that there* must *be a better way. As this recognition becomes more firmly established, it becomes a turning point. This ultimately reawakens spiritual vision, simultaneously weakening the investment in physical sight. The alternating investment in the two levels of perception is usually experienced as conflict, which can become very acute. But the outcome is as certain as God.* (CH2, III, 3)

The Real Nature of Forgiveness

After categorizing the problems caused by forgiveness-to-destroy, "The Song of Prayer" describes the nature and process of the genuine item, which it identifies as "Forgiveness-for-Salvation." The student is reminded always to ask for spiritual guidance in the process of forgiving because, however practiced one may become in the process of releasing grievances, it remains an essentially mysterious and miraculous means of transformation that cannot be rationally planned or driven by egocentric motivations. The aim of Course-style forgiveness is not to settle scores, excuse transgressions, or broker temporary peace treaties. Its aim is the liberation of human consciousness, which is also the end of alienation and despair.

> *Forgiveness-for-Salvation has one form, and only one. It does not ask for proof of innocence, nor pay of any kind. It does not argue, nor evaluate the errors that it wants to overlook. It does not offer gifts in treachery, nor promise freedom while it asks for death. Would God deceive you? He but asks for trust and willingness to learn how to be free. He gives His Teacher to whoever asks, and seeks to understand the Will of God. His readiness to give lies far beyond your understanding and your simple grasp. Yet He has willed you learn the way to Him, and in His willing there is certainty.*

"What should I do for him, Your holy Son?" should be the only thing you ever ask when help is needed and forgiveness sought. The form the seeking takes you need not judge. And let it not be you who sets the form in which forgiveness comes to save God's Son. The light of Christ in him is his release, and it is this that answers to his call. Forgive him as the Christ decides you should, and be His eyes through which you look on him, and speak for Him as well. He knows the need; the question and the answer. He will say exactly what to do, in words that you can understand and you can also use. . . .

And what is it He speaks to you about? About salvation and the gift of peace. About the end of sin and guilt and death. About the role forgiveness has in Him. Do you but listen. For He will be heard by anyone who calls upon His Name, and places his forgiveness in His hands. Forgiveness has been given Him to teach, to save it from destruction and to make the means for separation, sin and death become again the holy gift of God. Prayer is His Own right Hand, made free to save as true forgiveness is allowed to come from His eternal vigilance and Love. Listen and learn, and do not judge. It is to God you turn to hear what you should do. His answer will be clear as morning, nor is His forgiveness what you think it is. (SOP 2, III, 1–6)

 CHAPTER 6

From Special to Holy Relationships

Although many of the ideas in *A Course in Miracles* may strike students as startling or difficult to understand, perhaps none of them is quite as disconcerting as what the teaching has to say about what it calls "special relationships." The topic is a hot-button issue for most students, and it connects with several major themes of the Course teaching: the illusory nature of the ego-self, the destructive use that ego usually makes of relationship, and the role of forgiveness in transforming relationships to a "holy" condition.

To be frank, almost every kind of relationship we can imagine would qualify as "special" in Course terms, because human beings normally perceive themselves as separate from one another and unique in their histories, personalities, hopes, and preferences. Thus we must relate in a different or special way to everyone we encounter. Although we may occasionally pay lip service to the idea that "we are all one," it's difficult, if not impossible, for most people to imagine consistently relating to each other from that perspective. Yet ACIM insists that a spiritual "oneness" is our true condition. The everyday perception of ourselves as separate beings encased in physical bodies is not only mistaken, says the Course, but also the cause of all the suffering inherent to human experience.

The body is a tiny fence around a little part of a glorious and complete idea. It draws a circle, infinitely small, around a very little segment of Heaven, splintered from the whole, proclaiming that within it is your kingdom, where God can enter not.

Within this kingdom the ego rules, and cruelly. And to defend this little speck of dust it bids you fight against the universe. This fragment of your mind is such a tiny part of it that, could you but appreciate the whole, you would see instantly that it is like the smallest sunbeam to the sun, or like the faintest ripple on the surface of the ocean. In its amazing arrogance, this tiny sunbeam has decided it is the sun; this almost imperceptible ripple hails itself as the ocean. Think how alone and frightened is this little thought, this infinitesimal illusion, holding itself apart against the universe. The sun becomes the sunbeam's "enemy" that would devour it, and the ocean terrifies the little ripple and wants to swallow it. . . . (CH18, VIII, 2–3)

Do not accept this little, fenced-off aspect as yourself. The sun and ocean are as nothing beside what you are. The sunbeam sparkles only in the sunlight, and the ripple dances as it rests upon the ocean. Yet in neither sun nor ocean is the power that rests in you. Would you remain within your tiny kingdom, a sorry king, a bitter ruler of all that he surveys, who looks on nothing yet who would still die to defend it? This little self is not your kingdom. . . . (CH18, VIII, 7)

Nonetheless, the human condition is rooted in the belief that we are indeed "little selves," and we are acutely aware of the incompleteness that we feel in our physical and emotional isolation. Thus we turn to other people (or even certain objects, ideas, or rituals) in the hope of finding what we keenly miss within ourselves. Although special relationships between human beings can be of any form—including parent-child, friendship, boss and employee, and so on—the dynamics of the special relationship are usually felt most keenly in the adult romantic relationship. "Falling in love" is the entrée to the kind of special relationship that people seek with the highest possible expectations, and suffer over acutely when those expectations are dashed.

Despite the near-universal longing for special relationships, ACIM's commentary on the subject is almost unrelentingly harsh:

The special relationship has the most imposing and deceptive frame of all the defenses the ego uses. Its thought system is offered here, surrounded by a frame so heavy and so elaborate that the picture is almost obliterated by its imposing structure. Into the frame are woven all sorts of fanciful and fragmented illusions of love, set with dreams of sacrifice and self-aggrandizement, and interlaced with gilded threads of self-destruction. The glitter of blood shines like rubies, and the tears are faceted like diamonds and gleam in the dim light in which the offering is made.

Look at the picture. *Do not let the frame distract you. This gift is given you for your damnation, and if you take it you will believe that you* are *damned. You cannot have the frame without the picture. What you value is the frame, for there you see no conflict. Yet the frame is only the wrapping for the gift of conflict. The frame is not the gift. Be not deceived by the most superficial aspects of this thought system, for these aspects enclose the whole, complete in every aspect. Death lies in this glittering gift. Let not your gaze dwell on the hypnotic gleaming of the frame. Look at the picture, and realize that death is offered you.* (CH17, IV, 8–9)

Why So Tough?

"The Course is incredibly tough on special relationships," admits Robert Perry, a prominent Course philosopher and cofounder of the Circle of Atonement study center in Sedona, Arizona, who has authored nineteen books and hundreds of articles on ACIM. "But I don't know how different that is from modern psychological perspectives, which are often critical of romantic relationships for some of the same reasons. In ACIM's view, special love is something very different from what it appears to be. It's really hate dressed up as love, although the hate may not surface until the bitter end. The Course also says that this kind of relationship is actually *taking* dressed up as *giving*. Finally, the special relationship is isolation dressed up as joining—in other words, it's actually no relationship at all.

"The reason that we're so attracted to special love is that we see it as joining and giving," adds Perry, "which the Course says is just a veneer over opposite qualities. Because of its real, underlying content, the special relationship must eventually result in suffering. It may seem to deliver happiness in the short term, but sooner or later the inherent logic plays out and the payload of suffering is dropped on your head. We think the suffering results from choosing the wrong partner, yet in fact it results from the thought system that guides our own participation in the relationship."

So when people "fall in love," what is actually happening in the Course point of view? Perry cites a section titled "The Choice for Completion" in chapter 16 of the Text:

> *Most curious of all is the concept of the self which the ego fosters in the special relationship. This "self" seeks the relationship to make itself complete. Yet when it finds the special relationship in which it thinks it can accomplish this it gives itself away, and tries to "trade" itself for the self of another. This is not union, for there is no increase and no extension. Each partner tries to sacrifice the self he does not want for one he thinks he would prefer. And he feels guilty for the "sin" of taking, and of giving nothing of value in return. How much value can he place upon a self that he would give away to get a "better" one?*
>
> *The "better" self the ego seeks is always one that is more special. And whoever seems to possess a special self is "loved" for what can be taken from him. Where both partners see this special self in each other, the ego sees "a union made in Heaven." For neither one will recognize that he has asked for hell, and so he will not interfere with the ego's illusion of Heaven, which it offered him to interfere with Heaven. Yet if all illusions are of fear, and they can be of nothing else, the illusion of Heaven is nothing more than an "attractive" form of fear, in which the guilt is buried deep and rises in the form of "love."*
>
> *The appeal of hell lies only in the terrible attraction of guilt, which the ego holds out to those who place their faith in littleness. The conviction of littleness lies in every special relationship, for only the deprived could value specialness. The demand for specialness, and the perception of the giving of specialness as an act of love, would make love hateful. The real purpose of the special relationship, in strict accordance with the ego's goals, is to destroy reality and substitute illusion. For the ego is itself an illusion, and only illusions can be the witnesses to its "reality."* (Ch16, V, 7–9)

As Perry summarizes, "People are actually falling in love with their own *thought* that another person has a self which is very special, probably more special than themselves. I think that if I can take ownership of that self, wrest it away from the other person, then that special self becomes mine. And the promise of possessing that self, possessing its specialness, results in the giddy feeling of falling in love."

That raises the question of whether the specialness we seek to take from another is really there, or a figment of our own imagination.

"I think it's both," Perry muses. "Obviously we project a lot onto the other person that idealizes him or her. The Course, however, would say that even when those special qualities are actually in the other person, they are part of a false self. The self we are falling in love with is an illusion which masks the real nature of the other person. The Course calls that illusion an *idol*."

Is the end of romance, then, not really "heartbreak" over conflict or rejection by a love partner, but the inevitable failure of our own idolization?

"The expectations that we set up for a special person adds up to a role we expect them to fulfill," explains Perry. "What we're loving is the role that we think someone's going to fulfill, and when he or she doesn't do that, then we're heartbroken and disillusioned." Indeed, this is the crucial moment in many relationships when the beloved suddenly seems to have changed into someone undesirable, uninteresting, or even threatening. The search for someone who seemed to answer all our needs will seem to have failed again, and the restless ego will set forth on another quest for perfect love.

Toward a Truly Collaborative Venture

Despite all the bad news about the special relationship as the Course defines it, there is a cure for this existential dilemma: the "holy relationship." In his teaching experience, Robert Perry has observed that ACIM students tend to talk more about the problems of the special relationship than about the qualities of the holy relationship, although the Course itself gives more attention to the latter. He points out that ACIM deals with special relationships mostly in chapters 15, 16, and 17 of the Text, whereas the holy relationship is treated extensively in chapters 17 through 22.

"Different teachers treat the subject differently," Perry observes, "and most students tend to think a relationship has become holy when one person is in a holy place about it, that is, deciding to be loving or forgiving. Then the *relationship* isn't holy so much as one person's approach is. Because of a prevailing mindset that the Course is only about what's going on in one's own mind, we don't expect the Course to say that a holy relationship is a truly collaborative venture between two people. We expect it to say that my relationship is holy when *I'm* holy about it. But without exception ACIM characterizes the holy relationship as *mutual*. A relationship becomes holy when there is a 'holy instant' between two people, in which they dedicate the relationship to the Holy Spirit. They do that by joining in a truly common purpose."

Is the common purpose always the same in all holy relationships? Perry thinks not: "For Helen Schucman and Bill Thetford, their common purpose was to find a better way of working in their academic environment, in which people would cooperate rather than compete. Their aim was simply to get along; they weren't trying to be spiritual. But when they joined in that purpose of finding a better way, their relationship was made holy."

Perry points out two other examples of finding a common purpose. One occurs in the Manual for Teachers, in a discussion of student and pupil joining to learn the same spiritual path:

When pupil and teacher come together, a teaching-learning situation begins. For the teacher is not really the one who does the teaching. God's Teacher speaks to any two who join together for learning purposes. The relationship is holy because of that purpose, and God has promised to send His Spirit into any holy relationship. In the teaching-learning situation, each one learns that giving and receiving are the same. The demarcations they have drawn between their roles, their minds, their bodies, their needs, their interests, and all the differences they thought separated them from one another, fade and grow dim and disappear. Those who would learn the same course share one interest and one goal. And thus he who was the learner becomes a teacher of God himself, for he has made the one decision that gave his teacher to him. He has seen in another person the same interests as his own. (MANUAL, 2, 5)

In this example, a relationship becomes holy when two people "join together for learning purposes"—more specifically, to "learn the same course," the same spiritual path.

In another example from the "Psychotherapy" pamphlet channeled by Helen Schucman, Perry cites a discussion of how therapist and patient must eventually resolve divergent goals:

> *At the beginning, then, the patient's goal and the therapist's are at variance. The therapist as well as the patient may cherish false self-concepts, but their respective perceptions of "improvement" still must differ. The patient hopes to learn how to get the changes he wants without changing his self-concept to any significant extent. He hopes, in fact, to stabilize it sufficiently to include within it the magical powers he seeks in psychotherapy. He wants to make the vulnerable invulnerable and the finite limitless. The self he sees is his god, and he seeks only to serve it better.*
>
> *Regardless of how sincere the therapist himself may be, he must want to change the patient's self-concept in some way that he believes is real. The task of therapy is one of reconciling these differences. Hopefully, both will learn to give up their original goals, for it is only in relationships that salvation can be found. At the beginning, it is inevitable that patients and therapists alike accept unrealistic goals not completely free of magical overtones. They are finally given up in the minds of both.* (Psychotherapy, 2, 3–4)

Because it's their special love relationships that most people would be concerned with making holy—or at least healthier—is there a common spiritual purpose for romance, in the view of *A Course in Miracles?*

"Perhaps there's a common essence to different kinds of joining," suggests Perry. "Rather than a couple joining to raise their status in the world—'let's have the best house on the block,' which would be a common goal of shoring up two egos—it would be about two people joining in an inner transformation, in which they become more healthy, whole, loving, and kind inwardly, and thereby become a benefit to others around them. That's probably the common essence of any goal that two people can join in for a holy purpose."

When Holy Doesn't Look That Way

Although Perry cites the relationship of the Course scribes Schucman and Thetford as one made holy by their joining of intent, it's been widely reported that their own relationship was never visibly healed. Does that mean that a relationship can be made holy but still appear to be troubled on a daily basis?

"Well, yes," Perry admits. "The Course sketches an entire journey that a holy relationship goes through. For a time, and that can be a very long time, the relationship may appear to be holy in name only. That's because joining in a common goal invites holiness to enter the relationship and heal it, but that healing initially takes place at a deep unconscious level. That unconscious healing, or holiness, then has to rise and displace the surface patterns of specialness. And that is a long process indeed. Helen and Bill entered the initial stages of that process, which the Course calls the 'period of discomfort.' [CH20, VII, 2] That's an understatement, by the way; it's really more like living through hell."

As the Course describes this difficult period:

The holy relationship, a major step toward the perception of the real world, is learned. It is the old, unholy relationship, transformed and seen anew. The holy relationship is a phenomenal teaching accomplishment. In all its aspects, as it begins, develops and becomes accomplished, it represents the reversal of the unholy relationship. Be comforted in this; the only difficult phase is the beginning. For here, the goal of the relationship is abruptly shifted to the exact opposite of what it was. This is the first result of offering the relationship to the Holy Spirit, to use for His purposes.

This invitation is accepted immediately, and the Holy Spirit wastes no time in introducing the practical results of asking Him to enter. At once His goal replaces yours. This is accomplished very rapidly, but it makes the relationship seem disturbed, disjunctive and even quite distressing. The reason is quite clear. For the relationship as it is, *is out of line with its own goal, and clearly unsuited to the purpose that has been accepted for it. In its unholy condition,* your *goal was all that seemed to give it meaning. Now it seems to make no sense. Many relationships have been broken off at this point, and the pursuit of the old goal re-established in another relationship. For once the unholy relationship has accepted the goal of holiness, it can never again be what it was.*

The temptation of the ego becomes extremely intense with this shift in goals. For the relationship has not as yet been changed sufficiently to make its former goal completely without attraction, and its structure is "threatened" by the recognition of its inappropriateness for meeting its new purpose. The conflict between the goal and the structure of the relationship is so apparent that they cannot coexist. Yet now the goal will not be changed. Set firmly in the unholy relationship, there is no course except to change the relationship to fit the goal. Until this happy solution is seen and accepted as the only way out of the conflict, the relationship may seem to be severely strained. (CH17, V, 2–4)

"So even in a relationship that has been changed by a decision to join in a common purpose," explains Perry, "people will have the same old attachments to their purposes of specialness, and they don't want to let those go. Then they look at the war going on between themselves, and between their two purposes, and think, 'This is a joke; we're ridiculous, hopeless.' That's the period of discomfort, and people can only leave that as they slowly shift their minds over to the new goal. It seems that with Helen and Bill, that shifting never went far enough to become evident in their daily relationship."

The Course advises against moving on to find ego-gratification when the period of discomfort becomes intense:

Now the ego counsels thus; substitute for this another relationship to which your former goal was quite appropriate. You can escape from your distress only by getting rid of your brother. You need not part entirely if you choose not to do so. But you must exclude major areas of fantasy from your brother, to save your sanity. Hear not this now! *Have faith in Him Who answered you. He heard. Has He not been very explicit in His answer? You are not now wholly insane. Can you deny that He has given you a most explicit statement? Now He asks for faith a little longer, even in bewilderment. For this will go, and you will see the justification for your faith emerge, to bring you shining conviction. Abandon Him not now, nor your brother. This relationship has been reborn as holy.* (CH17, V, 7)

Nonetheless, even spiritual people break up, get divorced, and find new partners. Can holy relationships continue even when they apparently end?

"Yes, I think so," says Perry. "The most helpful discussion of this issue is in the third section of the Manual for Teachers, where it talks about three levels of teaching. The context given is a teacher-pupil relationship, but what's said there can be generalized to all relationships. People get together because of the potential to learn something from each other. Since that's why they're together in the first place, when they reach a point where they no longer can learn from each other, they part, and sometime later—maybe even thousands of years later—they're brought together again when they have that readiness to realize their holy relationship."

In fact, the Manual refers to a "perfect" learning-teaching relationship that may actually be characterized by hostility:

> *The third level of teaching occurs in relationships which, once they are formed, are lifelong. These are teaching-learning situations in which each person is given a chosen learning partner who presents him with unlimited opportunities for learning. These relationships are generally few, because their existence implies that those involved have reached a stage simultaneously in which the teaching-learning balance is actually perfect. This does not mean that they necessarily recognize this; in fact, they generally do not. They may even be quite hostile to each other for some time, and perhaps for life. Yet should they decide to learn it, the perfect lesson is before them and can be learned. And if they decide to learn that lesson, they become the saviors of the teachers who falter and may even seem to fail. No teacher of God can fail to find the Help he needs. (MANUAL, 3, 5)*

Avoiding the Special Use of Holiness

The whole issue of special versus holy relationships can become so charged for Course students that they may turn the pursuit of holiness into "something special." Robert Perry confirms that he has seen this problem among students he has taught and advised. "It's really crucial to not want to claim the title of Holy Relationship," he comments. "So many Course students want to claim that they've made their relationship holy before there's been any joining in a common goal. They seem more interested in claiming the title than in actually meeting the qualifications. And that can become just another trophy to add to the ego's shelf.

"It's less important to think about special or holy than to think that we're in relationship to learn how to love, to truly give without strings, to forgive those who aggravate or frustrate us, and to learn great patience. We have to think about being in relationship in order to become a different person, who's genuinely loving and joyful. Then it doesn't matter whether you call your relationships special or holy."

What, then, is the key element for transforming special relationships?

"Of course it's forgiveness," says Perry, "because the special relationship is all about expecting the other person to play the right role for you. Invariably he or she messes up their lines and the relationship goes downhill. So what's the method for cleansing our relationships of the burden of anger over accumulated screw-ups on both sides? It has to be some way of letting go of resentment over transgressions that are inevitable in special relationships."

As noted in the previous chapter, the ultimate level of Course forgiveness is to forgive each other for "what did not occur" in terms of our spiritual reality. Since it seems unlikely that most people can get that far on a daily basis—"I forgive you for saying that terrible thing because I recognize that nothing actually happened"—is there a more practical level of forgiveness that still works to heal relationships?

"Realistically, people have to be regularly doing the kind of practices that the Workbook teaches," Perry recommends. "That means watching your mind throughout the day for upsets, judgments, and resentments, and when those happen, doing what the Course calls 'responding to temptation'—using Workbook practices to dispel your negative feelings. Perhaps you remove yourself from the heat of conflict for five or ten minutes and do your exercises to authentically shift your perception.

"For instance, the idea that I'm practicing today is 'forgiveness is the only gift I give, because it is the only gift I want, and everything I give I give myself.' That means I'm letting another person off the hook, and by giving that gift to them, letting my own guilt slide off my shoulders. That last part's a big motivator because, let's face it, we always carry around guilt about our closest relationships. Unless we're keeping these practices on our mind daily, hopefully starting the morning with them, then there's not going to be much hope of dealing with the tough stuff as it comes up."

A Different Premise

In chapter 22 of the Text, the Course offers some clear distinctions between the conditions of special and holy relationships:

> *For an unholy relationship is based on differences, where each one thinks the other has what he has not. They come together, each to complete himself and rob the other. They stay until they think that there is nothing left to steal, and then move on. And so they wander through a world of strangers, unlike themselves, living with their bodies perhaps under a common roof that shelters neither; in the same room and yet a world apart.*
>
> *A holy relationship starts from a different premise. Each one has looked within and seen no lack. Accepting his completion, he would extend it by joining with another, whole as himself. He sees no difference between these selves, for differences are only of the body. Therefore, he looks on nothing he would take. . . .*
>
> *Think what a holy relationship can teach! Here is belief in differences undone. Here is the faith in differences shifted to sameness. And here is sight of differences transformed to vision.* (CH22, INTRO, 2–4)

At such moments of vision, says the Course, we experience a "holy instant": a timeless moment in which anyone can realize his true nature as eternal spirit, a realization that ACIM refers to as "Atonement." Many spiritual paths teach that such a moment of transcendence or enlightenment is possible, but it is often thought of as a solitary achievement attained only after much time spent in disciplined meditation. Indeed, the most popular image of an enlightened being is probably that of an ascetic loner living in a cave, coming to an "Aha!" moment after years of cross-legged contemplation with virtually no human contact.

A notable paradox of *A Course in Miracles* is that although it is often referred to as a "self-study" curriculum (a description not made in ACIM itself), its teachings are fully activated only in relationship. The Course certainly recognizes the self-serving snares, misunderstandings, and outright delusions that characterize virtually all ordinary relationships; indeed, that's what makes them "special." But through the disciplines of self-confrontation and forgiveness, one gradually learns to turn over the conduct of relationships to the inner agency of wisdom that the Course calls the Holy Spirit. And it is in this surrender of the ego to spirit—which may have to be repeated countless times in the daily flow of life—that relationships are transformed, paving the way to a *mutual* enlightenment that extends even beyond each relationship made holy:

It is no dream to love your brother as yourself. Nor is your holy relationship a dream. All that remains of dreams within it is that it is still a special relationship. Yet it is very useful to the Holy Spirit, Who has a special function here. It will become the happy dream through which he can spread joy to thousands on thousands who believe that love is fear, not happiness. Let Him fulfill the function that He gave to your relationship by accepting it for you, and nothing will be wanting that would make of it what he would have it be.

When you feel the holiness of your relationship is threatened by anything, stop instantly and offer the Holy Spirit your willingness, in spite of fear, to let Him exchange this instant for the holy one that you would rather have. He will never fail in this. But forget not that your relationship is one, and so it must be that whatever threatens the peace of one is an equal threat to the other. The power of joining its blessing lies in the fact that it is now impossible for you or your brother to experience fear alone, or to attempt to deal with it alone. Never believe that this is necessary, or even possible. Yet just as this is impossible, so is it equally impossible that the holy instant come to either of you without the other. And it will come to both at the request of either.

Whoever is saner at the time the threat is perceived should remember how deep is his indebtedness to the other and how much gratitude is due him, and be glad that he can pay his debt by bringing happiness to both.

Let him remember this, and say:

I desire this holy instant for myself, that I may share it with my brother, whom I love.
It is not possible that I can have it without him, or he without me.
Yet it is wholly possible for us to share it now.
And so I choose this instant as the one to offer to the Holy Spirit, that his blessing may descend on us, and keep us both in peace.
(CH18, V, 5–7)

 CHAPTER 7

Living in an Unreal World

The basic philosophical premise of *A Course in Miracles* is stated in simple yet cryptic language in the brief Introduction preceding the main Text, in which it is asserted that the entire teaching can be summed up in these words:

Nothing real can be threatened.
Nothing unreal exists.
Herein lies the peace of God.

Because everything in the world of matter can be threatened by change, decay, or destruction, the Course is asserting here that everything we see in physical reality does not actually exist. This philosophical claim is not new, being prefigured in the Hindu notion of *maya* (a Sanskrit word referring to the physical world as an illusion that veils the Brahman, or Unitary Self) and in various strains of Western Gnosticism.

This fundamental aspect of the Course teaching also bears a remarkable similarity to the "immaterialism" of the eighteenth-century philosopher George Berkeley, Bishop of Cloyne, generally credited as one of the three great empiricists of his time (along with John Locke and David Hume). Despite his conventional career in the Church, Berkeley shocked his contemporaries with the assertion that "*esse is percipi*" (to be is to be perceived), and by noting that the "opinion strangely prevailing amongst men, that houses, mountains, rivers, and in a world all sensible objects have an existence natural or real, distinct from being perceived" is "a manifest contradiction."[1] In other words, Berkeley asserted that the reality we experience every day consists entirely of our *ideas* about what we are seeing, rather than all things and people having an objective reality independent of our perceptions.

In the Course, "*esse is percipi*" is restated by such Workbook Lessons as "I have given everything I see . . . all the meaning that it has for me" (3) and "I have invented the world I see" (32). In fact, the initial Course lessons focus on the habitual ideas we have developed about the world around us, starting the student along a path of questioning and surrendering these ideas in order to "see things differently":

> *When you say, "Above all else I want to see this table differently," you are making a commitment to withdraw your preconceived ideas about the table, and open your mind to what it is, and what it is for. You are not defining it in past terms. You are asking what it is, rather than telling it what it is. You are not binding its meaning to your tiny experience of tables, nor are you limiting its purpose to your little personal thoughts.*
>
> *You will not question what you have already defined. And the purpose of these exercises is to ask questions and receive the answers. In saying, "Above all else I want to see this table differently," you are committing yourself to seeing. It is not an exclusive commitment. It is a commitment that applies to the table just as much as to anything else, neither more nor less.* (LESSON 28)

But the claim that "nothing real can be threatened" calls for more than a new perception of objects. ACIM is also implying that any state of mind driven by fear is a false consciousness. Indeed, the Course regards the ego—the normal human "sense of self"—as a fear-driven complex of illusions that makes the world in its own image: "What I see is a form of vengeance" (LESSON 22); "I can escape from the world I see by giving up attack thoughts" (LESSON 23).

Far from being a dry philosophical abstraction with no impact on one's everyday life, our identification with an unreal world is posited by the Course as the source of all our suffering. The human condition is likened to a form of homesickness in the following poignant passages:

> *The world you seem to live in is not home to you. And somewhere in your mind you know that this is true. A memory of home keeps haunting you, as if there were a place that called you to return, although you do not recognize the voice, nor what it is the voice reminds you of. Yet still you feel an alien here, from somewhere all unknown. . . .*
>
> *No one but knows whereof we speak. Yet some try to put by their suffering in games they play to occupy their time, and keep their sadness from them. Others will deny that they are sad, and do not recognize their tears at all. . . . Yet who, in simple honesty, without defensiveness and self-deception, would deny he understands the words we speak?* (LESSON 182)

If the everyday world is not our real home, then where is it? *A Course in Miracles* generally describes the "real world" not as a place but as a state of mind that surpasses human consciousness, referred to by the Course as "knowledge." We begin the journey toward knowledge whenever we start changing the way we look at the everyday world:

> *This world of light, this circle of brightness is the real world, where guilt meets with forgiveness. Here the world outside is seen anew, without the shadow of guilt upon it. Here are you forgiven, for here you have forgiven everyone. Here is the new perception, where everything is bright and shining with innocence, washed in the waters of forgiveness, and cleansed of every evil thought you laid upon it. Here there is no attack upon the Son of God, and you are welcome. Here is your innocence, waiting to clothe you and protect you, and make you ready for the final step in the journey inward. Here are the dark and heavy garments of guilt laid by, and gently replaced by purity and love.* (CH18, IX, 9)

In other instances, ACIM does offer descriptions of spiritual reality in cosmological terms.

Beyond the body, beyond the sun and stars, past everything you see and yet somehow familiar, is an arc of golden light that stretches as you look into a great and shining circle. And all the circle fills with light before your eyes. The edges of the circle disappear, and what is in it is no longer contained at all. The light expands and covers everything, extending to infinity forever shining and with no break or limit anywhere. Within it everything is joined in perfect continuity. Nor is it possible to imagine that anything could be outside, for there is nowhere that this light is not. (CH21, I, 8)

Although this description bears some resemblance to Christian views of heaven as a bright and shining place where saved souls live eternally, the two cosmologies are quite different. The Course does not posit an afterlife because it asserts that we are now asleep and dreaming in the midst of the real, ongoing life of the spirit. Thus we do not have to die in order to reach heaven; instead, we need to wake up in order to recognize that we are already home in God, inside a light that "covers everything." We do not see this light now only because we willingly block it with our grievances: "My grievances hide the light of the world in me," says Workbook Lesson 69.

Likewise, from the Course point of view the world is neither "fallen" nor evil, nor does it serve as an existential proving ground where we must recognize and admit our sins in order to be saved and thus qualify for a heavenly reward after death. Rather, the body, the world, and the entire physical universe are simply fictions in which nothing really lives *or* dies. The body is often described in ACIM as "neutral," and we need only surrender our attachment to it ("I am not a body. I am free." [LESSON 199]) to recognize our true condition, which is innately divine and eternal: "There is one life, and that I share with God." (LESSON 167)

Struggling with Unreality

Needless to say, the surrender of everything we believe to be real—our bodies, the natural and constructed world, and the vast cosmos beyond our own planet—is difficult to negotiate for most people. A woman who said she had been studying the Course for more than a year expressed it this way in a posting to an online ACIM discussion group:

If we are supposed to view the world differently, if what we see is not real, how do we go about our everyday activities? Do we quit our jobs and sit and contemplate? Do we actively fill every free moment with passages and practices of the course?

Why are there babies dying every day from poverty and violence? Are we supposed to see this as not real? . . . I truly am confused and in my quest for salvation, by turning to God, have sought out these questions and have gotten no answers. It's almost impossible to pretend that we are not who we are. Try as I may, I still have to work to pay bills, yet I find it hard some days to get up in the morning, to prepare myself for the day knowing that all the things I am doing in the eyes of the Lord are not real and, moreover, meaningless. . . . I really feel like this is an obsession that leads to depression, especially when so much time is invested in understanding the concepts of ACIM.

To this message an online correspondent answered, "I'm with you. I threw my ACIM books out"—a reaction not uncommon among beginning students of ACIM. As Casey Kington, a twenty-two-year veteran of Course study, commented to me, "The metaphysics screwed up my studies so much I threw the damn books in the trash. And I burned my second set in a campfire. Unfortunately, my last copy is still on my nightstand and no matter how much I pray, it just won't disappear."

For students who hang on, the initial disorienting effect of the Course metaphysics eventually softens, changing their way of being and relating in the world in a positive if unexpected manner. Sofia Pizano, an Hispanic American living in northern California, recalls that early in her Course study she became "very dissociated from the world around me. I lost desire and passion for life as I used to know it. . . . Nothing seemed to matter except studying and experiencing the teachings of the Course. I wasn't depressed, just numb. Eventually I experienced a subtle shift where I began to feel more comfortable around all kinds of people, even strangers in public places. I began to love talking and being present with everyone I met. Overall I'm still not interested in what's happening in the world, but I am interested in sharing and 'being' a part of the world, if that makes any sense."

Pizano's experience describes the path to the paradoxical spiritual goal, sometimes attributed to the Sufi tradition, of being "in the world but not of it." This condition is a kind of caring detachment, in which one learns to respond to the undeniable tragedies and cruelties of life on earth with a practical, resilient compassion rather than an embittered and eventually exhausting attachment. As psychiatrist and philosopher Roger Walsh (see chapter 8) related to me, "There has long been a fear among some people—perhaps Karl Marx is the best known example—that spiritual seeking merely perpetuates social pathology and inequality, and may occasion a permanent withdrawal from the concerns of the world. However, many spiritual seekers withdraw for a while and return to share what they have learned in order to help the world. This is what historian Arnold Toynbee calls 'the cycle of withdrawal and return.' He discovered that it was a characteristic feature of the lives of those people who have contributed most profoundly to human well-being."

Regardless of the difficulty of adjusting to the notion of an immaterial world, it's a challenge that may soon have to be faced not just by students of *A Course in Miracles*, but by humanity at large. For it's precisely this challenge that is being predicted by advances in the science of physics, which has traditionally sought for the building blocks of physical reality—a search recently producing assessments of reality that sound increasingly metaphysical.

Welcome to the End of Time

On January 1, 2004, the *New York Times* published an editorial titled "The Time We Thought We Knew" by physicist Brian Greene, author of the popular science titles *The Elegant Universe* and *The Fabric of the Cosmos*. Had Greene's piece not been sequestered in the newspaper's parlor room of opinion pieces, it might well have served as front-page news of the greatest historical import:

Today's scientists seeking to combine quantum mechanics with Einstein's theory of gravity (the general theory of relativity) are convinced that we are on the verge of another major upheaval. . . . Many believe this will involve a radically new formulation of natural law in which scientists will be compelled to trade the space-time matrix within which they have worked for centuries for a more basic "realm" that is itself devoid of time and space. . . . As outrageous as it sounds, to many researchers, including me, such a departure of time and space from the ultimate laws of the universe seems inevitable.

It should be noted that Greene is not a New Age physicist with correspondence-school credentials. He holds a chair in mathematics and physics at Columbia University (where two psychology professors secretly recorded ACIM decades before him), and he does not venture into any spiritual or psychological meanings that might be drawn from his work. Like the late Carl Sagan, who popularized astronomy and cosmology for the masses, Greene displays a showman's enthusiasm and a contagious sense of wonder about his explorations while displaying little interest in their nonscientific implications.

Interestingly, one of the persistent criticisms of the work that he and his peers are doing in quantum physics, particularly the specialty of string theory, is that these rarefied scientific pursuits resist "real-world" experimentation and laboratory proofs. So far these theories have proved themselves only on the basis of mathematics—that is, in the intangible, Berkeleyan realm of ideas instead of the tangible, material realm. Nonetheless, the work of Greene and his peers clearly represents the leading edge of a fundamental science, not merely a speculative offshoot.

And as Greene often points out, his challenges to the status quo of reality are not even new, having been first issued by Albert Einstein a century ago and amplified since by contributory advances in physics. Both science and human culture at large have simply not caught up to Einstein's groundbreaking insights that time and space are not fixed and immutable, but circumstantial and relative. In other words, we use the ideas of time and space to organize our reality, but they are not realities in themselves.

For instance, most of us still live every day by the assumptions of Isaac Newton, who asserted in the seventeenth century that "time flows equably without reference to anything external"—or as if, as Greene put it, "the universe is equipped with a kind of built-in clock that ticks off seconds identically, regardless of location or epoch." Because that fundamental perception of time is reliable unless you are traveling near the speed of light or vacationing near a black hole—where everything starts to change in some very weird ways—"nature lulls us into believing Newton's rigid conception," says Greene. Still, he adds, "the cost of adhering to Newton's description of time is high. Like believing the earth flat or that man was created on the sixth day, our willingness to place unjustified faith in immediate perception or received wisdom leads us to an inaccurate and starkly limited vision of reality."

A Course in Miracles would agree, although its realm of thought is not scientific and it is focused on healing human suffering rather than furthering the evolution of grand universal theories. But if Greene is right in suggesting that science will eventually have to surrender our belief in space and time, then it's up to nonscientists to start asking what the ramifications may be for the rest of human culture.

For instance, what difference will this profound shift in perception make in psychology and religion? When it becomes obvious that human beings can no longer define themselves within the old parameters of fixed time and measurable space, how then will we see ourselves? From the "starkly limited vision of reality" that we now entertain, can we even begin to imagine how our existence may be redefined by a profoundly greater vision of truth?

Veteran students of ACIM will likely agree with the proposition that the Course is introducing our minds to just such an advanced vision and furthermore providing a kind of "boot camp" training in the state of awareness required to inhabit that vision. If our existence is in fact not bound by time and space as we now believe—meaning that our awareness need not be constrained by the body nor the customary limits of "life and death"—then it may be a simple statement of fact that "nothing real can be threatened, and nothing unreal exists." The logic of the Course concludes that within this realization lies "the peace of God." This has traditionally been called "the peace which passeth understanding," a dynamic union with the creative power of the universe itself.

Toward a Copernican Revolution of the Psyche

Before Copernicus, it was inconceivable to most people that the planet Earth was not the center of the universe, and that the affairs of humanity were not the overriding concern of an all-powerful, watchful Creator who had decided to make some mortal and quite fallible beings in His own image, for reasons unknown. (As the English songwriter David Knopfler has mused, "If God could make angels, why in hell make man?"[2])

Although religion has generally resisted the progress of scientific perception, it is science that has gradually enlarged our view of the physical universe until we've come to accept that the Earth is but an infinitely tiny speck in a vast and fantastic cosmos. Science has also been fast transforming our view of the universe as a single, measurable fabric of space, time, and matter, to an infinite and multidimensional play of energetic, mutable light, unbounded by space and time. In this developing vision, we may eventually comprehend that we are not the tiny, separated beings we have always imagined ourselves to be, bound by gravity and grief to finite life spans that seldom give us time to comprehend ourselves before our individual consciousness is snuffed out.

Instead, we may learn to grasp that we are forever part of that infinite play of light, and that our minds—profoundly limited by our senses, prejudices, and expectations—are presently asleep to a vastly greater awareness. However limited and problematic it seems now, our consciousness nonetheless presents us with the opportunity to peer beyond our current, seemingly inescapable limitations and synchronize ourselves with the timeless truth of creation.

Thus we may be on the verge of a new Copernican revolution of the psyche, in which we will become aware that the ego is not the center of consciousness and the body is not the limit of our existence—and that in such a heightened state of mind lies the healing of our historic sufferings. Along the way to this selfless awareness we have to solve all the problems that arise from believing so fiercely in our existential imprisonment, our current condition of perceiving ourselves as separated from the rest of creation and doomed to die alone. But ACIM suggests that all these problems are the same.

No one could solve all the problems the world appears to hold. They seem to be on so many levels, in such varying forms and with such varied content, that they confront you with an impossible situation. Dismay and depression are inevitable as you regard them. Some spring up unexpectedly, just as you think you have resolved the previous ones. Others remain unsolved under a cloud of denial, and rise to haunt you from time to time, only to be hidden again but still unsolved.

All this complexity is but a desperate attempt not to recognize the problem, and therefore not to let it be resolved. If you could recognize that your only problem is separation, no matter what form it takes, you could accept the answer because you would see its relevance. Perceiving the underlying constancy in all the problems that seem to confront you, you would understand that you have the means to solve them all. And you would use the means, because you recognize the problem. (LESSON 79)

Although the Course suggests that a "final step" to the end of separation lies beyond forgiveness, that is not a step that we make on our own. Rather, it is the continual work of forgiving the world we see that will make us ready:

Yet even forgiveness is not the end. Forgiveness does make lovely, but it does not create. It is the source of healing, but it is the messenger of love and not its Source. Here you are led, that God Himself can take the final step unhindered, for here does nothing interfere with love, letting it be itself. A step beyond this holy place of forgiveness, a step still further inward but the one you cannot take, transports you to something completely different. Here is the Source of light; nothing perceived, forgiven nor transformed. But merely known.

This course will lead to knowledge, but knowledge itself is still beyond the scope of our curriculum. Nor is there any need for us to try to speak of what must forever lie beyond words. We need remember only that whoever attains the real world, beyond which learning cannot go, will go beyond it, but in a different way. Where learning ends there God begins, for learning ends before Him Who is complete where He begins, and where there is no end. It is not for us to dwell on what cannot be attained. There is too much to learn. The readiness for knowledge still must be attained. (CH18, IX, 10–11)

What *A Course in Miracles* calls "knowledge" other traditions have called enlightenment, nirvana, or being at one with the Tao. Although the Course does not present itself as a superior spiritual path—calling itself part of a "universal curriculum" that will lead everyone to the same conclusion via different paths—it does suggest that serious students will progress by its discipline faster than by any other method. (Among a number of references to the time-saving aspects of ACIM are mysterious claims such as "The miracle substitutes for learning that might have taken thousands of years." [CH1, II, 6])

In fact, one of the difficulties presented by the Course is that in the first decade or so of study one often gets the feeling of being pushed unfairly hard toward a spiritual goal that seems too costly, requiring the total surrender of one's favorite prejudices, well-worn grudges, and cockeyed worldviews. Despite the fact that our narrow perceptions and beliefs cause much of our existential pain, most of us are incredibly stubborn about surrendering our skewed logic and questionable decision-making processes to another way of thinking. As the Course suggests,

Tolerance for pain may be high, but it is not without limit. Eventually everyone begins to recognize, however dimly, that there must *be a better way. As this recognition becomes more firmly established, it becomes a turning point. This ultimately reawakens spiritual vision, simultaneously weakening the investment in physical sight. The alternating investment in the two levels of perception is usually experienced as conflict, which can become very acute. But the outcome is as certain as God.* (CH2, III, 3)

Thus, *A Course in Miracles* represents a contemporary, psychologically sophisticated guide to the reawakening of spiritual vision without the dogma, rituals, or social requirements of an established religion. Students can achieve that life-changing vision through the courageous and consistent application of forgiveness, not primarily because forgiving is morally right or divinely approved, but simply because it works better than anything else to heal our hearts and get our heads on straight. What proceeds from forgiveness may be a different kind of miracle than the sort we are used to hearing about in the news or at a revival meeting. But it is the kind of miracle that we can actually "work" on our own if we are willing. And as one begins to sense, with repeated applications and growing effectiveness, it's the kind of miracle that just might change our view of everything.

✑ ENDNOTES ✑

1. George Berkeley, "A Treatise concerning the Principles of human knowledge . . ." See full text online at www.siue.edu/~evailat/principles.html.
2. David Knopfler, "If God Could Make the Angels," *Wishbones* album, Tru Note Records, 2001. See www.knopfler.com.

PART III

A PROVOCATIVE LEGACY

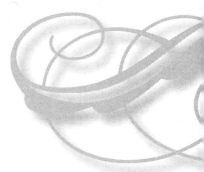

 CHAPTER 8

Where Psychology Meets the Perennial Philosophy

Roger Walsh was completing his psychiatric training in 1976 when he first saw *A Course in Miracles*, handed to him by his future marriage partner Frances Vaughan. "I opened it, saw the words God and Holy Spirit, then immediately shut the book and refused to have anything to do with it for two years," says Walsh. "But I kept meeting people I respected who respected the Course. The final straw was meeting Bill Thetford, who made a presentation at a meeting of the American Orthopsychiatric Association in 1978. I remember thinking, 'If this guy's interested, then I'm interested.' I started reading the Course again, and it took me about three months to get through my resistance to the language. Then it suddenly shifted from being obnoxious to being beautiful, and the teaching really opened up for me. My serious study of the Course has continued ever since."

Walsh, a professor of psychiatry, anthropology, and philosophy at the University of California at Irvine, and Vaughan, a therapist in private practice and past president of the Association for Transpersonal Psychology, represent a contingent of Course students that belies the skeptical view of it as a lightheaded love doctrine (see chapter 10). Considering that this contingent of intellectuals with high-powered academic degrees and psychological training included Helen Schucman and Bill Thetford, it is arguably more representative of ACIM's lineage than any other faction.

Although Walsh and Vaughan are not primarily identified as Course teachers, they are reliable sources on two major aspects of ACIM's philosophical heritage: its continuity with psychotherapy and its commonality with certain core aspects of the world's great religious traditions, or what has been called the *perennial philosophy*. Authors of fifteen books between them on such subjects as therapy, intuition, and shamanism, Walsh and Vaughan also edited a compilation of Course excerpts titled *Gifts from A Course in Miracles* (Tarcher/Putnam, 1995).

Growing up Episcopalian, Frances Vaughan says she became interested in comparative religion while an undergraduate at Stanford University. There she studied under Frederick Spiegelberg, who provided her first exposure to Eastern thought. She was a student of Buddhism with some experience in Zen meditation when she encountered the Course in 1975, receiving a photocopy of the original manuscript from Jerry Jampolsky. "I was going through a divorce in 1975," Vaughan recalls, "and the Course was tremendously helpful to me in dealing with guilt and anger."

Unlike many students who came to the Course after departing from their Christian upbringing, Vaughan found the Course philosophically similar to her Episcopalian training. "The core message that I got as an Episcopalian was that Jesus taught 'God is love.' The good news of the Gospel of the New Testament was that sins are forgiven. The rest of the message was 'Know the truth and the truth shall make you free.' That was it. And that's totally consistent with the Course."

Having sampled a number of spiritual paths before ACIM, Vaughan "liked the fact that you didn't have to join anything, belong to a group, or swear allegiance to a teacher" to undertake the Course discipline. "You simply had the material available and could study it on your own." Although she experienced some difficulty at first with its masculine tone, Vaughan says she "felt very much at home with the Course" before long.

Walsh, a native Australian for whom the Church of England constituted his earliest religious influence, says that he was "pretty much of an agnostic" by the time he arrived at Stanford University for his psychiatric training. "I was a hardcore neuroscientist oriented toward behavior-modification therapy and a related outlook on life."

A major turning point in Walsh's life occurred when he entered psychotherapy in 1974, "opening up a whole new world of inner feeling and imagery that I'd been totally out of touch with." Sampling a wide variety of trainings and workshops while pursuing psychiatric training and then his postdoctoral psychiatric research, Walsh found himself gravitating toward meditation practice and contemplative traditions—"although I didn't know exactly why, since I still regarded religion as the opiate of the masses."

Then came another turning point. "I experienced a blinding moment of insight," recalls Walsh, "when I realized that the contemplative core of the world's great spiritual traditions offered technologies for the induction of transcendent states of mind."

As Walsh points out in his book *The Spirit of Shamanism* (Tarcher, 1991), such "altered states of consciousness" (ASCs) were largely regarded as pathological disturbances by psychologists until the last few decades. Since then humanistic, transpersonal, and Jungian psychologies have accorded more respect to such ASCs as dreaming, meditation, and mystical experiences. As Walsh writes, "The net result is that Western psychology is now better positioned to understand and appreciate, rather than to pathologize and denigrate, religious experiences in general . . ."

From this perspective, the mid-1970s arrival of *A Course in Miracles*—with its unique blend of psychological and spiritual language plus an explicit discipline for "mind training"—could not have been more perfectly timed. But in Roger Walsh's view, what makes the Course so effective is not only its modernity but also some core characteristics that it shares with the world's most ancient and revered religious traditions.

"Higher Grades of Significance"

Common Boundary, a national magazine formerly published in Bethesda, Maryland, explored the meeting ground of psychotherapy and spirituality. Its advisory board included both Walsh and Vaughan. In January 1989 *Common Boundary* featured a cover story by Roger Walsh about *A Course in Miracles*, a story that would later spark a hostile reaction by a prominent psychologist in the same magazine (see chapter 10). Walsh's review of the Course was consistently glowing.

"One of the hallmarks of a profound teaching is that when you go through it again, you find what philosophers call 'higher grades of significance,'" wrote Walsh. "This seems to happen each time I go through the Course. I'm now at the point where I feel it's on a par with any other material or discipline I've seen. . . . I'm inclined to think that this document may be a spiritual masterpiece."

Walsh went on to delineate three contemporary advances in the understanding of comparative religion that help clarify how the Course fits in with the world's major spiritual traditions. The first advance involves what is sometimes sardonically called the "spiritual supermarket" that opened in the late twentieth century—the unprecedented modern exposure, particularly in the West, to a worldwide variety of spiritual paths and perspectives. "A few hundred years ago, there were no tapes, not much in the way of books, and people were usually exposed to only one religion," Walsh observed. "Trying to bone up on another was not terribly popular and could land one on a funeral pyre."

The second change was the discovery in 1945 of the Gnostic Gospels, or Nag Hammadi Library, revealing the existence of a number of early schools of Christian mystics who generally took a more metaphysical view of Christ and his teachings than the traditional school that came to dominate Western religious thought. Citing Elaine Pagels' popular work *The Gnostic Gospels*, Walsh summarized some major points of the Gnostic teachings that will sound familiar to any Course student:

The implications for Christianity are extraordinary. First, the [Gnostic] picture of Jesus is not of someone claiming to be forever unique or in any way ontologically distinct and forever set apart from the rest of humankind. Rather, he simply says he has arrived at a state that is latent within all of us. He speaks not of sin and guilt, but of endarkenment and illusion. He speaks of himself as having awakened and speaks of those who imbibe his words and practices as becoming like Him, one with Him: "He who will drink from my mouth will become as I am." So suddenly, for the first time, we have a picture of Christianity consistent with the mystical forms of other religions.

The final advance is psychology's improving opinion of ASCs—from considering them states of mind invariably viewed as delusional to seeing them as states that may sometimes provide unique access to extraordinary insight and wisdom. As Walsh observed, "This means that the deepest spiritual wisdom may not be fully comprehensible to us unless we too train ourselves to experience appropriate states of mind"—through such traditional spiritual technologies as meditation, yoga, contemplation, and devotional practices.

In fact, Walsh believes that the world's spiritual traditions were inspired in part by the altered-states experiences of the great teachers and prophets such as Jesus, Buddha, and Mohammed. If so, it's ironic that religion is often used today as a protection against extraordinary experiences. (Growing up Methodist in North Carolina, I was always bemused by the neighboring fundamentalists' proscriptions against social dancing—surely one of the milder inducements of altered states.)

In Walsh's view, then, authentic spiritual traditions are "those capable of inducing appropriate altered states, transcendence or higher development." *A Course in Miracles*, he says, shares at least four similarities with older teachings:

- How the teachings are revealed
- What the teachings say about the human condition
- What the teachings say about our potential
- What the teachings say about the means for realizing our potential

(In the remainder of this chapter, the remarks of Roger Walsh are taken from either an original interview or his taped lecture, "The Universal Course," available from Miracle Distribution Center.)

How the teachings are revealed. "I'm still terribly embarrassed to be associated with something channeled," confesses Walsh, "as were Bill Thetford and Helen Schucman. But as far as I can see, religions have usually been produced from very unrespectable sources. Jesus was condemned as a common criminal, Lao-Tzu wandered off into the desert as a total unknown, Confucius couldn't hold a job, and Mohammed was a suspect camel driver whom a lot of people waged war on."

Walsh admits that there's an "enormous amount of nonsense to be found in channeled material. The problem is that there's also some good stuff. It's much rarer, but it defies common-sense explanations. It seems pretty clear that some of the Bible was produced this way, as well as part of the Koran. In Judaism there have been scores of mystics who produced works by the process of inner dictation, and in Buddhism, many Indian and Tibetan texts were produced this way." Even in the West, Walsh adds, "the Greek oracle of Delphi—actually a series of priestesses who supposedly spoke on behalf of the god Apollo—stayed in business for nine hundred years."

Walsh is particularly impressed by the "voice" of the Course in comparison to other channeled teachers he has sampled. "If I try to sense the mind of Emmanuel, for instance, I feel a wonderful, compassionate presence, but there's still a feeling of individuality. By contrast, the mind behind the Course feels boundless."

What the teachings say about the human condition. Perhaps the most common feature of the great spiritual traditions is that they take a dim view of the human condition in its everyday, unspiritual state. "The teachings make it clear that things aren't good and there's an enormous amount of suffering going on," says Walsh. "They point to the sorrows and shortness of life; the inevitability of sickness, old age, and death; the ever-present confrontation with meaning, purpose, and the questions of relationship and aloneness; and the uncertainty and fickleness of fate." The first Noble Truth of the Buddha points to the inevitability of suffering in life, which Walsh cites alongside a passage from Psalms: "In the immensity of the universe we seem as dust. Our lives are but toil and trouble; they are soon gone. They come to an end like a sigh; like a dream. What person can live and not see death?"

"*A Course in Miracles* agrees completely," remarks Walsh. "It says this is an insane world of sorrow and death, and it is not where you ultimately belong. Then why are we here? Both ACIM and the contemplative core of the great traditions say that the problem the world represents is really the state of our minds. We're driven and dominated by unhealthy desires and fears, obsessed by wanting to get more variations and intensities of sensation and feelings. Plus, we're dominated by egocentric concerns, driven by the twin powers of addiction and aversion. From these spring the seven deadly sins of Christianity, the hindrances of Buddhism, the pain-bearing obstructions of yoga—different names for similar afflictions."

Buddhism and the Course are very similar in their suggestions that our way of thinking literally creates the world we see, says Walsh. The message of ACIM is that "you're so insane you don't know you're insane. You're suffering from a shared, unhappy, psychotic dream, and the Course offers an alternate thought system you can substitute for that dream.

"This point about dreaming is very important," continues Walsh, "because a lot of the deeper meaning of the great traditions is hidden unless you get the implications of this message: that what we ordinarily take to be a fully wakened state is actually a dream." Walsh feels that the following Course explanation of our waking hallucinations is among the best available in the world's traditions:

Dreams show you that you have the power to make a world as you would have it be, and that because you want it you see it. And while you see it you do not doubt that it is real. Yet here is a world, clearly within your mind, that seems to be outside. . . . You seem to waken, and the dream is gone. . . . And what you seem to waken to is but another form of this same world you see in dreams. All your time is spent in dreaming. Your sleeping and your waking dreams have different forms, and that is all. (CH18, II, 5)

What the teachings say about our potential. "We can get some sense of our true nature if we look at the opposite of our unenlightened condition as it usually is," comments Walsh. "Instead of finitude and limits, we find descriptions of infinity and boundless being. In place of time and change we find descriptions of the eternal and the changeless. In place of birth and death we have the unborn and the deathless. In place of angst and fear we have love, bliss, and joy."

Likewise, says Walsh, the great traditions suggest an enormous potential for the mind. Enlightened mind is said to be free of the ravages of fear, greed, hatred, and anger. Christ called it the "peace which passeth understanding"; for the Buddha it was nirvana, for the yogi it's the bliss of *samadhi*. As the Course says, "A tranquil mind is not a little gift." (MANUAL, 20, 4) The universal message here is that to the extent we quiet the raucous activity of our untrained minds, to that extent we will find our true self, a place of boundless peace and bliss. This is the Buddha's recognition of *anatta*, the awareness that the ego was an illusion all along. It's the goal of yoga, which means "union of self with Self." It's Taoism's alignment with the Tao, and for Christian mystics it was deification, Christ-consciousness, or oneness with God. In the Course's words, it's "Let me remember I am one with God, at one with all my brothers and my Self, in everlasting holiness and peace." (LESSON 124)

"This all sounds like nice stuff," Walsh concludes. "The question is, how do we get there?"

What the teachings say about the means for realizing our potential. According to Walsh, authentic spiritual traditions offer not just a belief system but also an explicit guide to training the mind so that one becomes open to higher states of being and awareness. Thus, all great paths offer what Walsh calls a "technology of transcendence." Looking across all these paths, Walsh cites five common elements of such technology:[1]

1. Ethical training
2. Attentional training
3. Emotional transformation
4. Motivational change
5. The cultivation of wisdom

1. *Ethical training.* "The common thinking of religious morality is 'do this or God will get you,'" says Walsh. "This is not the perspective of the perennial wisdom, which views ethics as a means for training the mind. If we look closely we find that unethical behavior both arises from and reinforces painful and destructive mind states: anger, fear, greed, hatred,

and jealousy. On the other hand, ethical behavior tends not to reinforce these mind states, hence reducing them and cultivating their opposites: generosity, love, joyfulness. So one becomes ethical not out of fear or guilt, but simply because one recognizes that this is what leads to greater well-being for oneself and others. Ethics is a skillful strategy."

2. *Attentional training.* "Our minds are a mess!" declares Walsh. "If you've ever tried meditation, you know the experience of sitting down to concentrate on following your breath, then realizing twenty minutes later that while there was certainly some breathing going on, you weren't around for it. The Bhagavad-Gita says, 'Restless man's mind is. So strongly shaken in the grip of the senses, gross and grown hard with stubborn desire for what is worldly, how shall we tame it? Truly I think the wind is no wilder.' Ramana Maharshi said, 'All scriptures without any exception proclaim that for attaining salvation mind should be subdued.' And then we have the Course saying, 'You are much too tolerant of mind wandering . . .'" (CH2, VI, 4)

Regardless of the path, Walsh suggests, the method of attentional training is basically the same: "a continuous bringing-back of attention to a predetermined object. The yogi returns again and again to the breath. The Course Workbook asks us to come back to our thought for the day. The aim is to constantly recollect the mind, returning it to what we have decided to focus on—and this gives power.

"In Buddhism there are 'four imponderables,'" adds Walsh. "These are four things that you can't fathom, and they are: origination, or how the universe began; causation or karma, how things are caused; the scope of the mind of the Buddha; and finally, the power of the fully concentrated mind. Apparently a fully concentrated mind has awesome power at its disposal."

3. *Emotional transformation.* Walsh names two components of this element: the reduction of negative, "unskillful" emotions and the cultivation of positive, useful ones. As mentioned earlier, the perennial philosophy sees all unskillful emotions emanating from the obsessions of addiction and aversion.

"The Course has a variety of approaches to reducing our attachment to what it calls 'idols,' all the things we crave," says Walsh. "There is a whole series of Workbook lessons on this, including 'The world I see holds nothing that I want.'(Lesson 128) It's not that we can't live with joy and love here in the world; the Course and other traditions make it clear that we can. But as long as we think that fulfilling our desires is what will make us happy, we're actually destined for unhappiness."

Anger and hatred are the two chief emotions rooted in aversion, says Walsh, and he cites a pungent Buddhist image for the assessment of anger's value: "They say we should regard anger as stale urine mixed with poison. The Course maintains that '[A]nger is *never* justified. Attack has *no* foundation.' (Ch30, VI, 1) The Course's primary tool for reducing anger is forgiveness, and it provides an exquisitely detailed variety of approaches to forgiveness, more so than any other path I have found."

The second component of emotional transformation is the cultivation of positive or skillful emotions, believed to lead the spiritual aspirant toward states of unlimited love and compassion. "These states are what Buddhism calls the 'divine abodes,'" Walsh observes, "what Christianity calls *agape*, what the bhakti tradition calls divine love. In one lesson the Course likewise suggests 'God's will for me is perfect happiness.'" (Lesson 101)

4. *Motivational change.* Walsh believes that the perennial philosophy encourages a number of shifts in one's deepest motivations, chief among them being the shift from wanting to acquire things, attention, or power, to pursuing inner development as the only lasting means of satisfaction. Another shift is simply from getting to giving.

"Traditionally this has been called purification," reports Walsh. "Psychologists would recognize it as moving up Maslow's hierarchy of needs. For Kierkegaard it was epitomized in the saying, 'Purity of heart is to will one thing.' Jesus said, 'Seek ye first the kingdom of heaven and all else will be given to you.' What then is the highest motivation, the highest desire to focus on? In Mahayana Buddhism, we have the ideal of the *bodhisattva*: to awaken with the aim of using that awakening for the helping and healing of all beings. This may be the highest ideal the human mind has ever conceived, and in Buddhism it's believed to take place over many lifetimes in order to liberate all sentient beings."

A Course in Miracles is a bodhisattvic path as well, claims Walsh, "making it very clear that none of us are going to get out of this game until all of us get out of it. You can't clean up your mind only, because all minds are one and interconnected, according to the Course. It also makes clear that the work involved is in no way a sacrifice, because as one lesson says, 'All that I give is given to myself.'" (LESSON 126)

5. *The cultivation of wisdom.* Walsh identifies two kinds of wisdom that play a part in achieving our spiritual potential: initial and final. "Initial wisdom is what starts one on the path, trying meditation or reading the Course or whatever. One recognizes the suffering and unsatisfactoriness of the world and thinks, as Bill Thetford did, that there must be a better way. In Buddhism it's the recognition of *duhkha*, that unenlightened living does indeed lead to suffering.

"Final wisdom is a profound insight into the nature of mind, self, and reality," Walsh continues. "This is a direct, transcendental intuition, not of the mind or intellect. In the East it's called *prajna*, in the West *gnosis*, and in the Course *knowledge*. This wisdom is also known to be profoundly empowering and liberating. In Christianity it's 'the Kingdom of Heaven is within you'; in the Upanishads it's 'by understanding the Self, all this universe is known'; in Siddha Yoga it's 'God dwells within you as you.'"

Walsh concludes, "This is enlightenment, *satori, moksha, wu,* liberation, salvation—different words for the same realization. The message of the great traditions as well as *A Course in Miracles* can thus be summarized very simply: Wake up!"

Is the Course a Psychotherapy?

Very simply, the purpose of psychotherapy is to remove the blocks to truth. Its aim is to aid the patient in abandoning his fixed delusional system, and to begin to reconsider the spurious cause and effect relationships on which it rests. No one in this world escapes fear, but everyone can reconsider its causes and learn to evaluate them correctly. God has given everyone a Teacher Whose wisdom and help far exceed whatever contribution an earthly therapist can provide. Yet there are times and situations in which an earthly patient-therapist relationship becomes the means through which He offers His greater gifts to both. (Psychotherapy, 1, 1)

The preceding passage is taken from the pamphlet "Psychotherapy: Purpose, Process and Practice," one of two brief addenda to the Course proper that Helen Schucman scribed in the years following the completion of the Text, Workbook, and Manual for Teachers (see chapter 1). The existence of "Psychotherapy" strengthens the paradoxical association of the Course—unmistakably a spiritual discipline—with a healing methodology rooted in decidedly antireligious theories of human behavior, including those of Sigmund Freud. The mainstream of psychology has historically been devoted to fathoming the mysteries of our minds and behavior in strictly scientific terms, although practitioners of the "harder" sciences with longer histories have often looked askance on the entire psychological enterprise.

That's due in part to the fact that spirituality always seems to be lurking behind psychology's door, evanescent but undeniable as a shadow. Trace the semantic roots of the word *psychotherapy*, for instance, and you find the meaning of "soul healing." Freud's greatest student, Carl Jung, broke with his teacher over essentially spiritual questions. And for many, the purely analytic mode of therapy leaves something to be desired in terms of changing human behavior and relationships for the better. Real change, when it occurs, often follows an experience of "surrender" to a previously unrecognized source of wisdom—a wisdom that's internally realized and yet unmistakably distinct from one's previous, ordinary range of consciousness.

This recognition generally marks a transition from psychological self-exploration to the spiritual search. Only in recent decades has psychology begun to study this transitional arena, and then primarily in the progressive branch generally identified as "transpersonal"—in which the study of the ego crosses over into the study of soul, spirit, and even more surpassing forms of consciousness. As Frances Vaughan comments in her book *The Inward Arc* (Shambhala, 1986):

Traditionally, psychological growth and the spiritual quest have been perceived as separate and fundamentally antagonistic pursuits. Most Western psychology has tended to dismiss spiritual searching as escapist, delusional, or, at best, a psychological crutch. Spiritual disciplines, on the other hand, have tended to regard psychology as an irrelevant distraction on the path of spiritual awakening. Here [in transpersonal psychology] these two apparently divergent approaches to the relief of human suffering are viewed as complementary and interdependent aspects of healing and the journey to wholeness.

Co-editors of an anthology titled *Paths Beyond Ego: The Transpersonal Vision* (Tarcher, 1993), Vaughan and Roger Walsh are both recognized as leading voices in what is sometimes called the "fourth force" of modern psychology (after Freudian psychoanalysis, behaviorism, and humanistic psychology). Partners in marriage as well as professional interests, they nonetheless have some disagreements on the finer points of the transpersonal outlook—one of these being whether *A Course in Miracles* constitutes a psychotherapy in itself.

When I queried them in person on this point, Walsh replied, "The Course is clearly designed not only to affect psychological healing, but also spiritual maturation beyond the levels that most psychotherapies aim for. One might say its major emphasis is cognitive, in that the teaching comes to us in books and words, but it also has a strong relational component, a service component, a bhakti component—it has all these different strategies. Thus it's one of the most broad-range therapies available."

"I have a different view on this," countered Vaughan. "In Jung's sense that 'all religions are therapies for the soul,' I would say the Course qualifies as therapy. But I see psychotherapy as being based on the relationship between two people. In that light the Course is an effective self-development methodology, not a psychotherapy. Also, although the Course talks a lot about releasing the past, it doesn't give you a lot of 'how-to'; I think that's a piece of the work that we do in psychotherapy, dealing in specifics with a necessity that the Course discusses in general."

The hanging-on to guilt, its hugging-close and sheltering, its loving pro-
tection and alert defense,—all this is but the grim refusal to forgive.
"God may not enter here" the sick repeat, over and over, while they
mourn their loss and yet rejoice in it. Healing occurs as a patient begins
to hear the dirge he sings, and questions its validity. Until he hears it,
he cannot understand that it is he who sings it to himself. To hear it is
the first step in recovery. To question it must then become his choice.
(PSYCHOTHERAPY, 2, VI, 1)

Although Vaughan's own style of therapy is derived from many influences, her description of it echoes the principles found in "Psychotherapy."
In place of the classic "transference" of psychoanalysis—a process in which
the patient is allowed and even encouraged to develop a dependency on
the therapist that is not unlike a child-to-parent relationship—Vaughan
sees the process of therapy "as something that the client and I do together,
a mutual exploration to see what is needed for healing in each particular
case. It's important for me to meet a person heart to heart, and to be as
fully present and transparent as possible. I don't do anything to the client,
in terms of applying psychological tricks or techniques. I try to allow something to happen between us that allows people to change, grow, and heal."

Ideally, psychotherapy is a series of holy encounters in which brothers meet
to bless each other and to receive the peace of God. And this will one day
come to pass for every "patient" on the face of this earth, for who except a
patient could possibly have come here? The therapist is only a somewhat
more specialized teacher of God. He learns through teaching, and the
more advanced he is the more he teaches and the more he learns. But
whatever stage he is in, there are patients who need him just that way.
They cannot take more than he can give for now. Yet both will find sanity
at last. (PSYCHOTHERAPY, 2, I, 4)

Does Vaughan ever explicitly introduce the idea of "inner guidance" to
clients, or explicitly recommend spiritual disciplines such as the Course?
"I don't introduce spirituality unless people ask for it," says Vaughan, "or
introduce it themselves. Mostly I try to listen; I do very little initiating as

a therapist. When I write books or give lectures, that's when I'm taking the initiative. But in individual therapy I let the client lead, in terms of telling me what he or she needs. As far as the Course goes, I'll support someone's curiosity about it, in terms of answering their questions, but I wouldn't recommend it to anyone not already expressing an interest. As Bill Thetford used to say, this course is not for everyone."

> *The patient need not think of truth as God in order to make progress in salvation. But he must begin to separate truth from illusion, recognizing that they are not the same, and becoming increasingly willing to see illusions as false and to accept the truth as true. His Teacher will take him on from there, as far as he is ready to go. Psychotherapy can only save him time. The Holy Spirit uses time as He thinks best, and He is never wrong. Psychotherapy under His direction is one of the means He uses to save time, and to prepare additional teachers for His work. There is no end to the help that He begins and He directs. By whatever route he chooses, all psychotherapy leads to God in the end. But that is up to Him. We are all His psychotherapists, for He would have us all be healed in Him. (*PSYCHOTHERAPY, I, 5)

"One of the ideas from the Course I've found most useful in psycho-therapy is 'Let all things be exactly as they are' (LESSON 268)," remarks Vaughan. "Fritz Perls used to say that the greatest obstacle to change is wanting to change. As long as you're trying to get reality to match your pictures of how things are supposed to be, you're in a lot of trouble. The aim of psychotherapy is first of all to accept things as they are, and then, as the Serenity Prayer says, to accept the things you can't change and work to change the things that you can. One thing you can change is the sense of separation, realizing that you are not separate from God."

But, Vaughan continues, "Concepts of God vary enormously. I don't try to impose a belief or tell people what's wrong. A spiritual teacher might say, 'This is how things are'; a psychotherapist asks, 'How are things for you?' It's by joining with the client that I may enable her to see things differently, to change what she can change and to accept what she cannot. The work proceeds in the direction of self-forgiveness. When clients begin to heal their own feelings of guilt, then they're able to become more compassionate, loving, and forgiving of others."

> *No one who learns to forgive can fail to remember God. Forgiveness, then, is all that need be taught, because it is all that need be learned. All blocks to the remembrance of God are forms of unforgiveness, and nothing else. This is never apparent to the patient, and only rarely so to the therapist. The world has marshalled all its forces against this one awareness, for in it lies the ending of the world and all it stands for.* (PSYCHOTHERAPY, 2, II, 3)

Because *A Course in Miracles* makes an uncompromising connection between forgiveness and a radical shift in perception, should it perhaps not be taken on unless one has therapeutic experience?

"I wouldn't say that anyone should not work with the Course," replies Vaughan, "but I certainly think psychotherapy helps. It's often said that it's better to have a strong ego before undertaking any spiritual practice, that you have to be somebody before you can learn to be nobody. And it's advantageous to have completed the developmental tasks of growing up, so that you don't get tempted by a 'spiritual bypass' that might gloss over unresolved psychological issues."

Roger Walsh notes that research in psychotherapy has shown that "people who do best are the people who need it least. Anecdotally speaking, this seems to be the same in spiritual practice. The more skills and maturity you bring to it, the more you're likely to gain, although that seems somewhat unfair.

"But how people progress is very difficult to predict," Walsh muses. "Bill Thetford always said that he was amazed how many people got so much out of the Course, when his initial assumption was that it was too intellectual to have mass appeal. He was astounded to find relatively uneducated people thriving on it, sometimes doing better than students with a stronger intellectual or psychological background."

Frances Vaughan concludes that the Course works for many because, regardless of its language or difficulty, "it does help people reduce fear, guilt, and anger, and increase their experience of peace, love and joy. I've never met anyone in any culture who didn't want to be able to give and receive more love. The Course is simply one effective way of helping people do that."

> *No one is healed alone. This is the joyous song salvation sings to all who hear its Voice. This statement cannot be too often remembered by all who see themselves as therapists. Their patients can but be seen as the bringers of forgiveness, for it is they who come to demonstrate their sinlessness to eyes that still believe that sin is there to look upon. Yet will the proof of sinlessness, seen in the patient and accepted in the therapist, offer the mind of both a covenant in which they meet and join and are as one.*
> (PSYCHOTHERAPY, 2, VI, 7)

✍ ENDNOTES ✍

1. For an expanded discussion of transcendental technologies, see Roger Walsh, *Essential Spirituality* (Wiley, 2000).

CHAPTER 9

Why the Course Is Not Christian—Or Is It?

The Christianized language of *A Course in Miracles*, which makes frequent references to God the Father, His Son, and the Holy Spirit, has been a source of substantial confusion about its message and orientation. Casual readers and surface-skimming critics have mistaken the Course for a contemporary restatement of traditional Christian theology. And there's no doubt that some novice students have happily taken it to church only to find that it receives a less than warm reception from their ministers or church elders.

That's because the superficial resemblance of Course language to biblical prose rapidly disintegrates as soon as one comes across certain statements proposing complete reversals of contemporary Christian thought. Add to this the fact that the voice making such radical propositions claims to be that of Jesus Christ himself, and there's a wrenching surprise in store for any traditional Christian who decides to give this thick blue book, usually printed on familiarly thin "Bible" paper, a serious look.

Compare, for instance, the message of a familiar Bible verse memorized by generations of Sunday school students to ACIM's treatment of the same subject in the following passages.

For God so loved the world that he gave his only begotten Son, that whoever believes in him shall not perish but have eternal life. —JOHN 3:16

You will not find peace until you have removed the nails from the hands of God's Son, and taken the last thorn from his forehead. The Love of God surrounds His Son whom the god of crucifixion condemns. Teach not that I died in vain. Teach rather that I did not die by demonstrating that I live in you. For the undoing of the crucifixion of God's Son is the work of the redemption, in which everyone has a part of equal value. God does not judge His guiltless Son. Having given Himself to him, how could it be otherwise? (CHI I, VI, 7)

These claims by the Jesus of the Course that he "did not die" and that everyone has an equal part in "undoing" the crucifixion are just two of many startling theological departures that ACIM takes from biblical orthodoxy. As the Reverend Jon Mundy commented to me, "There are lots of points on which the Course doesn't work in a traditional Christian context. The Course says there's no hell and no devil. The whole concept of the Atonement is different. The whole thing about the cross and the Resurrection is different. It just doesn't work as traditional Christianity."

But that didn't prevent Mundy from giving it a try. From the time he encountered the Course in 1975 until he resigned from his Methodist pulpit in 1989, Mundy attempted to share the new teaching of the Course with his congregation. "That was a long time to hang in there," he recalls, "and I was very actively teaching the Course from the pulpit. I didn't make any bones about where my information was coming from; I was very clear about it." But what brought an end to Mundy's experiment presenting the Course in a Christian church was not his own realization that the two perspectives were incompatible. "What happened was that some fundamentalists moved into my church and realized that I was not speaking their language. And that was the end of it."

To evangelical Christian critics of *A Course in Miracles*, such a turn of events doubtless sounds just and satisfying. In the future it is likely that fundamentalists will have many more opportunities to dislodge an encroaching

Course from the pews and pulpits of mainline churches. But any evangelical crusade against Course followers homesteading on Christian territory will have to acknowledge an unexpected ally. Because the leading philosopher of the Course movement, Kenneth Wapnick, PhD, doesn't think *A Course in Miracles* belongs in church either.

Remarks from a Gentlemanly Debate

In 1989 Wapnick sat down with Father W. Norris Clarke, a Jesuit priest and philosopher, to have a long and polite discussion about the doctrinal differences between the Course and biblical Christianity. Clarke, whom Wapnick credits with "an open-minded and non-judgmental approach to non-Catholic teachings," spent thirty-one years as a professor of philosophy at Fordham University before his retirement in 1985, founding and editing the *International Philosophical Quarterly* for two and a half decades. Clarke, a friend of Wapnick's for many years, also appeared in the 1987 film documentary *The Story of* A Course in Miracles, elucidating a few of the major contrasts between the Course and the Bible.

The 1989 dialogue was videotaped for distribution by the Foundation for *A Course in Miracles*, but a technical hitch prevented its reproduction, and Wapnick published the transcript as a hundred-page FACIM book in 1995. *A Course in Miracles and Christianity: A Dialogue* stands as an intriguing debate between a gentle Catholic elder—who sounds bemused by the sheer differentness of a radical new teaching—and an articulate heretic, equally gracious in tone but confident in the validity of a radical new spiritual path.

In the introduction to *Dialogue*, Wapnick outlines four major thematic contrasts between the Bible and *A Course in Miracles*:

1. *A Course in Miracles* teaches that God did not create the physical universe, which includes all matter, form, and the body; the Bible states that He did.
2. The God of *A Course in Miracles* does not even know about the sin of separation (since to know about it would make it real), let alone react to it; the God of the Bible perceives sin directly . . . and

His responses to it are vigorous, dramatic, and at times punitive, to say the very least.

3. *A Course in Miracles'* Jesus is equal to everyone else, a part of God's one Son or Christ; the Bible's Jesus is seen as special, apart, and therefore ontologically different from everyone else, being God's only begotten Son, the second person of the Trinity.

4. The Jesus of *A Course in Miracles* is not sent by God to suffer and die on the cross in a sacrificial act of atonement for sin, but rather teaches that there is no sin by demonstrating that nothing happened to him in reality, for sin has no effect on the Love of God; the Jesus of the Bible agonizes, suffers, and dies for the sins of the world in an act that brings vicarious salvation to humanity, thereby establishing sin and death as real, and moreover clearly reflecting that God has been affected by Adam's sin and must respond to its actual presence in the world by sacrificing His beloved Son.

Shortly concluding that there is "no way" to reconcile biblical and Course theology, Wapnick concedes that "it is a continual source of amazement . . . for one to observe how frequently this reconciliation is attempted." Thus, far from attempting to hitchhike the Course onto the established institutions and broad reach of Christianity, Wapnick makes it clear that he, for one, is trying to make sure the Course blazes its own trail.

Dialogue presents discussion between Clarke and Wapnick on a number of specific issues, including the origin of the world, the nature of Jesus, the meaning of the Eucharist, and differences between the Course and Christianity on everyday challenges of living in the world. Two of these issues are summarized here.

One is the problem of evil, about which the Course has been criticized elsewhere. In his collection of lectures titled *Further Along the Road Less Traveled* (Touchstone, 1998), the late Christian psychotherapist M. Scott Peck cited the Course as "a very good book, filled with a lot of first-rate psychiatric wisdom" while also dunning it as a spiritual "half-truth" that fails to deal with the problem of evil. In *Dialogue*, Clarke and Wapnick compare the biblical and Course approaches to evil in the following exchange:

CLARKE: Let us be perfectly honest. The problem of evil is indeed one filled with mystery for our limited human minds, and not one possible for us to crack with our own limited vision of world history and what God is planning for beyond death. But Christian faith can shed considerable light on it, I think. First, the moral evils of the world, deriving from the free evil moral decisions of human beings and their consequences, such as hatred, selfishness, exploiting of others, etc., are our own responsibility and not due to God at all, who only permits this so as not to override our freedom and remove our possibilities of doing moral good, too. Freely given love and service by human beings is such a lofty good that God is willing to run the risk of our free choice of evil instead of good. . . .

There is also the further mystery, which human experience bears out, I think, to all of us who have lived long enough, that somehow the full depth and richness of human character is simply not reached by embodied spirits like us unless by passing through the challenge, purification, and transformation of suffering. Herein lies the mystery of the Cross and the passion of Jesus himself.

WAPNICK: . . . In terms of creation, there cannot be both good and evil in the Course's view of reality, because there is only one God. The phenomenon of opposites exists only in the illusory world of perception and matter, which God did not create. And as *A Course in Miracles* says in the Introduction to the text, "The opposite of love is fear, but what is all-encompassing can have no opposite." And so the Course's non-dualistic God of creation is only Love, which means that evil does not exist because there can be nothing but the Love of God.

However, evil, which in *A Course in Miracles* is equated with the belief in sin and separation from our source—God—most definitely does exist in the dualistic, post-separation world of dreams. But since all this occurs only within the collective and individual dreams of the world, sin and evil cannot and do not truly exist, because only a misthought in a dreaming mind believes it can will in opposition to the Will of God, and bring into existence a world of multiplicity. Therefore within his fevered dream of sin, the Son actually believes that he has destroyed the oneness of Reality, which he judges to be an evil act deserving only punishment.

Thus although Clarke and Wapnick agree that evil *happens* in the everyday world, their perspectives offer different views as to its ultimate nature. And what is to be done about evil? Depending on how conservative or liberal one's brand of Christianity is, a sinner may be forgiven or punished by God for his free choice of evil. But the sinner certainly runs the risk of punishment, including an afterlife in hell, if he remains unrepentant. According to the Course, the discipline of accepting and extending forgiveness is what everyone must undertake in order to awaken from the dream in which evil (not to mention time, space, and matter) *seems* so real. (It should also be noted that in the view of the Course, the only hell is the one the unforgiving ego constantly creates for itself: a nightmare of separation from God, albeit a nightmare spiced with just enough pleasure and temporal love to keep most people addicted to it.)

On another point, *Dialogue*'s discussion of the Eucharist reveals a dramatic difference between the Course and Christianity (particularly Roman Catholicism) on the significance of symbolism and ritual:

CLARKE: According to this doctrine, traditional from the earliest days of the Christian Church, the Eucharistic liturgy is the reenactment in symbolic form of the original redemptive sacrifice of Jesus, in imitation of Jesus' own initial enactment at the Last Supper, which he asked his followers to keep doing in memory of him. This is done when the ordained priest, speaking in the name of Christ the High Priest, eternally living now as risen and present at every Mass, pronounces the "words of consecration" in imitation of Jesus, which really and truly transform the inner reality of the bread and wine into the body and blood of Jesus, but veiled in mystery under the remaining appearances of bread and wine. . . . Then at the Communion service following, the believers partake of the body and blood of the sacrificed and now risen Christ under the appearances of bread and wine, in obedience again to Jesus' command, "Unless you eat my body and drink my blood you shall not have life in you . . ." (John 6:53) . . .

WAPNICK: From the point of view of *A Course in Miracles*, seeking outside oneself for salvation is a principal characteristic of specialness . . . The special love relationship is one in which we believe someone or some object outside ourselves has something we lack: the capacity to make us happy and peaceful, or the capacity to save us. And so we seek to take these special persons or objects in and make their holiness or power our own, thereby completing our inherent incompleteness with something outside us and therefore truly not our own. In this sense, a special relationship would hold whether one is considering a love object, food, alcohol, or the body of Jesus. Thus, listening to the voice of specialness, we would believe that we lack the holiness and innocence of Christ, our true Self, but Jesus has what is missing in us. Therefore, if we are to have it, we must get it from him by partaking in the sacrament of the Eucharist, a process that only reinforces this lack, but does not undo or heal it.

. . . Jesus is no different from us, but rather he urges us to choose like him, joining with his mind, and not his body. So from the Course's point of view, it would make no sense for Jesus to share his illusory body with us in communion.

It should be added that the Course takes a similar position in regard to all rituals, whether they be Christian, Buddhist, Islamic, or New Age in character: "Your claim to miracles does not lie in your illusions about yourself. It does not depend on any magical powers you have ascribed to yourself, nor on any of the rituals you have devised. It is inherent in the truth of what you are." (LESSON 77) Thus *A Course in Miracles* stakes out a position that differs from common religious belief: that no ritual or spiritual practice has any meaning in itself; rather, its value depends entirely on whether it helps the practitioner change his or her mind about reality.

Despite the many doctrinal differences they inventory, Father Clarke and Ken Wapnick end *Dialogue* on a note of religious brotherhood:

CLARKE: As Jesus said, I came that you might have peace; I came to give you my peace.

WAPNICK: The Jesus of *A Course in Miracles* would echo that too, certainly.

CLARKE: So we differ on much, but also agree on much. Let me give one last quotation from Charles Morgan, the novelist: "There is no surprise more magical than the surprise of being loved; it is God's finger on man's shoulder."

WAPNICK: That's wonderful. If I could add something relevant to that: *A Course in Miracles* would say that there is no greater joy in this world than the joy of knowing that one is forgiven, and that forgiveness can only come through experiencing the Love of God through Jesus or the Holy Spirit.

If this genial discussion between a kindly priest and a spiritual psychologist truly summed up the schism between the Course and contemporary Christianity, the debate would be a decorous one indeed. But *A Course in Miracles* has drawn the attention of some Christian critics decidedly less liberal than Father Clarke.

Unmasking "The Jesus of the Course"

The Spiritual Counterfeits Project (SCP) is the sort of organization that's hard to imagine materializing anywhere besides its politically contentious home base of Berkeley, California. In what might be called an expression of the "counter-counterculture," SCP is composed largely of evangelical Christians who share a background of familiarity or firsthand experience with Eastern religions or New Age spirituality and have returned to the Bible as the touchstone of truth.

SCP sounded the first warning about ACIM to its constituency with a critique by Frances Adeney in its newsletter of June/July 1981, noting some of the "inroads into the Christian Church" that the Course was making—including the appearance of Jerry Jampolsky on evangelist Robert Schuller's *Hour of Power* television show. "Schucman's new, do-it-yourself spirituality is actually not new at all," commented Adeney. "The Hindus have been saying for centuries that the world is illusion, that all is one and that escape from pain is realized by denying its reality. . . . The 'voice' that speaks in those volumes may or may not be the voice of Helen Schucman," concluded Adeney. "It is definitely not the voice of Jesus Christ."

But SCP didn't really bear down on the Course until 1987, when an SCP journal titled *Spiritism: The Medium and the Message* devoted most of its pages to several substantial articles about ACIM by SCP researcher Dean C. Halverson. His work included a lengthy interview with Ken Wapnick, an interpretive essay titled "Seeing YourSelf as Sinless," and a chart comparing passages from the Course with Bible verses. (See "Charting the Course," pages 162–163.)

Halverson's research into the Course was meticulous and included a sort of collaboration with Wapnick that began well before their interview. Several years prior to writing his articles for the journal, Halverson had sent Wapnick a manuscript critical of the Course, which Wapnick felt was "way off base" in its representation of the principles of ACIM. He recalls that he replied at length, suggesting several points on which he thought Halverson "could legitimately criticize the Course from a fundamental Christian perspective. After that, Dean responded with a very nice letter asking further questions."

Halverson, who told me he filled two notebooks with Course excerpts before drafting the manuscript he sent to Wapnick, later attended a workshop led by Ken and Gloria and interviewed them during a lunch break. When he discovered later that his tape recorder had malfunctioned, he asked Ken for a repeat interview, which was granted and appeared in the journal. The printed interview was cordial, and Halverson seemed chiefly intent on drawing Wapnick out on the principles of the Course. At one point, however, he challenged Wapnick on his selective quoting of the Bible in one of his books, *Forgiveness and Jesus*, which bears the subtitle *The Meeting Place of A Course in Miracles and Christianity*. The following exchange occurred in response to Halverson's charge that Wapnick was avoiding Bible passages that did not fit his mapping of that "meeting place":

WAPNICK: Absolutely right. In my book I was selective. I picked and chose. Anything consistent with the Course, I took as valid, and anything that wasn't, I took as invalid. . . . Some parts of the Bible have the Holy Spirit as their source. Other parts are from the ego. Any passage that speaks of punishment or hell, I understood as being from the ego. Any passage that speaks of forgiveness and love, the unreality of the body, etc., I took as an expression of the Holy Spirit. I did not take the Bible as being totally true or totally false. I said here are some things that I feel are valid, here are some that are not valid.

HALVERSON: You reinterpreted it?

WAPNICK: Yes. There's no question. That is what I did.

Replying to Halverson's articles, a letter by Wapnick in the succeeding edition of the journal applauded Halverson's "sincere attempts at fairness in presenting material which you so strongly disagree with." Despite their disagreements, Wapnick and Halverson seemed to enjoy a high degree of mutual respect; the Christian writer described the Course editor to me as "a very gracious person. He and I hit it off pretty well." Wapnick remembered Halverson in person as a "very nice, serious, gentle guy—not what I expected of the Spiritual Counterfeits Project."

But Halverson's challenge to the Course itself was less gentle. In the conclusion to "Seeing YourSelf as Sinless," Halverson suggested that the Course's view of reality, sin, and redemption is dangerously flawed:

Sin, according to the Course, is the false belief in separateness, which is unreal. It is this false belief that gives rise to the physical world. It is also this false belief that gives rise to personhood. For to be a person is to be an individual, separate and distinct from others and from God. By affirming separateness as illusory, the Course abolishes the value of both the physical world and personhood. By declaring all personhood to be unreal, the God of the Course commits the severest form of judgment. . . .

The God of the Bible, however, offers genuine good news: not that salvation is a restored union with an impersonal Mind but that salvation is a restored communion with a personal God. It is only because God is personal and distinct that our existence as distinct persons has value and meaning. . . .

The God of the Bible solved the problem of sin not by annihilation but by reconciliation, not by obliterating separateness but by restoring a relationship. In the Course, the problem is perceptual, the solution impersonal. In the Bible, the problem is relational, the solution interpersonal. Scripture, thus, affirms the value of personhood. Biblical reconciliation seeks to restore and preserve the worth of the person.

Halverson's final judgment on ACIM was that its source was neither Jesus Christ nor Helen Schucman:

The good news of the Course, upon closer inspection, turns bitter. But that should come as no surprise. For the Jesus of the Course is not the Jesus of the Bible, but an angel of death and darkness masquerading as an angel of life and light (2 Cor. 11:14).

The table on the following pages comparing Course passages to Bible verses is excerpted from a longer version originally published by the Spiritual Counterfeits Project. The table was compiled and titled by Dean C. Halverson.

"Stabbed in the Back"

A more personal critique of the Course appears in *The Light That Was Dark: A Spiritual Journey* (Northfield, 1992; Lighthouse Trails, 2005) by Warren Smith, who acknowledges the assistance of the Spiritual Counterfeits Project and the inspiration of SCP president Tal Brooke. Smith's spiritual memoir ranges over a variety of New Age influences and involvements, including a flirtation with the freewheeling spiritual movement surrounding the iconoclastic guru Bhagwan Shree Rajneesh, and consultations with psychics and channelers. By 1981, Smith had become a certified massage practitioner with the Sacramento Holistic Health Institute in California, certainly a solid New Age credential.

Smith first learned of Course principles through Jerry Jampolsky's book *Love Is Letting Go of Fear*, which he credited with producing "an instant and profound effect on me. . . . He [Jampolsky] emphasized that only as I cleared up my old negative thought system would I start to experience

CHARTING THE COURSE

compiled by Dean C. Halverson

The Course	The Bible
GOD AND THE UNIVERSE	
The world you see is an illusion of a world. God did not create it, for what He creates must be as eternal as Himself. MANUAL, CLARIFICATION OF TERMS, 4, 1	In the beginning God created the heavens and the earth. GENESIS 1:1
JESUS	
There is nothing about me [Jesus] that you cannot attain. CH1, II, 3	At the name of Jesus every knee should bow . . . and every tongue confess that Jesus Christ is Lord. PHILIPPIANS 2:10–11
THE CHRIST	
Christ waits for your acceptance of Him as yourself . . . CH11, IV, 7	Jesus answered: "Watch out that no one deceives you. For many will come in my name, claiming, 'I am the Christ,' and will deceive many." MATTHEW 24:4–5
Is [Jesus] the Christ? O yes, along with you. MANUAL, CLARIFICATION OF TERMS, 5, 5	[John the Baptist] did not fail to confess, but confessed freely, "I am not the Christ." JOHN 1:20
THE ATONEMENT	
I [Jesus] was not "punished" because *you* were bad. The wholly benign lesson the Atonement teaches is lost if it is tainted with this kind of distortion in any form. CH3, I, 2	For what I [Paul] received I pass on to you as of first importance: that Christ died for our sins according to the Scriptures. 1 CORINTHIANS 1:5–3
THE SOURCE OF SALVATION	
My holiness is my salvation. WORKBOOK LESSON 39	Salvation is found in no one else [but Jesus Christ], for there is no
My salvation comes from me. It cannot come from anywhere else. LESSON 70, 7	other name under heaven . . . by which we must be saved. ACTS 4:10–12; CF. JOHN 3:14–19, 14:6

THE MESSAGE OF THE HOLY SPIRIT

The Holy Spirit dispels [guilt] simply through the calm recognition

When [the Holy Spirit] comes, he will convict the world of guilt in regard to sin. JOHN 16:8–9

The Holy Spirit dispels [guilt] simply through the calm recognition that it has never been. CH13, I, 11

HUMANITY'S SPIRITUAL IDENTITY

The recognition of God is the recognition of yourself. There is no

They exchanged the truth of God for a lie, and worshipped and served created things rather than the Creator. ROMANS 1:25

The recognition of God is the recognition of yourself. There is no separation of God and His creation. CH8, V, 2

You are part of Him Who is all power and glory, and are therefore

In the pride of your heart you say, "I am a god. . . ." But you are a man and not a god. EZEKIEL 28:2

You are part of Him Who is all power and glory, and are therefore as unlimited as He is. CH8, II, 7

SIN

All our sins are washed away by realizing they were but mistakes.

If we claim to be without sin, we deceive ourselves and the truth is not in us. If we confess our sins, he is faithful and just and will forgive us our sins and purify us from all unrighteousness. If we claim we have not sinned, we make him out to be a liar, and his word has no place in our lives. JOHN 1:8–10; CF. ROMANS 3:23; 6:23; EPHESIANS 4:18

All our sins are washed away by realizing they were but mistakes. LESSON 98, 2

. . . all your sins have been forgiven because they carried no effects at all. And so they were but dreams. MANUAL, CLARIFICATION OF TERMS, 5, 4

No one is punished for sins, and the Sons of God are not sinners. CH6, I, 16

CONDEMNATION

The wrath of God is being revealed against all the godlessness and wickedness of men who suppress the truth by their wickedness. ROMANS 1:12

You have condemned yourself, but condemnation is not of God. Therefore it is not true. CH8, VII, 15

THE END TIMES

When the Lord Jesus is revealed from heaven in blazing fire with his powerful agents [then] he will punish those who do not know God and do not obey the gospel of our Lord Jesus. 2 THESIANS 1:7–8

The Second Coming means nothing more than the end of the ego's rule and the healing of the mind. CH4, IV, 10

The Final Judgment on the world contains no condemnation. WORKBOOK, PART II, COMMENTARY 10, 2 love and inner peace. Only as I learned to let go of fear would I stop experiencing the attacks that I perceived as coming from the world but which were actually a result of my own negative thoughts." In the spring of 1982 Smith joined a Course study group, which became the "focal point" of each week for him for the next two years. Smith's romantic partner, Joy, another massage practitioner, soon joined the study group, and they began to look forward to a life together devoted to spirituality.

It was not long, however, before Joy began to have disturbing experiences that would ultimately shake the couple's faith in metaphysical pursuits. In the fall of 1982 Joy began to feel "an awful, sinister male presence" around her, first sensed while in a state of relaxation at home and later distinctly connected to a massage client who had "a twisted smile on his face and a strange look in his eyes." She later confronted the client about his "out-of-body harassment," but he protested his innocence. Refusing to treat or see the client again did little good, as Joy came to conclude that:

> . . . the man was *very* proficient in astral projection and was continuing to use it in a negative way. . . . We tried every metaphysical and spiritual technique we had ever learned—we repeated our *Course in Miracles* lessons, did visualizations, prayed as best we knew how, sent the spiritual intruder blessings, and kept the whole situation surrounded in white light—but none of it had any effect. We had to wait it out. The spiritual presence was calling the shots.

For Warren and Joy, the key to escaping this sinister spiritual presence came from Trudy, a cofounder of their Course study group, who startled them by insisting that they needed to take the idea of the devil seriously:

> We were all caught completely by surprise, and I asked her, "Trudy, what in the world are you talking about?"
> "Ephesians 6:10. It's in your Bible. We wrestle not against flesh and blood but against spiritual wickedness in high places." She was now looking at us with wide-eyed conviction.

"Trudy," I said, "*A Course in Miracles* doesn't even believe in darkness or a devil." I still couldn't understand what she was saying.

"I don't care what it says, the devil is real!" she said with absolute determination.

This encounter, plus a reading of Johanna Michaelsen's *The Beautiful Side of Evil* (Harvest House, 1982) convinced Smith that he needed to do a comparative reading of the Bible and the Course. Although he and Joy read both spiritual texts together, they continued to experience spiritual attacks from presences or people they perceived as evil, and received no support for their perceptions of these attacks from the rest of their Course study group. Joy became convinced that the Jesus of the Course was not authentic; Smith, reluctant to go that far, did conclude that when it came to dealing with evil, the Course "clearly missed the mark."

Finally Smith spent the better part of a week taking notes on both Scriptures and the Course, determined to resolve the confusion he felt about the two perspectives:

> My conclusions were inescapable and shocking. . . . Joy was right. *A Course in Miracles* was not from God. And the Jesus of the Course was not the real Jesus. Who would have ever guessed that the metaphysical/new-age gospel that came in the name of Christ would actually end up denying Christ? As I sat there thinking about how much I had trusted the Course, I felt as if I had been stabbed in the back by one of my closest friends.

"Seven Years of Demonic Dictation"

According to the biographical statement in her book *Ransomed from Darkness: The New Age, Christian Faith and the Battle for Souls* (North Bay Books, 2005), Moira Noonan was even more in the thick of the New Age movement than Warren Smith. For more than twenty years she was active in the ministry of Religious Science, developing expertise in hypnotherapy, past-life regression, astrology, the Course, Reiki, channeling, crystals, and other esoteric practices. But after a series of experiences pointing her back to the Catholic faith of her youth, Noonan rejected all her New Age influences. By the mid-90s she was "witnessing and evangelizing, explaining the deeper meaning and influences of the New Age movement."

Noonan devotes three short chapters of *Ransomed from Darkness* to *A Course in Miracles*, noting that:

> Seven years of demonic dictation cannot be summarized in a few pages. Suffice it to say that the Course in Miracles is the Evil One's mockery and mimicry polished to perfection for the New Age. People are looking for deliverance from sin; the Course offers that. People are looking for control over their life, and the manifestation techniques taught by the Course are fulfilled often enough to give it credibility. Among Christians, a twenty-first century, information age interpretation of the Gospel is an inviting idea, and, as in every age, the appeal of miracles is hard to resist.

Despite its appeal, Noonan cites several major flaws of the Course that convince her its source is evil. For instance, ACIM's insistence on the unreality of the world means that problems such as "crime, poverty, homelessness, war—they are ultimately not real. They are our own creations in this dream world we inhabit. Social justice is a waste of time." But equally important to Noonan is the fact that:

> The Course completely denies the existence of Satan. Utterly rejected are the ideas of spiritual warfare, the battle for the soul and the need for salvation. The only evil is our separation from God, which is an illusion we have created. There are no legions of fallen angels, like the Bible teaches, who wreak havoc among human beings on earth and work to win over our souls. You can imagine how pleased the Evil One is with this. As people read this, they fall farther and farther from their faith, from the belief that they need the help of a loving savior. In embracing the Course in Miracles they join forces with those who are against them. In seeking salvation they risk losing their souls.

The concerns of Warren Smith and Moira Noonan are echoed in other criticisms of the Course published or posted online by such Christian organizations as Christian Research International (which characterizes the Course as "glossed Hinduism for the masses"), the Watchman Fellowship, and the Catholic Resource Network. Yet part of the reason that such evangelical and apologetics organizations are concerned about the Course is the fact that it has proved appealing or useful to mainstream Christians who do not necessarily adopt all of ACIM's philosophy. And contrary to some critics' accusation that the Course offers quick, simplistic solutions to people's problems or philosophical dilemmas, one aspect of Course study to which practically all of its followers would certify is the challenge of sticking with its disciplines of personal responsibility and forgiveness over the long term. So if the Evil One is indeed behind *A Course in Miracles*, the method he has chosen to draw believers into his grasp is anything but a simple seduction.

A Universal Experience?

There's a story that Jung once surveyed the diverse field of research and therapy that his pioneering work had spawned and said, "Thank God I am Jung and not a Jungian." One may well wonder whether Jesus Christ might say something to the same effect were he to reappear today and survey the vast collection of beliefs, practices, and undeniable distortions that have arisen from his original teaching and now coexist under the very broad umbrella of "Christianity"—many of these approaches claiming to be the one true interpretation of his creed.

"*Christian* is one of the fuzziest words in existence," opines Course teacher Robert Perry, pointing out that "even the Course uses the words 'real Christian' to characterize someone thinking along its lines." Of course there is considerable disagreement not only about proper interpretations of the message and example of Jesus Christ but also about the validity and historicity of many parts of the Bible. Richard Smoley, a scholar of Western spiritual traditions who is both a student and a critic of the Course (see appendix II), asserts that "few of the fundamentalist teachings have much to do with the Christianity of the New Testament, based as they often are on distorted translations of the original. I've read parts of the Bible in Greek and Hebrew, and every time I've found myself exclaiming, 'My God! Does it really say *that*?'"

Interpretive variations and doctrinal schisms have arisen in every major spiritual tradition as soon as—and sometimes before—the originator or first prophet of a tradition passes away. At this writing significant differences in interpretation of *A Course in Miracles* already exist, and the teaching is only three decades old. Robert Perry observes that "the Course's attitude toward Christianity and the Bible is multi-faceted," noting that some other Course experts regard Ken Wapnick's position on the Course's discontinuity with Christianity as extreme.

But the Course itself suggests that all theological differences have a limited significance:

> *All terms are potentially controversial, and those who seek controversy will find it. Yet those who seek clarification will find it as well. They must, however, be willing to overlook controversy, recognizing that it is a defense against truth in the form of a delaying maneuver. Theological considerations as such are necessarily controversial, since they depend on belief and can therefore be accepted or rejected. A universal theology is impossible, but a universal experience is not only possible but necessary. It is this experience toward which the course is directed.* (MANUAL, CLARIFICATION OF TERMS, INTRO, 2)

What might be the nature of the "universal experience" toward which Course students are directed? Jon Mundy, the reverend who finally resigned from his Methodist pulpit, says that when the time came for him to choose between church orthodoxy and Course teaching, he chose the Course because, for him and many others he knows, "It works. It transforms people's lives. You really do begin to look at things differently. You begin to see that what's important is honesty, patience, and forgiveness, and you let all the other stuff go."

 CHAPTER 10

Secular Critiques of the Course

O ne of the challenges of assessing the social impact of *A Course in Miracles* derives from how little has been written about it by objective observers in secular and academic circles. Although evangelical Christian critics such as Dean Halverson (see previous chapter) might be suspected of bringing foregone conclusions to their study, they have generally done their homework and judged the Course from a largely accurate understanding of what it says. Informed secular criticism, on the other hand, is rare. The scarcity of intelligent reviews from mainstream academia or theology most likely stems from a widespread perception of the Course as a light-headed New Age doctrine not deserving of consideration by serious scholars.

Yet in the primary scholarly assessment of ACIM that is available at this writing, this perception is characterized as a case of mistaken identification. Writing in *New Age Religion and Western Culture: Esotericism in the Mirror of Secular Thought* (SUNY Press, 1998), Wouter J. Hanegraaff, a religious studies research fellow at Utrecht University in the Netherlands, comments:

> If we were to select one *single* text as "sacred scripture" in the New Age movement, the sheer awe and reverence with which *The Course*—as it is fondly called—is discussed by its devotees would make this huge volume the most obvious choice. Indeed, it is among those channeled

texts which refute the often-heard opinion that channeling results only in trivialities. . . . Large numbers of people profess to have been deeply influenced by the teachings. Many small groups have emerged in which the *Course* is respectfully studied, and an extraordinarily large number of commentaries have been published.

Later, in summing up the central themes of New Age thinking, Hanegraaff observes that

This-worldliness, particularly of the weak variety, characterizes the attitude of New Age believers to experiential reality. In this respect, a text such as *A Course in Miracles*, though often regarded as belonging to the New Age movement, is decidedly atypical. . . .

Although repeated allusions in New Age sources to the importance of the unitive experience of ultimate reality might make one expect otherwise, true other-worldliness is very rare in the New Age movement. The only unambiguous example in our corpus is *A Course in Miracles*. According to this text—which has correctly been characterized as a Christianized version of non-dualistic *Vedanta*—our world is just an illusory chimera, which has nothing to offer but violence, sorrow and pain. We must awaken from the bad dream of separation, and reunite with God. . . . Although many other New Age sources routinely use the Oriental concept of "maya" and refer to the world of space-time as ultimately illusory, they seldom come close to the uncompromising world-rejection found in the *Course*.

The "uncompromising world-rejection" expressed by the Course— coupled with its equally uncompromising emphasis on forgiving the world as we experience it—figures into the next secular criticism we will consider. Unlike Hanegraaff, the independent scholar who issued this controversial assessment chose a highly emotional language.

The Course as "Omnipotent Fantasy"

"I hate *A Course in Miracles*, and I'm coming out to do something about it." These words were spoken by the most prominent critic of the Course to date, and they characterize the extreme if not always well-informed reactions that ACIM occasionally inspires in critics. In early 1989, *Common Boundary* magazine (no longer in print) published an essay by Roger Walsh summarizing the Course philosophy (see chapter 8)—an essay that drew the attention of James Hillman, author of a score of books including the best seller *The Soul's Code* and *The Force of Character*. Hillman is widely respected as one of the most original and provocative interpreters of the Jungian legacy of depth psychology.

Hillman responded to Walsh's essay with a piece of his own: "A Course in Miracles: Spiritual Path or Omnipotent Fantasy?" published in the Fall 1989 issue of *Common Boundary*, in which Hillman made his feelings about the Course known in no uncertain terms. It should be noted that the Hillman article originated not as a written piece but as a conversation with *Common Boundary* contributing editor Barbara Goodrich-Dunn, and consisted entirely of Hillman's reactions to statements by Roger Walsh. As my subsequent inquiries revealed, it is uncertain whether Hillman ever examined the Course firsthand.

Describing himself as "shocked and enraged" that *Common Boundary* "would publish an article that has no common boundary with psychology," Hillman charged that Walsh's presentation of Course ideas contained "old-fashioned, self-deluding Christianity," adding that "the roots of fascism exist within [the Course] philosophy. . . . Everybody would like to make the world as he or she would like it. But trying to get the power to make the world that way is a form of insanity. This is also what Mussolini and Hitler had: an omnipotent fantasy."

Hillman also maintained that the Course promotes the extinction of strong emotions and passionate convictions. Noting that Walsh had suggested that the Course, like other spiritual traditions, advocates the relinquishing of fear, anger, jealousy, and hatred, Hillman then issued a defense of each of these emotions.

Fear is absolutely essential to staying alive. If my fear were extinguished, I had better not go out and cross the street because I'd get run over immediately. If jealousy were extinguished, I would lose all coupling and mating emotions which exist in animals and birds. Jealousy belongs with feelings of closeness. If I were to lose my anger I would lose my social sense. I would have no sense of justice, of abuse, of political terror, because I wouldn't be angry any more. I wouldn't notice. If I were to lose hatred, I would lose culture because culture is not only based on love, but on hatred, too. . . . So if the Course is going to extinguish those emotions, what have we got left? Hallmark feelings? Safe, mediocre, passive emotions? Sanitized pain relievers?

Partly as a result of discouraging strong feelings, concluded Hillman, "the Course keeps us from being political. It keeps us from protesting because the mess 'out there' is merely a cognitive illusion. . . . *A Course in Miracles* is Republican right-wing politics in the guise of spiritual reformation. It's not even good conservatism. It's reactionary."

Although a lively round of letters followed in the succeeding issue of *Common Boundary*, the response from Roger Walsh printed alongside Hillman's article in the same issue was brief. "Unfortunately, the critique by James Hillman is not informed and seriously misrepresents the Course," wrote Walsh. "The positions he attributes to it are not only incorrect in most cases, but in many cases are diametrically opposite to what it says."

Hillman's scholarship on the Course, directly challenged by Walsh, is difficult to assess because Hillman refused to document his study. Replying to a 1990 letter in which I requested a telephone interview and asked for specific Course text references to illustrate some of his assertions, Hillman sent a note saying, "I don't want to do this. I've said what I wanted to say and have nothing to add." Barbara Goodrich-Dunn told me at the time that she did not know the extent of Hillman's Course study, but did say she knew he was "not displeased about the controversy" their article generated.

"I know that Hillman is very concerned about the lack of critical thinking in a lot of New Age psychology," explained Goodrich-Dunn. When I relayed that remark to Roger Walsh, he remarked, "Well, I certainly have no disagreement with him about that."

While researching the 1997 edition of this book I wrote to James Hillman requesting a follow-up to his critique of the Course. Noting that his 1989 remarks remained the most prominent hostile review of ACIM in print, I asked him again to substantiate his major criticisms—either with quotations from the Course itself or with other evidence he had gathered before or since his published statements. I specifically inquired if he could cite instances of the Course being used to promote fascistic ideas or programs, if he knew of a significant number of Course students who are passive and apolitical, and if he could identify any prominent or influential right-wing Republicans who espouse the Course teaching.

Hillman's written response was succinct: "I have no answers to your questions and do not have the interest to pursue them. You may make of that fact what you will."

The Course as "Masked Authoritarianism"

A more focused critique of *A Course in Miracles* appeared in a widely reviewed book titled *The Guru Papers: Masks of Authoritarian Power* (Frog, 1993), by Diana Alstad and Joel Kramer. Alstad, an instructor in humanities and women's studies with a doctorate from Yale, and Kramer, a yoga adept and former instructor at Esalen Institute, wrote their book to expose the "authoritarian structure" they feel is "interwoven and disguised in most arenas of human interaction, including religion, morality, power, institutions, the family, intimacy, and even sexual relations and personal problems, such as addiction."

For the most part, *The Guru Papers* eschews criticism of particular institutions, movements, or individuals, instead providing a more general analysis of such topics as "The Seductions of Surrender," "Fundamentalism and the Need for Certainty," and "Love and Control." Two exceptions to their "essentially structural" critique are a five-page commentary on the Reverend Jim Jones and the 1978 mass suicide at Jonestown—and ten pages on *A Course in Miracles*.

Kramer and Alstad focused on the Course "because it purports to be non-authoritarian, while claiming to be channeled by no less an authority than the spirit of Jesus Christ. . . . We single it out because it is a classic example of programming thought to renunciate beliefs." Most of the ensuing critique focuses on the Workbook of the Course, which in Kramer and Alstad's view pursues a kind of brainwashing proceeding along three routes:

1. Promulgating detachment from the world by denying its reality
2. Decreeing forgiveness and the letting go of grievances to be the only route to love and salvation
3. Promising immortality and the elimination of all negativity through identifying only with what is delineated as the god aspect within oneself

The authors also note that the avowed purpose of the Workbook is to "eventually bring forth one's 'Internal Teacher' which in turn, without any external authorities, will lead one to truth. . . . This claim is worth examining because under the guise of presenting objective truth that any seeker can find, what is actually going on is the age-old ploy of authoritarian indoctrination: A worldview is presented by an unchallengeable authority as the truth to be found. . . . Nothing could be more authoritarian, for who could argue against a disembodied spirit with the credentials of a traditional God?"

Who could argue? An obvious answer is Helen Schucman, the Course channel who argued with the voice of a disembodied spirit in her own head until the end of her days (see chapters 1 and 2). Kramer and Alstad's charge about the authoritarianism of the Course is further weakened by two facts. First, most authoritarian systems rely on an organization or embodied figure of authority rather than an implicit imperative. Second, many Course students do in fact argue with its voice even as they study the message.

Many contemporary students—including such leading proponents as Jerry Jampolsky, Marianne Williamson, Ken Wapnick, and Judy Skutch—come from Jewish backgrounds and thus were not particularly inclined to regard the voice of Jesus as a divine or unimpeachable authority in the first place. Possibly a majority of students are veterans of other spiritual disciplines—including more traditional and overtly authoritarian structures—who report that what they like about the Course is its "take it or leave it" accessibility. Still others with agnostic orientations tell stories like that of Roger Walsh (see chapter 8), who shut his copy of the Course as soon as he encountered its claim of spiritual authorship and did not reopen it for two years—until consistently positive reviews by respected peers convinced him to take another look. As Ken Wapnick relates, "I've heard countless stories of the Course sitting on people's bookshelves for several years before they happen to read something in it that suddenly makes sense."

Thus Kramer and Alstad's critique incorporates little knowledge of what Course students are really like or what they have to say about how the teaching actually affects them. Their critique cites no direct comments from interviews with Course teachers or students. And even when Kramer and Alstad rely on a student's own written words to draw an interpretation of the Course's effects, their methodology and conclusions are decidedly questionable.

"He Feels Better"

To illustrate their contention that "those willing to be programmed get programmed," Kramer and Alstad assert that it is necessary to examine not only the Course's Workbook exercises "but also the nature of the mind that is willing and able to do them daily for an extended time."

> As an example we will paraphrase and quote an enthusiast and teach-er of the Course. We use this person's words only to represent a posi-tion which we (and he, too) believe is similar to that of many others. Consequently, we do not think the identity of the person matters. He initially states that before doing the Course, he was very disap-pointed in life because he saw that ideals important to him would not or could not be achieved in this world. "The more I faced the 'real world,' the less real I felt." He had "a divided sense of self that didn't measure up to anything"; and his "fragmented idealism" was "contaminated by conflicting ambitions."
>
> Here is a person who wanted the world to fit into what were most probably ideals of purity, where non-violence, compassion, selfless-ness, and love would reign supreme. It is not surprising this man

would gravitate toward a worldview that presented these four items as in fact reigning supreme, this being done by denying the reality of the world where they do not reign supreme. This same person went on to say, "After years of thrashing about in a senseless world that seemed to oppose my highest aspirations, I have simply forgiven that world . . . I'm no longer concerned with defining what the "real world" is—perhaps, as the Course asserts, there is no world at all, but I do know I have gained a personal sense of authenticity." He then concluded that he now feels better than he ever felt before.

The danger of this kind of feeling better, Kramer and Alstad explain, is the "great illusion . . . that through denial one can transcend what one is afraid of, whether it be death or isolation. . . . What all renunciate world-views such as *A Course in Miracles* really create are internally divided people who need an external authority to help keep control of their unwanted parts."

Kramer and Alstad did not acknowledge or footnote their source, making it difficult for readers to follow up their research or challenge their conclusions. Reading their critique as a journalist, I decided that I would try to contact the quoted student myself. Beginning to read his excerpted statements a second time, I realized that this wouldn't take much footwork—because the increasingly familiar language of this "programmed" student was my own.

In fact, the quotations Kramer and Alstad excerpted originally appeared in my first personal essay about *A Course in Miracles*, published in 1988 by *The Sun: A Magazine of Ideas*. To offer my own interpretation of what I wrote—about which I can be reasonably authoritative—it is necessary to reproduce the entire passage edited by Kramer and Alstad. Italics indicate material they deleted or did not include:

After years of thrashing about in a senseless world that seemed to oppose my highest aspirations, I have simply forgiven that world *by realizing that it was largely defined and limited by my own pessimism.* I'm no longer concerned with defining what the "real world" is—perhaps, as the Course asserts, there is no world at all—but I do know that I have regained a personal sense of authenticity. *I know that I am here to learn and, through writing, to teach whatever I can discover, record, and synthesize. No other definition of myself is needed.*

This essay, written during recovery from a prolonged illness during which I encountered and completed my initial study of *A Course in Miracles*, represented a sort of personal "coming out." In it I was exploring how what I had recently learned might be usefully extended to a world from which I had felt sequestered for several years by an intense struggle of physical suffering, psychological self-confrontation, and spiritual crisis.

By learning how to relinquish longtime habits of pessimism and cynicism, I felt that I was "loosing the world," as the Course puts it in Lesson 132, from my demands and judgments. I no longer expected the *world* to fit ideals of "non-violence, compassion, selflessness, and love," as Kramer and Alstad suggested; rather, I had come to realize that fulfilling and communicating such worthy ideals were *my* responsibility. To pursue them I needed to rely on a greater sense of instinctive guidance than my habitual ego-self. *A Course in Miracles* was invaluable in helping me discover and contact such a sense of guidance.

I should add that in the process of learning to access that guidance, my relationship to the Course was never that of unquestioning obedience to an "unchallengeable authority." I have argued inwardly with the voice of the Course for more than two decades of study, and I probably always will. It is the testing of Course principles against my own prior assumptions and prejudices that has validated the usefulness of the teaching to me. I have never particularly cared about the nature of the Course authorship, but only whether its discipline delivered results of positive change.

While examining *The Guru Papers*, I became curious as to why anti-authoritarian writers like Kramer and Alstad would take the liberty of interpreting my writing without contacting me to discuss their perspective in a fair and egalitarian manner. (Reaching me would have been easy enough; my address was published with *The Sun* essay, and responses from readers were explicitly invited.) I also wanted to discuss with Kramer and Alstad my reactions to their work. In my letter requesting their cooperation, I advised Kramer and Alstad that they would have the opportunity to preview what I wrote about them in manuscript, correct any factual inaccuracies, and discuss any points on which they might feel misrepresented before publication. In a written response Diana Alstad stated that "we are truly sorry if you feel misrepresented." But she declined to be interviewed, stating that "we are not interested in involving ourselves in a dialogue about the value of *A Course in Miracles*." This refusal to engage in discussion about the Course is ironic, since Kramer and Alstad remark in *The Guru Papers* that they "have a surety and confidence in what we are saying. But confidence need not be authoritarian in itself if one is truly open to being shown wrong. The essence of ideological authoritarianism is unchallengeability, not confidence."

Not Exactly Easy Reading

A frequent criticism of the Course by its own students and others who have examined it is that its patriarchal, Christian, and just plain difficult language puts up a formidable barrier to study. The late Rick Fields, a prominent writer in American Buddhism and my editor at *Yoga Journal* during the 1990s, probably spoke for untold thousands when he told me that "the Christian language was just too much for my taste."

Course student and psychotherapist Frances Vaughan (see chapter 8) says that the consistently masculine tone of the teaching "was not something I liked about the Course at first, and I would translate terms like *Son of God* to *Child of God* as I read it. I'd also substitute *enlightenment* for *salvation*, and so on. What worked for me was to take what fit, and let pass the things that didn't." Over time, however, Vaughan says that her technical difficulties with the Course terminology diminished to the point of irrelevance.

Charles T. Tart, PhD, is a senior research fellow at the Institute of Noetic Sciences and a retired psychology professor from the University of California at Davis who edited the landmark book *Altered States of Consciousness* (Wiley, 1969), a rare best seller among scientific anthologies. He remembers that the Course presented special difficulties for a mind trained in the scientific approach to reality.

"The Course really came in at a right angle to most of my professional work," Tart remarks. "I could find a lot of stuff in there that fit my understanding of how we 'live in illusion'—that is, how we use psychological defense mechanisms that distort our perceptions and create trouble for us. But basically the Course goes right for the heart, and the heart is not a standard part of scientific discipline. So it was tough for me."

Echoing Ken Wapnick's frequent assertions that *A Course in Miracles* should not be mistaken for an easy path to personal fulfillment or spiritual enlightenment, Course publisher Judy Skutch says, "I don't think serious students find it easy at all. We're all involved in a worldly thought system that is a direct antithesis to the Course. Some people come to it looking for a reinforcement of their feelings for peace, love, and light, and that's what they'll find. But their eyes may glaze over when they come to the Course definition of the ego as a murderer. There are many paths that will tell you of your perfection in spirit, and that you are loved. The Course does that too, but it may not be the best place to go for it."

The most cogent published summary of the difficulties engendered by Course study appeared in the Fall 1987 issue of *Gnosis*, the former "journal of the Western inner traditions" published in San Francisco. Writer Richard Smoley revealed in his essay "Pitfalls of A Course in Miracles" that he had worked with the Course for a number of years, finding it to be "an effective tool for spiritual growth. It seems to be especially useful for intellectuals who feel the need to deepen qualities of love and compassion. . . . Yet, like all spiritual paths, the Course has its pitfalls."

One of these, says Smoley, paradoxically derives from a Course virtue: its encouragement to students that they listen for the voice of the Holy Spirit within. "The independence permitted by this approach is wonderful for developing a sense of responsibility for oneself," allows Smoley. But he points out that the destructive voice of ego can easily be mistaken for authentic spiritual guidance, thus leading the Course student astray. Smoley comments:

> Normally if this happens, some kind of balance is restored by the response of others. But the Course emphasizes very strongly that we are not to judge others: "In order to judge anything rightly, one would have to be fully aware of an inconceivably wide range of things, past, present, and to come. . . . Who is in a position to do this? Who except

in grandiose fantasies would claim this for himself?" (MANUAL, 10, 3) Thus, any criticism offered by somebody else can be immediately turned against him or her: "You're judging me!"—which, among Miracles students, often closes the book on the issue, though rarely satisfactorily. In my experience, this has caused legitimate questions and problems to fester into something really quite bad, whereas they might have been settled easily if one student had permitted himself to listen to the other's "judgment."

Partly for this reason, Smoley feels that *A Course in Miracles* may not be a strong foundation for organizations trying to use its principles to achieve their goals. As he writes, "A group or organization that is trying to live by the Course's teachings may arrive at a decision by consensus. Yet a member chosen to carry it out may do exactly the opposite, on the grounds that the Holy Spirit directed him otherwise later on. And who's to say he's wrong?"

Smoley's concerns about the misidentification of divine guidance seem valid. One doesn't have to visit Course study groups or electronic discussion forums for long to hear the Holy Spirit cited frequently as the internal broker of every conceivable decision, intuition, or lucky break, from deciding to divorce or pull up stakes to finding a wished-for parking space. There is generally less discussion over whether it's truly the Holy Spirit at work in all these occasions; short-term benefits are often taken for proof of divine guidance.

Ken Wapnick observes that one of the key misperceptions that arises for Course students is "the idea that it's the easiest thing in the world to hear the Holy Spirit—that a little light meditation is all that's required to get the Holy Spirit to tell you what to do. But the reason the Course as a whole exists is to help us clear out the interference that blocks the Holy Spirit. That interference is huge, and it's not a simple matter to get rid of it. The ego won't dissolve immediately simply because you begin to think you want it to dissolve."

Richard Smoley also suggests that Workbook Lessons such as 97, "I am spirit," and 199, "I am not a body. I am free" can encourage Course students to lose "a firm grounding in the physical. . . . Often one does sense in

Miracles students a lack of a firm foundation, an ethereal or dreamy quality that can be pleasant to be around but may also represent a spiritual dead end." Wapnick identifies this quality as a tendency among novices. "It's true that many students new to the Course have a tendency to get dreamy and spaced-out. A friend of mine calls them the 'bliss ninnies.'"

Wapnick further notes, "I find that I often have to tell people, *Don't forget to be normal.* Students can end up thinking that they shouldn't lock their doors at night because the Course tells them to trust, they should cancel their insurance because the Course says not to plan the future, and they should feel guilty for sneezing because the Course says, 'Sickness is a defense against the truth.' (LESSON 136) So I have to remind them to be normal. Of course, be sympathetic to someone who's sick. Don't preach to them about their illness being a defense.

"What people tend to do is deny where they are," Wapnick explains, "or they try to reinterpret their current behavior along the intellectual lines of the Course rather than change themselves according to inner guidance. The Course doesn't ask us to deny our feelings and experiences—in fact, it does just the opposite. It says we should look clearly at our feelings in order 'to bring them to the truth.' You can't do the second without the first, without being fully aware of what you feel."

The tendency to deny one's flaws and contradictions and evade uncomfortable truths is arguably a universal expression of the human condition and so by no means unique to Course students. But it is clear that some students exploit the Course's ideas about forgiveness and the illusory nature of the world as novel mechanisms of denial. When confronted with one's mistakes, it becomes all too easy to say that "everything's an illusion anyway" or "we've all been forgiven." Neither of these excuses would carry much weight outside Course circles. But as Richard Smoley has pointed out, the culture inside study groups can become rarefied to the extent that such protestations can effectively short-circuit discussion and confrontation. The result is that truth and genuine understanding may be sacrificed to a false harmony and cloying religiosity.

But to the extent that Course students resort to denial and evasion, they are also evading explicit directives of the Course itself, as in the following passages.

Honesty does not apply only to what you say. The term actually means consistency. There is nothing you say that contradicts what you think or do; no thought opposes any other thought; no act belies your word; and no word lacks agreement with another. Such are the truly honest. At no level are they in conflict with themselves. Therefore it is impossible for them to be in conflict with anyone or anything. . . . Conflict is the inevitable result of self-deception, and self-deception is dishonesty. (MANUAL, 4, II, 1–2)

Every thought you would keep hidden shuts communication off, because you would have it so. It is impossible to recognize perfect communication while breaking communication holds value to you. Ask yourself honestly, "Would I want to have perfect communication, and am I wholly willing to let everything that interferes with it go forever?" If the answer is no, then the Holy Spirit's readiness to give it to you is not enough to make it yours, for you are not ready to share it with Him. . . .

You will not be able to accept perfect communication as long as you would hide it from yourself. For what you would hide is hidden from you. (CHI 5, IV, 8–9)

A Merciless Teaching?

The extraordinary demands that the Course seems to make of its students have been noted in criticism by Anton van Harskamp, a researcher at the Blaise Pascal Institute, Vrije Universiteit Amsterdam and a professor at the same university teaching on religion, identity, and civil society. In an eight-thousand-word online essay titled "A Modern Miracle," Dr. Harskamp summarizes the history of the Course and asserts that it is a "variant of the old gnosticism" before coming to these conclusions:

We have to remind ourselves that "The Course" says two things at the same time. On the one hand the book repeats over and over again that all experiences of suffering and misery, within and outside us, are the result of suffering that we subject ourselves to. That is de facto an exceptionally heavy accusation to each of us. On the other hand, however, "The Course" does tell us that each and every one of us has the capacity to see through the suffering and get rid of it. It is exactly this combination that imposes on us a truly frightening responsibility. Imagine: every time we fail on the road to happiness, and of course we will fail a number of times, we will have to blame ourselves and only ourselves. And this is what we may call merciless. . . .

Many students of "The Course" consider themselves people who have bade farewell to or have abandoned the burden and pressure of a church-oriented Christianity. But what has replaced this? A religious ideology that in the form of an extremely optimistic view on man, places an incomparably greater burden and pressure on the individual. It is the burden of creating life ourselves. Paradoxically by letting go of our own ego, but nevertheless with our own strength and potential. The pressure results from the realization that we have to blame ourselves for every second that we have not reached complete happiness. This all renders "The Course" in my opinion "uncanny" and merciless. So: what should we think about this development to a "new-old ideology"? These words come to mind: bewildering and sad.[1]

The Problem of Ultimacy

It is undeniable that ACIM's fundamental challenge to the reality of all that we see, hear, and feel in our ordinary state of consciousness can have a bewildering effect on some students—an effect that may not be quickly resolved. To understand why a purportedly beneficial spiritual teaching can throw its students for a loop, it's necessary to understand the difference between the effects of conventional religion and an authentic mystical path.

According to San Francisco State University philosophy professor Jacob Needleman, author of the classic *The New Religions* (Doubleday, 1970) and more recent titles such as *The American Soul* (Tarcher/Putnam, 2002) and *Why Can't We Be Good?* (Penguin, 2007), the world's great religious traditions have always consisted of an outer shell of moral teachings and prescribed beliefs and an inner core of more demanding transformative practices. As Needleman explains,

Christianity, Judaism, and Islamic belief all provide people with moral precepts: ways of living meant to be obeyed by the masses. Any such way of living is based on a particular vision of human nature and society, and is intended to give balance and steadiness to our experience. It's not intended to transform us, to give us nirvana or God-realization. But if kept authentically, it can bring a few people who are seeking more to "the path" in relatively good shape. Their psyches are not torn apart or so terribly neurotic. This is the point of the exoteric function of the great religions—what Islam calls the *shariat*, its laws, customs, and traditions. It's a very important part of balancing human life, and at their best these rules provide guidelines for handling our various energies with compassion for one another.

Within the *shariat* is the *tarikat*: the way or the path. In Islam, this esoteric function is embodied by the Sufis. Many great teachers have said that the esoteric work is only for those who have been through the exoteric, and have achieved the necessary balance. It's true that the message of the great esoteric traditions is that only an inner change can genuinely infuse outer actions with truth, love, and power. But most of these transformative techniques were intended for people who had lived in balance with a tradition. What we're getting recently in the West is a lot of information about inner practice, available to people who haven't really had an outer practice.[2]

What can happen to people who encounter a transformative inner practice if they haven't had much of an outer one? Says Needleman, "If a spiritual practice is too intense, it 'blows your mind' and becomes overly fascinating, or leads you into fantasy. You could compare the esoteric core of a religion to a very pure, high-octane fuel. Put it into an old Volkswagen, and the car will go like hell for a mile before it blows apart."[3]

This vivid image may explain a lot about the disorienting effect of the Course on its students (and perhaps even about its combustive effect on some critics). What is startling about the Course in view of Needleman's analysis is that it appears to be a transformative inner practice that has come to us without an accompanying outer practice—that is, no commandments for moral behavior and no simple, direct judgments about various challenges of daily life.

Thus one of the greatest difficulties of *A Course in Miracles* might be called the problem of ultimacy—the fact that it operates as an ultimate teaching about the nature of consciousness and reality in a world in which so many people need simpler, more direct answers to their everyday problems. In my own experience, the Course is not sufficient as a troubleshooting guide to everyday life. No one should mistake it for a substitute for psychotherapy, peer counseling, or simple human communion in times of distress. Particularly in the early stages of study, the Course can be quite confusing and even distressing if one attempts to apply its teaching too literally to chronic or everyday problems.

The changes in consciousness that the Course can effect may be quite profound, but they come about in a subtle and gradual manner. Those people for whom the Course eventually works as a transformative path—truly connecting them to an internal agency of reliable, ego-surpassing wisdom—may indeed transcend the need for more specific forms of personal or moral guidance. This is the advanced state of instinctive morality that St. Augustine was probably referring to when he issued the mystical directive "Love and do what you will."

But all paths to such states are fraught with dangers and opportunities for delusion. Thus, anyone who undertakes a path like *A Course in Miracles* would be well advised to stay in touch with respected and caring peers who do not share the path, its assumptions, and its lingo. Reliable outsiders can provide invaluable reality checks to the esoteric seeker along his or her way—and sophisticated skeptics can provide some necessary tests of one's spiritual learning.

Of course, ACIM is not the only esoteric path available to seekers in the modern "spiritual supermarket." However dangerous it may be for people to take up an inner practice without preparation or guidance, it would appear that the growing social phenomenon of "inner seeking" is unlikely to reverse itself. Perhaps more people are lately drawn to esoteric spiritualities because the outer paths of the great religious traditions have been slow to adapt their exoteric guidance to the needs of a rapidly changing world—as witnessed, for example, by the stresses and strains to which the Catholic

Church is now subject. Or perhaps it's because the world's established religions have drifted too far from their inner, transformative core—a predicament that Jacob Needleman diagnosed three and a half decades ago when he wrote *The New Religions*. In discussing the central crisis of Western religion, he said:

> It is as though millions of people suffering from a painful disease were to gather together to hear someone read a textbook of medical treatment in which the means necessary to cure their disease were carefully spelled out. It is as though they were all to take great comfort in that book and what they heard, going through their lives knowing that their disease could be cured, quoting passages to their friends, preaching the wonders of this great book, and returning to their congregation from time to time to hear more of the inspiring diagnosis and treatment read to them. Meanwhile, of course, the disease worsens and they eventually die of it, smiling in grateful hope as on their deathbed someone reads to them yet another passage from the text. Perhaps for some a troubling thought crosses their minds as their eyes close for the last time: "Haven't I forgotten something? Something important? Haven't I forgotten actually to undergo treatment?"

Even as Needleman wrote those words, a "textbook" spelling out a spiritual cure to what ails us was being composed, and would shortly become available to the world. As this chapter has shown, we still lack any exhaustive, reasonably impartial assessments of the quality of this relatively new guide to transformation, although positive anecdotal reports continue to mount. The extent to which *A Course in Miracles* proves to be an effective esoteric therapy for the existential illness of humanity—whose painful symptoms include unhappiness, profound suffering, enmity, and oppression—remains to be seen.

∽ ENDNOTES ∽

1. For the full text of Prof. Harskamp's remarks, see www.bezinningscentrum.nl/
   teksten/anton_eng/mireng.htm.
2. Jacob Needleman, interview by D. Patrick Miller, "In the Spirit of Philosophy,"
   The Sun, June 1989.
3. Ibid.

 CHAPTER 11

The Presence of the Course

In *The Gnostic Gospels* (Vintage, 1989), Princeton University theologian Elaine Pagels lists some of the beliefs of Christianity that are widely accepted yet nonetheless "astonishing" on their face:

> The creed requires, for example, that Christians confess that God is perfectly good, and still, he created a world that includes pain, injustice, and death; that Jesus of Nazareth was born of a virgin mother; and that, after being executed by order of the Roman procurator, Pontius Pilate, he arose from his grave "on the third day."

The beliefs of the early Gnostics, although more in line with central elements of the "perennial philosophy" than modern Christianity, probably had no more face validity than those beliefs we now regard as orthodox. A central assumption of Pagels' book is that what came to be accepted as religious truth by most of the Western world had less to do with inherent validity than with politics and power struggles. As she concludes, "It is the winners who write history—their way."

Historical controversies aside, it is worth questioning why anyone ever adopts the astonishing beliefs that can be found in any religion—from the Western notion that the sacrificial death of a divine figure somehow pays for all the evil deeds of humankind, to the Eastern notion that the everyday world we see, hear, touch, taste, and feel is illusory. In a world in which most of the material and medical advancements of civilization are owed to science, not religion, why do so many people turn to belief systems that are plainly irrational? In short, why do people choose to believe any of these crazy mystical ideas?

One answer is that people raised in strong religious traditions simply never learn to question the creed that shapes their whole view of reality. But an answer that is more revealing of our culture's recent spiritual renaissance—and that certainly has more to do with the growing popularity of *A Course in Miracles*—stems from the inadequacy of rational materialism as a way of explaining our existence and providing personal guidance.

For however much science ultimately promises to dispel every last shred of mystery about nature and our lives on this earth, the fact remains that our lives are steeped in mystery at every moment. We do not know exactly what or who we are, why we feel what we feel from moment to moment, or why we behave in the ways we do. (Even when we learn that a specific gene may "determine" our proclivity to a particular disease or character trait, the questions remain: *How?* and *Why?*) In a sense, everyone who has ever been mystified is a mystic—and when it comes to answering the "big questions" of life, I suspect that most people are mystified throughout their lives.

A *spiritual awakening* can be seen as the recognition and acceptance of the mystery we live within. At their best, *spiritual beliefs* provide a meaningful roadmap through life's mystery. Finally, an authentic *spiritual discipline* is the means by which one learns to activate the potentials latent within the mystery of human consciousness. There are no statistically valid measures by which to plumb the potentials of mind, heart, and spirit, and no laboratory-approved safety regimens by which to utilize them. Everyone who ventures upon a spiritual path does so at personal risk. And although there are universal elements to all spiritual journeying, each individual's path is uniquely personal.

This chapter presents some concluding commentary on *A Course in Miracles* and about spiritual exploration in general. To further define my point of view and bias, I will share a brief travelogue of my own spiritual path—which usually looks to me like a faintly marked trail between the devil and the deep blue sea.

A Change of Course

My family was never very religious, and we stopped going to the neighborhood Methodist church regularly when I was about twelve. That was fine with me, as Sunday school hadn't held any appeal to me for a while. Ever since I had memorized John 3:16 in order to earn a wall plaque with the verse written on it in gilt lettering, I'd had the feeling that there was something amiss with churchgoing religion. I had first thought that Sunday school was the place one could ask the big questions of existence that weren't handled in regular school. But I soon learned that questions like *Where does the universe begin?* and *If God loves us and is in charge of everything, why does He let people get sick and die?* were answered either with befuddlement or with stern reminders to read more of the Bible until the urge to ask those big questions went away. By adolescence I had become largely agnostic, mostly in reaction to the fundamentalist and commercialized strains of Christianity that pervaded my hometown of Charlotte, North Carolina.

When I moved to California in my early twenties, I had set my sights on a career in investigative journalism with a special interest in environmental politics. But I didn't last long in the field, as I became increasingly troubled by my chosen profession's tunnel-vision grasp of reality. My editors and mentors encouraged me to look for people's base motives, but they were not at all interested in the investigation of deeper motivations. For them it was sufficient to document the greed of a crooked politician; I wanted to know what made him greedy.

It took me only a few years in investigative journalism to see that an entire career could be spent attempting to dislodge a few corrupt politicians from power, which looked like a zero-sum game to me. I wanted to have a distinctly positive effect on the world, not just eliminate a few of its negatives. Slowed by these professional doubts and distracted by personal anxieties, I backed off from journalism and for the next ten years simply tried to make a living working as a self-employed typographer, always intending to use any extra time to continue my writing career.

But I proved to be a break-even businessman at best, and by my early thirties I still didn't know what I wanted to write about. I was beginning to worry that I would never put together a fruitful life when I fell seriously ill with a mysterious, debilitating malady that was still a few years away from being medically identified as chronic fatigue syndrome (CFS).

That was when my rational grasp of the world began to suffer the slings and arrows of a prolonged "altered state" experience—lasting seven years from the sudden onset of CFS to the point at which I could consider myself completely recovered. My spiritual conversion came at the cost of great suffering and a hard-fought resistance every step of the way. Yet in retrospect I see that conversion as an uncovering of the spirituality that was always within me, rather than the wholesale adoption of a previously alien perspective.

Although my health crisis did not involve any kind of substance abuse, I look back on my experience with CFS as one of recovery from psychological addiction to guilt, cynicism, fearfulness, and suspicion—all of which I had long believed to be the most realistic, practical attitudes for dealing with a cruel world. The idea that one could see the world or govern one's own consciousness in any other way was completely foreign to me until I encountered *A Course in Miracles*. Like many other Course students, I have my own story of how an odd turn of events paved the way to that encounter.

In the first few months of my illness I was angry with my body's failure to perform as expected anymore, and I pursued purely medical solutions to a literally dizzying array of symptoms—frequent migraine headaches, traveling muscle pains, severe and continuous gastrointestinal distress, mental confusion, and overwhelming fatigue. But as increasingly vivid and poignant dreams surfaced in my prolonged sleeping sessions, I slowly began to entertain the possibility of psychological (and even deeper) roots to my condition, and I began reading widely in the fields of psychospirituality and consciousness. For the first time in my life I also entered psychotherapy, which consisted mainly of spilling out long-withheld emotional troubles to a very caring and attentive counselor.

Shortly after beginning therapy I came across a mention of *A Course in Miracles* in a book called *Higher Creativity* (Penguin, 1984) by Willis Harman, in which the healing power of affirmations was discussed. Increasingly willing to try anything that might restore my health, I had tried meditating with a few affirmations, but always ended up feeling silly for trying to change the way I thought or felt—much less trying to change my physical condition—simply by repeating positive ideas to myself.

However, a point that Harman made suddenly struck home for me: that an habitually unhealthy state of mind could be perpetuated by the semiconscious repetition of *negative* ideas to oneself. When I closely reviewed my habitual state of mind in the few years prior to the onset of CFS (looking to my personal journals as a "smoking gun"), the prominent role of such negative self-brainwashing was undeniable. I was profoundly shaken by the realization. Harman described the Course as a thorough "mind-training" in an opposite way of thinking, and I was intrigued.

I was also suspicious because the Course cost forty dollars in hardcover (for three separate volumes). Not knowing its length or density, compared with typical book prices at that time it sounded like a rip-off to me. On the next trip to my medical doctor I resolved to stop at the metaphysical bookshop across the street and peruse the Course long enough to form an opinion about it. (At that point, forming a quick and decisive opinion about things was still one of my major coping strategies.)

When I got to the bookstore, the first thing I saw was two entire shelves of the three-in-one paperback edition of *A Course in Miracles*, priced at twenty-five dollars. Startled, I asked the store owner how long he had carried the books. "I just shelved them," he replied. "The paperback was released recently and it came in this morning." For the first of countless times in my experience as a Course student, a soft *click* sounded in my head. I bought my first paperback copy.

Considering my immediate and visceral distaste for its Christian language, it is amazing how rapidly and intensively I undertook the Course Workbook and the daily reading of its Text. I was reading several other books at the time, and for a short while the Course seemed unremarkable in comparison, apart from its peculiar syntax.

But within weeks my dreams began to feature the blue book with regularity, and the daily Workbook lessons suddenly shifted from a curious chore to a compelling necessity. Somehow the crushing oppression of my illness and apparently failed life was lifting, at least inwardly. Something new was happening in my consciousness, and I wasn't sure what it was. At times this uncertainty provoked more than a little anxiety.

It was after one episode of such anxiety that I decided to tell my therapist of my new undertaking; I had otherwise kept the Course a secret from friends and helpers. I was also beginning to wonder where my therapy was heading, as I had vented most of my intimate anxieties over a couple of months and my counselor seemed to offer little more than patient listening and occasional words of kind encouragement. When I expressed my misgiving about the passivity of therapy and confessed my new esoteric adventure—wondering if my therapist might intervene or at least issue a warning about getting involved in strange religions—there were two surprises in store for me.

First, my counselor shared his observation that my illness had apparently forced me to confront myself to a greater degree than most of his clients who had been seeing him for much longer. "I spend most of my time trying to get people to face the kind of things you've come here and told me about," he said. Second, he added, "If you can handle the Course, you probably don't need me anyway." *Click*. Indeed, I soon left therapy with my counselor's blessings.

Although I would not recommend *A Course in Miracles* as a cure for any specific disease, I do credit my study of the Course as the central factor in my complete recovery from CFS. I used a wide variety of medical and psychological approaches, all of which played their part in resolving a diabolically creative disorder that, in its severest phase, could aptly be described as everything going wrong at once. But the Course helped me make sense of the process of healing, in ways too numerous and complex to describe here. The Course also strengthened my sense of intuition about which avenues of healing to pursue at different times.

CFS eventually cost me my livelihood, my financial resources, my closest relationships, and what I had formerly regarded as my "self-esteem." But in the process of a long and difficult recovery guided by the decidedly irrational influence of the Course, I gained a full-time profession in writing, better physical health than I had known before the onset of CFS, healthier ways of relating, and a powerful sense of inner calling to replace my old schemes of personal success.

In retrospect I wouldn't want my spiritual path to have followed any other route. But there were countless times when I seemed stuck in dead ends or unable to negotiate the next perilous hairpin turn. I honestly do not know what got me through it all except a growing sense of strength from a mysterious source that is somehow both within me and from beyond me—a source of strength that I can only call spiritual.

"To be fatigued is to be dis-spirited," suggests the Course, "but to be inspired is to be in the spirit. To be egocentric is to be dis-spirited, but to be Self-centered in the right sense is to be inspired or in spirit. The truly inspired are enlightened and cannot abide in darkness." (CH4, INTRO, 1)

Since the time of my recovery from CFS in the early 1990s, the Course has served as the central guide of my spiritual experience, although not the only input. ACIM has given me a sense of freedom in pursuing a variety of spiritual perspectives, including Jungian depth psychology and studies in the Enneagram, a mystical system of personality assessment and transformation. The Course has also given me a sense of freedom that allowed me to back away from its discipline at times and to question its validity during periods of intense personal challenge. Yet sooner or later I have always returned to ACIM as the touchstone of my spiritual life, in which I can always find extraordinary insights and a renewed sense of inspiration, regardless of how many times I have read the Text or worked the lessons.

Of Cults and Nuts

I initially completed the Text and Workbook of the Course relatively rapidly, within eighteen months. Except for a six-week discussion group I attended early in my study, my first experience with the Course was solitary. Thus I was a little surprised later on to learn the extent of the social phenomenon that ACIM has spawned. I am still of the opinion that the Course is primarily a self-study curriculum, and I tend to agree with fellow student Richard Smoley that the Course's inherent weaknesses can be inadvertently magnified by organizations who devote themselves to it.

That said, the problems that show up in Course groups are essentially no different from the problems that show up in other religious or tightly knit social organizations. Insular thinking, socially reinforced self-deception, presumptions of superiority, and cultish obeisance to questionable leaders are certainly not unique to Course groups. All these elements can be found in political parties, the military, government bureaucracies, and successful corporations.

By and large the Course community has avoided the development of cultish cliques; in the eyes of many Course veterans, Endeavor Academy in Wisconsin is the major exception to the rule. Yet even among ex-residents who have made their serious concerns about Endeavor public knowledge, one finds a genuine respect for the passion of that unique community.

From my own study of alternative religious groups over the years, I find that Americans in general—and the mainstream press in particular—have little understanding of the power and appeal of religious devotion, especially when it is focused on alternative paths or teachers. We tend to regard such devotion outside the religious mainstream as a bizarre, invariably destructive aberration in a culture that's supposed to be devoted to individual freedom above all. But in a society in which many individuals find themselves morally adrift in their unhappy freedom, we are likely to see a further proliferation of so-called cults that offer their members a deeply sought social identity, reliable rules of conduct, and an up-close focus for their spiritual passion.

Of course, a great deal depends upon how cults are defined; sometimes any phenomenon that's new or esoteric can have the "cult" tag hung upon it. Several times over my years of researching the Course I've encountered people who have said, "Oh, *A Course in Miracles*—isn't that a cult thing?" No doubt such free-floating impressions are due in part to ill-informed critiques of ACIM that have found their way into print and public notice. On the other hand, it's likely that some of the Course's bad rep could be sourced to people's encounters with overenthusiastic students slinging the Miracles lingo or an immature teacher glibly advertising ACIM as the latest spiritual snake-oil remedy. After surveying the field for more than two decades, however, I have concluded that the general population of Course students and instructors is no nuttier than humanity in general—and a significant proportion of Course followers have apparently achieved a remarkable reformation of their lives and characters.

Enlightenment Versus Delusion

Exactly how *A Course in Miracles* achieves this transformative effect is difficult to explain fully; even some of the most veteran students can only say, "It just works for me." I can't add much to that. I do know that I have experienced the Course as a remarkable discipline of confronting my worst internal enemies—what the Course calls "blocks to the awareness of love's presence"—and learning how to let them be replaced by less judgmental, more caring, and more truly objective attitudes. The Course is difficult only to the extent that self-confrontation is difficult. The resistance that many students experience along the way attests to the Course's consistency in facilitating a discipline of self-examination and surrender.

In terms of spiritual growth, exactly what one surrenders to is the crux of the matter. Anyone who has experienced a breakdown of his habitual personality and fundamental frame of reference is vulnerable to "conversion" to new spiritual or psychological orientations that may be much healthier—or tragically more destructive—than his old egocentrism. In their earliest stages the processes of enlightenment and delusion can be nearly indistinguishable. Both involve becoming "as a child" while the mind and heart open to substantially new feelings, perceptions, and world-defining concepts.

After this initial opening, however, maturing spiritual aspirants will become more sensible, if less rigid and narrow-minded. Their perceptions are less likely to be skewed by unresolved emotional disturbances, and they have a greater range of intuitive resources to draw upon. Conversely, a sure sign of progressive delusion among spiritual aspirants is an increasing illogic and vagueness—particularly a tendency to excuse inconsistencies of belief and behavior with references to one's supposedly superior advancement of consciousness. The general attitude goes like this: "If you were as enlightened as I am, everything I do would make sense to you."

A lot of counterfeit enlightenment has been passed off as authentic wisdom in this way, either by alleged spiritual masters or their devotees. Little if any such falseness would get by the Course's exacting requirements for its graduates, or "teachers of God"; in its Manual for Teachers, ACIM lists their identifying characteristics as trust, honesty, tolerance, gentleness, joy, defenselessness, generosity, patience, faithfulness, and open-mindedness.

Taken cumulatively, these qualities don't leave much room for greed, hubris, or obfuscation.

The advanced spiritual seeker will be able to explain himself or herself in simple, direct terms and admit to any unresolved contradictions in belief and behavior, embodying a sincere humility in place of presumed superiority. Gandhi, for instance, once observed that he had faced three great enemies in his struggle to bring about change: the first was the British government, on which he could claim some significant effect; the second was the Indian people, whom he found considerably more intractable; and the third great opponent—the one whom he despaired of ever changing for the better—he identified as himself.

Also, it has long been observed that great spiritual teachers can both enjoy and learn from the company of the "simplest" or most untrained people they encounter. They do not need to talk down to anyone or assert their own advancement. In Zen Buddhism the ultimate goal of meditation is to achieve the unfettered, nonjudgmental simplicity of "beginner's mind." Similarly, A Course in Miracles asserts that "complexity is of the ego, and is nothing more than the ego's attempt to obscure the obvious." (CH15, IV, 6)

Four Suggestions for Spiritual Pathfinding

The most salient question for new spiritual seekers—which so many modern Westerners are now becoming—is what safeguards they can employ to avoid veering off on paths of delusion or to at least avoid remaining on them past the point of their limited educational value (for sometimes it is undeniably valuable to experience disillusionment). Based on my experience as a researcher of many alternative spiritual viewpoints, I have four general guidelines to suggest. My explanation of each will use the Course for illustration.

1. Let your path "come to you." Philosopher Jacob Needleman once suggested that "an authentic spiritual path makes itself known, but does not attempt to persuade."[2] A great advantage of the modern spiritual supermarket is that a worldwide variety of spiritual paths and perspectives is now available to most people at their nearest bookstore or on the Web accessible by home computer. No longer do people have to accept the religious background of their family or native culture as the only proper spiritual path, particularly in the West. Thus it seems wise to survey as many paths as possible when attempting to find an appropriate discipline for self-transformation. After time and careful consideration, unsuitable paths and perspectives will fall away, and the "intuitive fit" of a particular discipline should become obvious.

Among its students, *A Course in Miracles* is legendary for "finding" them in unexpected ways, and for offering a strong intuitive appeal even when it seems bizarre or frightening. (My favorite report came from a student who claimed that a hardcover copy of the ACIM Text slipped off a towering stack of volumes in a used bookstore and literally hit her on the head.) On the other hand, untold numbers of people find no appeal in it whatsoever. Although some scattered teachers may proselytize it, neither the original publisher nor the most respected Course-teaching academies have been evangelical.

2. Make sure that your chosen path offers challenge without imprisonment. A disadvantage of the modern spiritual supermarket is that it offers people the opportunity to become spiritual dilettantes, identifying themselves with one or more transformative disciplines without ever actually undertaking any of them. Whether one chooses to focus on yoga, Zen, the Course, Christianity, or another path, it's important to actually follow the discipline(s) the path offers, and endure the inherent discomfort (and lifelong challenge) that a real spiritual discipline entails.

However, an important sign of an authentic path is that it will implicitly give you "permission" to quit, with no strings attached, whenever it no longer seems appropriate or productive. The Course is remarkable for its capacity to keep serious students engaged in its discipline even when it proves quite difficult—and to bring students back even after they have decided it was just too hard to continue. That it does this without recourse to external authority or social enforcement attests to a potent mystical quality embedded within the Course discipline.

But if one does decide to leave the training behind at any stage, the Course itself exacts no penalties, nor does it demand excommunication;

after all, it's just a book. (By the same token, Course students who feel that a study group or teacher is using the teaching to create a sense of enforcement or entrapment should question the validity of the situation.)

3. Look for results, not romance, from your chosen path. A sign of spiritual dilettantism is that it will produce only superficial changes of style in people's character and behavior. This is a frequent failing of various New Age fancies, in which people find it easier—and far more romantic—to, say, become a channel for the wisdom of the distant Pleiadians than to actually become wiser on their own.

Although one should grant oneself a "grace period" with a new spiritual discipline—during which personal problems may seem to get worse rather than better—after two years or so a dedicated commitment to a spiritual path should produce definite, observable improvements in one's character and consciousness. Such improvements are not to be confused with circumstantial or material benefits, which can neither be ruled out nor be expected to accompany inner changes.

Questions one can use to determine whether a spiritual path is really "paying off" include the following:

- Have I become more at peace within myself and in my relationships since undertaking this discipline?
- Do I blame less and have more compassion about my own difficulties and those of others?
- Do I experience more joy, empathy, and revelatory insight?
- Is my social and political conscience more informed and effective, regardless of how my forms of activism may have changed?
- Do I sometimes tap transcendent states of consciousness through the natural means of my own trained and focused awareness?

As this book has shown, many Course students will attest to the efficacy of their chosen discipline in bringing them very positive answers to these questions.

4. With experience, expect your spiritual practice to become "ordinary." The Dalai Lama of Tibetan Buddhism, one of the world's most respected spiritual and political leaders, often refers to himself as merely "an ordinary monk." This should be taken not as a sign of false modesty, but as a sign of advanced spiritual achievement, for it signifies a seeker who has learned to shed the temptations of what Tibetan teacher Chogyam Trungpa identified as "spiritual materialism."

There is no denying that *A Course in Miracles* can seem quite exotic to beginning students, and the first year or two of its study may feel like a prolonged "altered state" experience that seems to set the student off from other people and everyday reality. If study is sustained for a longer period, however, the Course points its students toward the ordinariness of spiritual mastery by its lack of emphasis on ritual and other religious trappings—a rare orientation among the world's major religions—and by emphasizing the spiritual equality of everyone, including Christ, within the "Sonship" of God.

That is not to say that veteran Course students never entertain inflated ideas of themselves and their path. But if one adheres faithfully to the Course discipline, it has a way of bringing one's hypocrisy and inflation up for conscious review on a regular basis. Over time, learning to catch one's own arrogance before it is translated into overbearing behavior becomes second nature—as do constructive and compassionate ways of thinking and behaving.

Sometimes I have been greatly startled to recall a typical moment of my "old" consciousness before I undertook the Course, and to notice the contrast between my self-awareness then and now. Although I have a ways to go to be entirely free of anger, cynicism, and selfishness, the degree to which I have been liberated from such self-defensive attitudes is remarkable. I believe it is a far greater degree of growth than I would have achieved through normal maturation without benefit of the Course. And yet my "new" consciousness does not strike me as an exalted state or a great personal achievement. Indeed, it seems like a normal way of life until I happen to recall how ordinary—but comparatively miserable—my pre-Course personality and beliefs felt to me.

The Uniqueness of the Course

In his book *Love Does Not Condemn* (FACIM, 1989), Ken Wapnick summarizes the major philosophical strains running through the massive mystical document he helped edit into its final form:

> Thus, we can see . . . how the Course is an amalgam of different approaches, yet a successful integration of them: It is Neoplatonic in terms of describing the downward progression (or projection) from the One; Gnostic in its clarity on the world not coming from the Divine at all, exposing the ego's trickery in back of it; and Christian, not only in its language, but through its recognizing a benevolent presence of God experienced in the world—the memory of His love (the Holy Spirit) in the split mind—not to mention the central place accorded to Jesus.

In a less scholarly vein I would add that the Course is decidedly *contemporary* in its exacting analysis of ego psychology, and uniquely *American* in its populist accessibility as a do-it-yourself, take-it-or-leave-it spiritual curriculum. Although major elements of the Course can be recognized in other spiritual perspectives and in modern psychology as well, the diverse yet well-integrated wholeness of the Course has not been preceded or replicated. Nor is its "forward momentum" matched by any other spiritual discipline or psychological perspective I have encountered.

What I mean by this is that the Course gives the serious student a dramatic sense of accelerated growth that is not limited to the particular insights and information of the teaching itself. For instance, most of my research into other psychologies and spiritual paths came after my initial study of *A Course in Miracles* and was in fact enabled by the sense of inspired curiosity that the Course awoke in me. While I still often consult the Course as a spiritual touchstone, in no way do I feel constrained to limit my investigations to the concepts or point of view it sets forth. In this way, too, I find that the Course promulgates a democratic open-mindedness.

Finally, perhaps the one quality of the Course I find most remarkable is its uncanny provision of a "presence" that I can only describe as wise companionship. Even though it is just a book, I often find myself regarding my copy of the Course as almost a living thing that might at any moment speak to me—no doubt with the same calm authority with which its Voice once silently requested of Helen Schucman, "Please take notes."

Considering how aggravating the Course can be at times, this sense of companionship is all the more uncanny. Yet it is merely the fulfillment of a promise that *A Course in Miracles* explicitly extends at the close of its Workbook of daily lessons:

> *This course is a beginning, not an end. Your Friend goes with you. You are not alone. No one who calls on Him can call in vain. Whatever troubles you, be certain that He has the answer, and will gladly give it to you, if you simply turn to Him and ask it of Him. He will not withhold all answers that you need for anything that seems to trouble you. He knows the way to solve all problems, and resolve all doubts. His certainty is yours. You need but ask it of Him, and it will be given you. . . .*
>
> *You do not walk alone. God's angels hover near and all about. His Love surrounds you, and of this be sure; that I will never leave you comfortless.*

☙ ENDNOTES ☙

1. Jacob Needleman, interview by D. Patrick Miller, "In the Spirit of Philosophy," *The Sun*, June 1989.

Appendix I

A Brief Guide to ACIM Study Centers, Teachers, and Online Resources

The following guide to resources for studying *A Course in Miracles* is not intended to be exhaustive, but rather to provide a representative sampling of some of the most established study centers, teachers, and online connections. All this information is subject to change after the printing of this book; whenever possible, check websites for current information.

For updates related to this book, see "The Continuing Story of the Course" online at www.fearlessbooks.com/ContStoryIndex.html.

Organizations in the United States

Foundation for Inner Peace (FIP)
PO Box 598, Mill Valley, CA 94942-0598
(415) 388-2060
www.acim.org
FIP is the original publisher of ACIM and remains the primary source for the standard edition, as well as eighteen translations and related video and audio media. In 2007 FIP released the third edition of ACIM, combining for the first time the three original volumes of Text, Workbook, and Manual for Teachers with the supplemental pamphlets "The Song of Prayer" and "Psychotherapy: Purpose, Practice, and Process."

Foundation for *A Course in Miracles* (FACIM)
41397 Buecking Drive, Temecula, CA 92590-5668
(951) 296-6261
www.facim.org
The sister foundation of FIP, FACIM is the home of the Institute for Teaching Inner Peace through *A Course in Miracles* and features workshops and seminars by Kenneth and Gloria Wapnick. A branch office is in La Jolla, California. Publishes *The Lighthouse* newsletter.

Miracle Distribution Center

3947 E. LaPalma Avenue, Anaheim, CA 92807

(714) 632-9005

www.miraclecenter.org

A long-established and reliable source for educational media related to ACIM, including an online directory of study groups worldwide. Publishes *The Holy Encounter* magazine and sponsors an annual conference in Anaheim.

Community Miracles Center

2269 Market Street, San Francisco, CA 94114

(415) 621-2556; toll-free (888) 621-2556

www.miracles-course.org

An ACIM-based church and teaching center that offers certified training for CMC ministers, as well as an exhaustive selection of Course-related books and other media and an online study group directory. Sponsors a biannual ACIM conference in San Francisco and publishes the *Miracles Monthly* newsletter.

Circle of Atonement

PO Box 4238, West Sedona, AZ 86340

(928) 282-0790

www.circleofa.org

Founded by Course teacher Robert Perry, this teaching center offers classes and workshops featuring the perspectives of Perry, Allen Watson, Greg Mackie, and Nicola Perry, as well as a variety of books and related teaching aids.

Pathways of Light

13111 Lax Chapel Road, Kiel, WI 53042

(800) 323-7284

http://pathwaysoflight.org

This center offers home study and correspondence courses and training for ACIM-inspired ministers and counselors, as well as onsite weekend workshops. An online store offers a variety of ACIM resources, featuring recorded workshops with popular Course author Gary Renard. A branch center has been established in London, England.

Endeavor Academy
PO Box 206, Lake Delton, WI 53940
(608) 253-6898
www.endeavoracademy.com
This ACIM-inspired residential community, teaching academy, and healing center focuses on the teachings of a so-called "Master Teacher" (Charles Anderson) and, unlike most other Course centers, has maintained an evangelical outreach over the years. Charges of cultism have been made by ex-residents.

The Quest Foundation
c/o Pauline Chiasson
97 Dodge Street, Nashua, NH 03064
(800) 879-2246
www.questfoundation.org
This service organization offers workshops, retreats, conferences, and seminars in the northeastern United States focusing on the principles of ACIM and Attitudinal Healing. Publishes the newsletter *The Spirit's Voice.*

One Mind Foundation
PO Box 11, Hastings-on-Hudson, NY 10706
www.onemindfdn.org
Managed by David Fishman and Linda Card, this organization maintains ACIM Gather Radio, an online teaching and discussion resource.

Course in Miracles Society
7602 Pacific Street, Suite 304, Omaha, NE 68114
(800) 771-5056
www.jcim.net
Publisher of the so-called "Original Edition" of the Course and other alternates to the standard edition.

Organizations outside the United States

Miracle Network UK
12a Barness Court, 6/8 Westbourne Terrace, London W2 3UW
Tel/Fax: (020) 7262 0209 www.miracles.org.uk

Miracles in Contact (The Netherlands)
www.miraclesincontact.nl

Miracle Studies Australia
www.miracle-studies.net.au

"Un cours en miracles": ACIM resources in French
www.connais.org/miraclef/

Canadian Foundation for the Awareness of Miracles
www.synapse.net/~awareness/

Clearmind International Institute
(Vancouver, Toronto, Stockholm, Dublin, London, Liverpool)
www.clearmind.com

Independent Teachers Online

DavidPaul and Candace Doyle, authors of the Course-inspired book *The Voice for Love.*
www.thevoiceforlove.com

Carol Howe, veteran ACIM-based consultant and lecturer, author of *Healing the Hurt Behind Addictions and Compulsive Behaviors.*
www.carolhowe.com

Jerry Jampolsky, author of best sellers such as *Love Is Letting Go of Fear* and *Good-bye to Guilt*, popular speaker with his wife, Diane Cirincione.
www.jerryjampolskyanddianecirincione.com
see also www.attitudinalhealing.org

Dan Joseph, author of *Inner Healing* and *Inspired by Miracles.*
www.quietmind.info

Jon Mundy, veteran teacher of ACIM, author of *Missouri Mystic* and *Awaken to Your Own Call* and publisher of *Miracles Magazine.*
www.miraclesmagazine.org

Gary Renard, popular speaker and author of *The Disappearance of the Universe* and *Your Immortal Reality.*
www.garyrenard.com

Marianne Williamson, popular speaker and author of such best sellers as *A Return to Love, Illuminata*, and *A Woman's Worth.*
www.marianne.com

Appendix II

A Comparison of Miracles

BY RICHARD SMOLEY

Among the controversies that have surrounded *A Course in Miracles* in recent years are the discrepancies in different versions of the Text. Students of the Course have found themselves wondering which of these versions is the most accurate and best reflects the author's intentions. Until comparatively recently, students of the Course had generally believed the material was verbatim as dictated by the unseen Voice (identified with Jesus Christ) to Helen Schucman. In the preface to the 1985 one-volume edition of the Course, we read this statement by Helen: "Only a few minor changes have been made. Chapter titles and subheadings have been inserted in the Text, and some of the more personal references that occurred at the beginning have been omitted. Otherwise the material is substantially unchanged."[1] But an examination of the two other versions currently circulating shows that the changes were somewhat greater than this statement might lead us to believe.

Three main versions of the Course are in question. The first consists of the original typescript made by Bill Thetford and Helen Schucman, almost all of this transcribed from Helen's shorthand notes of the Voice's dictation, with the rest dictated directly by Helen to Bill without the intermediary of shorthand. Produced in the seven-year period between September 1965 and September 1972, this version has been nicknamed the "Urtext" (from the German prefix *Ur-*, meaning "primordial").

The second version is an edited typescript given by Helen and Bill in 1972 to Hugh Lynn Cayce, son of the visionary Edgar Cayce and director of the Association for Research and Enlightenment (ARE) in Virginia Beach, Virginia. This version, a second retyping of the manuscript, differs from the Urtext partly in that, as Helen noted in the preceding quotation, "personal material was removed." This copy was entrusted to Cayce on the stipulation that it not be shared with anyone else except for his son, Charles Thomas Cayce. This version is sometimes called the "Hugh Lynn Cayce version" or the "HLC version."[2]

In late 1973, Kenneth Wapnick became involved with the technical editing of the Course, and after this point he worked closely with Helen on preparing it for publication. Several versions of this final redaction of the Course had begun to circulate by 1975. In 1976 the Course was published in a three-volume hardcover edition; single-volume hardcover and paperback editions would follow over the next decade. The 1976 version is the one most familiar to practically all Course students. (A second edition, published in 1996, incorporates some minor changes from the first, notably inserting numbers for each chapter, subsection, and sentence.) The discord over the discrepancies in the three versions does not, as a matter of fact, apply to the whole 1,200-page work. It is in the first five (of thirty-one) chapters of the Text that the discrepancies are most acute. Consequently, I shall focus on these.

Personal Material

As Helen herself admitted, the Urtext differs most from the later versions in omitting personal material that was interspersed with the more general principles that begin the Text. And there is a considerable amount of personal material. Some of it is purely personal: it comments directly on Helen's and Bill's situation, with only limited application beyond them. One example:

> (H[elen] S[chucman] meeting with Dr. Wise and Dr. Demrosch. Dr. D. permitted an opportunity for questioning in his capacity as chairman of the flu board for asking re B[ill]'s flu shot. This was an example of how miracles should work. You did not jump into the question yourself, and even though you DID rush for the phone on Red's advice, you exerted no pressure on B[ill]'s reluctance.)
>
> This gave ME a chance to let you leave it to the real expert, whom I sent to answer the question.[3]

This passage is so sketchy that it is possible to glean only a general idea of the situation. Obviously it was clear enough to Helen and Bill, but it is of limited interest to the general Course student.

In another instance, the Voice tells Helen, "You are still vacillating between recognizing the gift and throwing it away. B[ill] regards himself as too weak to accept it. You do not yet know its healing power. After you have passed the course, you will accept it and keep it and use it. That is the final exam, which you will have no trouble in passing. Midterm marks are not entered in the permanent record." (URTEXT, 5) (One notes in this last comment the wry humor that occasionally surfaces throughout the Course.)

As this passage suggests, a major issue in these personal asides is Helen's own resistance to transcribing this work. The Voice tells her, "Your earlier acute problem in writing things down came from a MUCH earlier misuse of very great scribal abilities. These were turned to secret rather than shared advantage, depriving it (?) of its miraculous potential, and diverting it into possession." (URTEXT, 49)

Occasionally, the Voice comments on the situation of people known to Bill and Helen. In regard to Rosie, a woman who was hired to clean her apartment, it counsels Helen, "Retain your miracle-minded attitude toward Rosie VERY carefully. She once hurt both of you, which is why she is now your servant. But she is blessed in that she sees service as a source of joy. Help her straighten out her past errors by contributing to your welfare now." (URTEXT, 51–52)

Because the preceding quotations are so personal and specific, from a purely editorial point of view it is quite clear why they were omitted, both from the HLC version and from the published edition. On the other hand, they raise an issue that occasionally comes up with these three different versions: what ideas do they imply, and how do these relate to the rest of the Course?

The passages about Rosie and about Helen's "scribal abilities" seem to presuppose an idea of which we see almost nothing in the published Course: karma, the idea that "whatsoever a man soweth, that shall he also reap" (Gal. 6:7). Indeed, at one point the Voice in the Urtext actually speaks of karma, telling Helen: "Your instability and his [Bill's] weakness have resulted from bad karmic choices." (URTEXT, 46)

Although the term itself comes from the Sanskrit, the concept of karma is almost universal in the world's religions, even in Christianity, as we see from the verse from Galatians I have just quoted. Some esoteric texts speak of it as the "law of cause and effect." The Course also speaks of cause and effect, but in a way that is somewhat different from what the preceding passages may imply. In the Course, thoughts are the causes; events are the results. "If I intervened between your thoughts and their results, I would be tampering with a basic law of cause and effect: the most fundamental law there is." (Ch2, VII, 1)

In the published Course, then, it is thoughts, not prior actions, that are causative. In fact, the Course goes to great lengths to emphasize that past events have no effect on the present. "The past is over. It can touch me not," we learn in the Workbook. (Lesson 289) Even quite early on, the Workbook emphasizes, "The mind's preoccupation with the past is the cause of the misconception about time from which your seeing suffers." (Lesson 8)

In short, it is difficult to reconcile the unstated implications of these passages in the Urtext with the Course's ultimate teaching. If we were to seek an explanation, we would have to conclude that either (1) the difficulty lay in Helen's ability to hear; or (2) the discrepancy has to do with two different levels: karma—the effect of prior actions on later ones—would apply in the ordinary world as we experience it every day, but in the ultimate reality toward which the Course is leading students, only thought is truly causative.

I tend to prefer the second explanation, if only because Helen's inability to hear could be used as a catchall explanation for anything. In any event, we also read in the Urtext: "God does NOT believe in karmic retribution at all. His Divine mind does not create that way. HE does not hold the evil deeds of a man against HIMSELF." (Urtext, 132)

In other cases, material in the Urtext that appears in a personal context is recast in the published version to have more a general application. Here is one striking example:

> *Bill, you can do much on behalf of your own rehabilitation AND Helen's and much more universally as well, if you think of the Princeton meetings in this way:*

I am here ONLY to be truly helpful.
I am here to represent Christ, who sent me.
I do not have to worry about what to say or what to do, because the one who sent me will direct me.
I am content to be wherever He wished [sic], knowing he goes there with me.
I will be healed as I let him teach me to heal. (URTEXT, PART2, 11)

In the published version, this reads:

You can do much on behalf of your own healing and that of others if, in a situation calling for help, you think of it this way:
   I am here only to be truly helpful.
   I am here to represent Him Who sent me.
   I do not have to worry about what to say or what to do, because He Who sent me will direct me.
   I am content to be wherever He wishes, knowing He goes there with me.
   I will be healed as I let Him teach me to heal. (CH2, V, 18)[4]

Sex and Fantasy

One personal subject that has been omitted from the later versions of the Course is sexuality. If you were to ask the typical Course student what the Course has to say about sex, very likely she would reply, "Nothing." And this is more or less true of the published version. Some might point to the statement that "the body cannot be used for purposes of union" (CH19, I, 4), but apart from this oblique comment, there is no reference to sex in the books as we have them. There is no listing for the words *sex* and *sexuality* in the compendious *Concordance of A Course in Miracles.*[5]

The Urtext, on the other hand, does contain some references to sexuality. In some cases this is personal, as when the Voice discusses Helen's sexual attraction to a man identified only as "Jack" ("Your mutual sexual attraction was also shared [*sic*]" [URTEXT, 34]). Some of the material, however, is more general in application—and much of it will no doubt surprise a number of Course students. Part of it is rooted in an issue I have already mentioned: the attempted use of bodies for union. "Indiscriminate sexual impulses resemble indiscriminate miracle impulses in that both result in body image misperceptions. The first is an expression of an indiscriminate attempt to reach communion through the body. This involves not only the improper self identification, but also disrespect for the individuality of others." (URTEXT, 31)

The chief misuse of sexuality, according to the Urtext, has to do with its use for a fictitious, ego-based sense of union, or of pleasure without union. "The 'sin of onan' was called a 'sin' because it involved a related type of self-delusion; namely, that pleasure WITHOUT relating can exist. To repeat an earlier instruction, the concept of either the self or another as a 'sex-OBJECT' epitomizes this strange reversal. As B[ill] puts it, and very correctly too, it IS objectionable, but only because it is invalid. Upside-down logic produces this kind of thinking."[6] (URTEXT, 39) Later on, the Voice says:

Sexual fantasies are distortions of perception by definition. They are a means of making false associations, and obtaining pleasure from them. . . . NO fantasies, sexual or otherwise, are true. . . . In a situation where you or another person, or both, experience inappropriate sex impulses, KNOW FIRST that this is an expression of fear. Your love toward each other is NOT perfect, and this is why the fear arose. Turn immediately to me by denying the power of the fear, and ask me to help you to replace it with love. This shifts the sexual impulses immediately to the miracle-impulse, and places it at MY disposal. (URTEXT, 48)

But perhaps the most astonishing point made in the Urtext about sexuality lies in the following passage: "Sex was intended as an instrument for physical creation to enable Souls to embark on new chapters in their experience, and thus improve their record."[7] (URTEXT, 37) Indeed, the Urtext goes on to say, "The only VALID use of sex is procreation. It is NOT truly pleasurable in itself. 'Lead us not into Temptation' means 'Do not let us deceive ourselves into believing that we can relate in peace to God or our brothers with ANYTHING external.'" (URTEXT, 38)

Given the general attitude about sex suggested in the sections mentioned above, it will not come as a great surprise that the Urtext shows some disapproval toward homosexuality—an issue that was likely to arise because Bill himself was homosexual. "Homosexuality is inherently more risky (or error prone) than heterosexuality, but both can be undertaken on an actually false basis. The falseness of the basis is clear in the accompanying fantasies. Homosexuality ALWAYS involves misperception of the self OR the partner, and generally both." (URTEXT, 52)

On the other hand, the Urtext is equally disapproving of the search for a perfect romantic partner in a heterosexual context. "The dream of the 'perfect partner' is an attempt to find EXTERNAL integration, while retaining conflicting needs in the self." (URTEXT, 52) The Voice is sharp in taking Helen and Bill to task in this area:

You and B[ill] both chose your present sex partners shamefully, and would have to atone for the lack of love which was involved in any case. You selected them precisely BECAUSE they were NOT suited to gratify your fantasies. This was not because you wanted to abandon or give up the fantasies, but because you were AFRAID of them. You saw in your partners a means of protecting against the fear, but both of you continued to "look around" for chances to indulge the fantasies. (URTEXT, 52)

These observations about choices of romantic partners, which reflect a situation that is perhaps more common in life than we may think, point ahead to the later discussions of the "special relationship" that occupy so much of later parts of the Text. They do not so much contradict the published Text as expand on it, bringing the Course's analysis of the difference between the "special relationship" and the "holy relationship" to bear on what are usually the most vexed and problematic of such relationships.

Both the HLC version and the published versions retain very little of the material about sexuality.[8] When they do, the point is considerably muted. Take, for example, this passage in the Urtext: "Inappropriate sex drives (or misdirected miracle-impulses) result in guilt if expressed, and depression if denied." (URTEXT, 37) The HLC renders this: "Inappropriate physical impulses (or misdirected attack impulses) result in conscious guilt if expressed and depression if denied." In the published version, it appears in this pared-down form: "Physical impulses are misdirected miracle impulses."(CH1, VII, 1)

What, then, are we to conclude from the missing passages on sexuality? Although they certainly cast an interesting light on an area about which the published Course is silent, they do not seem to recommend taking a radically different attitude toward sexuality than is implied by the published version. That is to say, they direct that we are not to judge or condemn anyone's behavior under any circumstances. Lesson 243 in the Workbook says, "Today I will judge nothing that occurs." As far as our own sexual and romantic choices are concerned, they are to be brought under the direction of the Holy Spirit, as all our actions are. This certainly is the most obvious meaning of the Course's long discourses on the transformation of the "special relationship" into the "holy relationship."

The Nature of the World

The Urtext claim that sex was intended for procreation, as a means of enabling souls to "improve their record," implies another idea that is relatively absent from the published Course: that the world as we know it is not the product of the distorted ego, but rather a kind of theater on which the drama of the Atonement can take place. (Similarly, we read in another passage: "The physical world exists only because man can use it to correct his UNBELIEF, which placed him in it originally"; URTEXT, 52). The status of the world in these passages thus differs subtly but importantly from those of the published version.

One notable omission made by the published version in this regard appears in a section that, in the Urtext, reads: "The acceptance of the Atonement by everyone is only a matter of time. *In fact, both TIME and MATTER were created for this purpose.* This appears to contradict free will, because of the inevitability of this decision. If you review the idea carefully, you will realize that this is not true" (URTEXT, 79; italics added). The published version has this as "The acceptance of the Atonement by everyone is only a matter of time. This may appear to contradict free will because of the inevitability of the final decision, but this is not so." (CH2, III, 3)

The published version thus omits the sentence "In fact, both TIME and MATTER were created for this purpose" (which is retained in the HLC version). This has led some commentators to claim that the published version displays a more negative attitude toward the world than do the earlier versions, because it suggests that the world we see is the consequence of the separation, rather than a place for correcting it. In this view, the earlier versions are seen as taking a more positive view of the world, in the sense that it was created to make the Atonement possible.

On the other hand, the published version also speaks of the world as a theater for Atonement: "God is lonely without His Sons, and they are lonely without Him. They must learn to look upon the world as a means of healing the separation." (CH2, III, 5) Still, the preponderance of the Text emphasizes the unreality of the world, as does the Workbook in numerous passages, including this one: "There is no world! This is the central thought the course attempts to teach." (LESSON 132)

The question of whether the world is ultimately the ego's handiwork or God's is an obvious cause for intellectual dispute—reminding us, as the Course notes, that "a universal theology is impossible." (MANUAL, INTRO, 2). Thus, individual students will take different views on the issue depending on their character and experience. Nonetheless, in practical terms the upshot of the Course is the same: whether the world is the product of the ego or created by God as a means of atonement, the only correct response is to forgive it.

Freud and Jung

Another remarkable difference between the Urtext and the later versions has to do with references to other authorities. The published Course makes no reference to any book outside itself except for the Bible. The early sections of the Urtext, however, contain a considerable amount of material referring to other writers and thinkers. Sometimes these references are brief and casual. At one point, the Urtext cites Mary Baker Eddy, the founder of Christian Science, in this context.

One translation of the Fall, a view emphasized by Mary Baker Eddy, and worthy of note, is that "a deep sleep fell upon Adam." While the Bible continues to associate this sleep as a kind of anaesthetic utilized for protection of Adam during the creation of Eve, Mrs. Eddy was correct in emphasizing that nowhere is there any reference made to his waking up. While Christian Science is clearly incomplete, this point is much in its favor. (URTEXT, SPECIAL MESSAGES, 49)

The published version makes the same point, but without mentioning Mrs. Eddy (CH2, I, 3).

In another instance, the Voice in the Urtext mentions Cervantes' Don Quixote in the context of fighting the Devil:

Destroying the Devil is a meaningless undertaking. Cervantes wrote an excellent symbolic account of this procedure, though he did not understand his own symbolism. The REAL point of his writing was that his "hero" was a man who perceived himself as unworthy because he identified with his ego and perceived its weakness. He then set about to alter this perception, NOT by correcting his misidentification, but by behaving egotistically. (URTEXT, 172)

But these references are comparatively brief. Most discussion of other thinkers is devoted, naturally enough, to those who were important to Helen and Bill. Foremost among these is Sigmund Freud. In the forty years since the Course was written, Freud has been demoted from his reputation as the greatest authority in the field of psychology to being considered, at best, a precursor of the modern discipline, many of whose central ideas remain unproven or are simply wrong. In the mid-1960s, it was not so. Freud's language and thought suffused the discipline of psychology, and many of his terms and ideas appear even in the published Course. The most important one, of course, is *ego* (a term coined by Freud's English translators as an equivalent for the more straightforward *Ich* or "I" of the German original).

The early sections of the Urtext discuss Freud at some length. (The HLC version retains much, though not all, of this material.) But the discussions are spotty and ad hoc, dispersed among other material, so it is not easy to summarize the Urtext's interpretation of Freud. Essentially, however, it deals with such issues as consciousness, the libido, and mechanisms of repression.

The Urtext agrees with Freud's view that there is a primordial energy, which Freud called the libido and more or less equated with sexuality. From the perspective of the Urtext, however, the libido is merely a displaced form of a deeper drive—the need for Atonement, sometimes called the *miracle-drive*:

> *Tension is the result of a building-up of unexpressed miracle-impulses. This can be truly abated only by releasing the miracle-drive, which has been blocked. Converting it to sexual libido merely produces further blocking. Never foster this illusion in yourself, or encourage it in others. An "object" is incapable of release, because it is a concept which is deprived of creative power. The recognition of the real creative power in yourself AND others brings release because it brings peace.* (URTEXT, 49)

Another key area in which the Urtext explicates (and differs from) Freud has to do with the repression of unconscious impulses. The Voice in the Urtext comments:

> *All psychoanalysts made one common error, in that they attempted to uncover unconscious CONTENT. You cannot understand unconscious activity in these terms, because "content" is applicable ONLY to the more superficial unconscious level to which the individual himself contributes. This is the level at which he can readily introduce fear, and usually does.*
>
> *Freud was right in calling this level pre-conscious, and emphasizing that there is a fairly easy interchange between pre-conscious and conscious material. He was also right in regarding the Censor as an agent for the protection of consciousness from fear. HIS major error lay in his insistence that this level is necessary at all in the psychic structure. If the psyche contains fearful levels from which it cannot escape without splitting, its integration is permanently threatened. It is essential not to control the fearful, but to ELIMINATE it.* (URTEXT, 105)

It is not easy to follow the argument here, and the editors understandably omitted it from the published version. The Voice evidently agrees with Freud in positing the existence of an unconscious or subconscious level of the psyche. But it differs with him, in the first place, in its attitude toward fear. Freud regarded fear as a natural or at any rate unavoidable part of the psyche. The Course, on the other hand, says fear is unnecessary. Moreover, it contends that the subconscious "content" of the psyche is a relatively superficial layer—the creation of its own unacknowledged fears. Below this level is the miracle-impulse, which Freud did not acknowledge, and which consists not of unconscious content, but of the ultimate libidinal urge: the drive toward Atonement.

To summarize, the Urtext seems to agree with Freud in positing that there is a fundamental source of energy in the psyche. Freud called this the libido and equated it principally with the sex drive; it is the thwarting of this drive by the superego, which cannot reconcile many of its impulses with its own self-picture, that causes anxiety and neurosis. The Urtext differs with Freud in stressing that the nature of this primordial drive is not sex or libido, but the drive toward Atonement. The repression mechanism consists of denying this power of the mind and pretending it does not exist.

The Voice's picture of Freud's religious attitudes is also noteworthy.

> *Freud's psyche was essentially a good and evil picture, with very heavy weight given to the evil. This is because everytime I mentioned the Atonement to him, which was quite often, he responded by defending his theory more and more against it. . . . Freud was one of the most religious men I have known recently. Unfortunately, he was so afraid of religion that the only way he could deal with it was to regard IT (not himself) as sick. This naturally prevented healing.* (URTEXT, 109)

This description accords with Jung's evaluation. Jung, who was close to Freud for several years, observes, "Freud's attitude toward the spirit seemed to me highly questionable. Wherever, in a person or in a work of art, an expression of spirituality (in the intellectual, not in the supernatural sense) came to light, he suspected it, and insinuated that it was repressed sexuality. Anything that could not be directly interpreted as sexuality he referred to as 'psychosexuality.'"[9]

As for Jung himself, the Urtext mentions him, but he does not receive as much attention as Freud. This is no doubt because Jung was a less looming figure among psychologists in general, but also because he did not deny the religious impulse, as Freud did.[10]

The Urtext's comments about Jung begin by acknowledging the validity of his concept of the archetypes—innate structural capacities in the mind of humanity that manifest in dream images, symbolism, and religious art—but then the text goes on to make a point that resembles its comments about Freud:

> *Jung's best contribution was an awareness of individual vs. collective unconscious levels. He also recognized the major place of the religious spirit in his schema. His archetypes were also meaningful concepts. But his major error lay in regarding the deepest level of the unconscious as shared in terms of CONTENT. The deepest level of the unconscious is shared as an ABILITY. As MIRACLE-MINDEDNESS, the content (or the particular miracles which an individual happens to perform) does not matter at all. They will, in fact, be entirely different, because, since I direct them, I make a point of avoiding redundancy.* (URTEXT, 104–05)

Although it is stated in a somewhat convoluted manner, the basic idea underlying these comments is clear enough. Essentially, the Voice is saying that the content of wrong-minded thinking is unimportant. All errors are versions of the same error: the belief that we can be separate from God. And these errors all merit the same correction. What is important is not unearthing the specific forms of error that each individual constructs for himself, but simply bringing them to the light and offering them up to the Holy Spirit. It is more important to resurrect the buried ability that lies hidden within the mind—the capacity to create its own reality and to acknowledge the Atonement—than to analyze any specific forms the error may take.

The Sleeping Prophet

Apart from Freud, the figure who receives the most attention in the Urtext is Edgar Cayce (1877–1945). Cayce, the celebrated American "sleeping prophet," was famed for his ability to go into a trance state, diagnose the ailments of individual patients, and prescribe treatments. Later on in his career, some of his followers tried to apply his talents more broadly by asking him questions about cosmic history and destiny, with uneven results.

At the time the Course was being written, Cayce's work was widely known in the United States, and transcriptions of his trance sessions were easily available in mass-market paperbacks (as they still are). Bill Thetford himself had an interest in Cayce, and had taken a reluctant Helen Schucman to visit the Association for Research and Enlightenment center in Virginia Beach in the early days of transcribing ACIM. So it is easy to understand why the Voice felt the need to address the Cayce material early on.

The Voice's view of Cayce is clearer and more easily summarized than its perspective on Freud is. The Voice praises Cayce and goes so far as to call his work "a major step in the speedup process" (that is, the Atonement [URTEXT, 142]). On the other hand, the Voice also goes into some detail about Cayce's errors.

The first references to Cayce appear early in the Urtext, in reference to the idea that miracles should not be performed indiscriminately: "While what he (Cacey [sic]) did came from Me, he could NOT be induced to ask me each time whether I wanted him to perform this PARTICULAR miracle. If he had, he would not have performed any miracles that could not get through constructively, and would thus have saved himself unnecessary strain. He burned himself out with indiscriminate miracles, and to this extent did not fulfill his own full purpose." (URTEXT, 18) Here the Voice alludes to Cayce's need to be under trance in order to giving healing advice to his clients, a stressful procedure that is generally believed to have caused his death.

Another issue concerning Cayce has to do with his "misperceptions of the need for sacrifice," which, the Voice suggests, ultimately led to his own exhaustion. In this connection we find an extremely interesting comment: "Anyone who is unable to leave the requests of others unanswered has not entirely transcended egocentricity." (URTEXT, 137) The Voice is presumably saying that the need to perform miracles whenever asked implies that one is doing them partly to reinforce one's self-image. By contrast, allowing Christ to decide in each instance (a process that is eventually supposed to become involuntary) enables the miracle worker to stand aside from this egotism and do only what is appropriate in each circumstance.

The Voice goes on to say that many of the errors and inaccuracies in Cayce's readings stemmed from this misunderstanding of the need for sacrifice: "Cayce could not see the Atonement as totally lacking in sacrifice at ANY level." Cayce realized that the mind and soul cannot be affected by the notion of sacrifice. "This left him only the body with which to invest his misperception. This is also why he used his own mind at the 'EXPENSE of his body.'" (URTEXT, 138)

One consequence of this error was that Cayce took the body as real, and that much of the readings were concerned with the body, "even though he usually concluded with the caution that the body cannot be healed by itself. It would have saved an enormous number of words if he had always begun with this." (URTEXT, 138)

Furthermore, Cayce "frequently engaged in a fallacy that we have already noted in some detail: namely, the tendency to endow the physical with nonphysical properties. . . . when Cayce attempted to 'see' the body in proper perspective, he saw physically discernible auras surrounding it. This is a curious compromise, in which the nonphysical attributes of the self are approached AS IF they could be seen with the physical eye." (URTEXT, 139) This comment is worth serious consideration by spiritual seekers, many of whom regard paranormal capacities as signs of advancement. The Voice warns that this is at best a "curious compromise," by which the evidence of the body's eyes is transcended to some degree, but not fully.

Finally, the Voice indicates, Cayce was unable to take the step of freeing himself from the past:

He looked to the past for an explanation of the present, but he never succeeded in separating the past FROM the present. When he said "mind is the builder," he did not realize that it is only what it is building NOW that really creates the future. . . . Because of his failure to accept his own perfect freedom FROM the past, Cayce could not really perceive others as similarly free. That is why I have not wholly endorsed the Cayce documents for widespread use. (URTEXT, 141)

The Voice concludes its discussion of Cayce with a qualified endorsement of his work, along with some suggestions for its future role:

I am heartily supportive of ARE's endeavor to make Cayce's singular contributions immortal, but it would be most unwise to have them promulgated as a faith until they have been purged of their essential errors. This is why there have been a number of unexplained set backs in their explication. It is also one of the many reasons why the Cayce material, a major step in the speedup, must be properly understood before it can be meaningfully validated.

Cayce's son has been wise in attempting to deal with reliability, which in Cayce's case is very high. There is a way of validating the material, and Hugh Lynn is perfectly aware that this must be done eventually. He is also aware of the fact that he is unable to do it. In the present state of the material, it would be most unwise even to attempt it. There is too much that IS invalid. When the time comes that this can be corrected to the point of real safety, I assure you it will be accomplished. In tribute to Cayce, I remind you that no effort is wasted, and Cayce's effort was very great.

It would be most ungrateful of me if I allowed his work to produce a generation of witch doctors. I am sorry that Cayce himself could not rid himself of a slight tendency in that direction, but fortunately I have a fuller appreciation of him than he had. (URTEXT, 142)

The HLC version retains none of the material about Cayce, which is not surprising, given its intended audience.

Terminology

A further difference between the manuscripts and the published versions of the Course has to do with terminology. "Soul" in the Urtext and HLC version is frequently changed to "spirit." The Urtext says:

The soul is in a state of grace forever.
Man's reality is ONLY his soul.
Therefore, man is in a state of Grace forever. (Urtext, 20)

Compare the published version:

Spirit is in a state of grace forever.
Your reality is only spirit.
Therefore you are in a state of grace forever. (Ch1, III, 5)

The terms *soul* and *spirit* have been used so widely and so vaguely through-out the history of the Christian tradition that anyone using them is to some extent required to define what he means by them.[11] The change just illustrated has presumably been made to accord with the later statement in the Teacher's Manual: "The term 'soul' is not used except in direct Biblical quotations be-cause of its highly controversial nature." The Manual goes on to define *spirit* as "the Thought of God which He created like Himself. The unified spirit is God's one Son, or Christ." (Manual, Clarification of Terms, 1, 1)

Another terminological change involves a general replacement of the Urtext's "spiritual eye" with the "Holy Spirit" of the published version. The Urtext reads, "The spiritual eye is the mechanism of miracles, because what the spiritual eye perceives IS truth." (Urtext, 22) The HLC version reads, "The Spiritual eye is the mechanism of miracles because what It perceives IS true." (HLC, 4) The published version simply says, "The Holy Spirit is the medium of miracles." (Ch1, I, 38)

In other instances, "spiritual eye" is replaced with "spiritual sight." The Urtext: "The REAL beauty of the Temple cannot be seen with the physi-cal eye. The *spiritual eye*, on the other hand, cannot see the building at all, but it perceives the altar within with perfect clarity." (Urtext, 78; italics added) The published version: "The real beauty of the temple cannot be seen with the physical eye. *Spiritual sight*, on the other hand, cannot see the structure at all because it is perfect vision. It can, however, see the altar with perfect clarity." (Ch2, III, 1; italics added)

Yet another difference in terminology has to do with coinages and ne-ologisms that appear in the Urtext and the HLC version but have been excised from the printed Text. One notable example is "distantiation," a term that the Voice defines thus: "Distantiation is a way of putting distance between yourself and what you SHOULD fly from." It is distinguished from *dissociation* and *detachment*, which the Voice defines in more negative terms. (Urtext, 70–71) Later on, we even find the verb *mis-distantiate*: "Tell B[ill] the reason why he was so strained yesterday is because he allowed himself a number of fear-producing attitudes. They were fleeting enough to be more will-of-the-wisps than serious will-errors, but unless he watches this kind of thing, he WILL find the notes fearful, and, knowing him well, will mis-distantiate." (Urtext, 122)

It is hard to criticize the editors for making these changes in wording. Some are clearly for the sake of consistency, others for the sake of style. From a literary point of view, *distantiation* is rather barbarous. The verb *distantiate* does appear in the *Oxford English Dictionary*, but it has the meaning of "to take the measure of"; the only cited use of it is from a textbook on surveying, dating from 1610. It would seem that as Helen became more comfortable with the channeling process, the need for such awkward locutions fell away. For the most part, the Course is quite careful in using only words found in ordinary English (though, as with terms like Atonement, ego, and Holy Spirit, it sometimes uses them in unconventional ways). The Course is often praised for its eloquence, and part of this eloquence is due to the comparative absence of psychological jargon.

Conclusions

It would be possible to go into more detail about differences between the earlier versions of the Course and the published edition, but the ones I have just sketched out are, I believe, the most salient and the most interesting to the general student. It remains only to draw some conclusions from this investigation.

In the first place, is the Urtext the "true" version of *A Course in Miracles*? The only way one could come to this conclusion would be by naively claiming that every word taken down as dictation from the Voice heard by Helen Schucman is Holy Writ, to be carved in stone forever. This position is hard to maintain. Much of the Urtext discusses difficulties in listening and transcribing, and the Voice often chides Helen for her resistance to the process, which, it says, results in a lack of clarity as well as actual errors. For example: "Contradictions in MY words mean lack of understanding, or scribal failures, which I make every effort to correct. But they are still NOT crucial." (URTEXT, 18)

Some contend that the HLC version, reflecting editorial changes before the involvement of Kenneth Wapnick, is the true version. The HLC version has some advantages in retaining some interesting material from the Urtext, while cutting out much of what is rough or superfluous. Even so, it is not a particularly polished piece of work on its own. It reproduces the frequent use of uppercase for emphasis in the Urtext, giving the book a strangely strident quality. On the whole, it is what it seems to be: a preliminary rough cut of the final version.

I could not go so far as to say that every editorial decision made by those who prepared the final version is the ideal one, but at this point we are entering areas of judgment and taste. In the process of editing, one comes to the stage where there are several possible decisions in such matters as terminology and sentence structure, any one of which may be just as good as any other. I do not know that "spiritual sight" is better than "spiritual eye," but it does not seem any worse, and it accords better with the usage in the later parts of the Course.

It is true that occasionally there are readings omitted from the published version that have their own beauty and power, such as a statement at the very beginning of the Urtext that says, "You should begin each day with the prayer 'Help me to perform whatever miracles you want of me today.'" (URTEXT, 1) There is also the striking assertion, "Miracles do not matter. They are quite unimportant." (URTEXT, 1) The published version recasts this as, "Miracles as such do not matter. The only thing that matters is their Source, Which is far beyond evaluation." (CH1, I, 2) (The HLC version accords with the published version in these two instances.)

In the end, we may be forced to throw ourselves on pragmatic considerations. The Course has enjoyed an astonishing success. In the thirty-plus years it has been available to the general public, it has established itself as a seminal work in the development of a new and freer spirituality. It is arguably the greatest spiritual text of the twentieth century, even if it has yet to be recognized as such by mainstream theology. Moreover, it is rightly praised for its eloquence and for the rhythms of its prose. Although the editing process may have produced certain changes in emphasis and nuance, it can hardly be said to have done violence to the Course's intrinsic message, and it has, in most instances, increased its resonance and accessibility.

I myself see no reason to go back to the beginning and recast a new edition out of the earlier manuscripts, or to publish one of these manuscripts as a "truer" version of the Course. There are good reasons for not doing so. A proliferation of different versions would simply muddle the picture and create controversies over what are, for the most part, minor issues. As the Course itself reminds us, those who are seeking controversy can always find it.

Nonetheless, these earlier versions are readily available; it is easy to go on the Internet and download copies of both the Urtext and the HLC version or find the alternate versions in print. What is the typical student to do with all this? Does one need to immerse oneself in these variorum readings in order to understand the Course?

Speaking personally, I don't think this is necessary. I would recommend that a beginning student who is serious about working with the Course take any one of the versions published by the Foundation for Inner Peace and work with that. I prefer the earlier editions, which do not have the numbering for sections and sentences that were inserted in the 1996 edition. Although this numbering was presumably intended to make reference to the Course easier—the *Concordance of A Course in Miracles* has been keyed to this edition as well as all the translations—it is perfectly feasible to use the *Concordance* to find a passage even in earlier editions that are not numbered. To me, from a purely visual point of view, the numbers for chapter and verse give the Course a dismayingly ecclesiastical flavor. Others may feel differently.

For more advanced students—those who have done the Workbook once or twice and have read the Text and Teacher's Manual to the point of having a working grasp of them—the Urtext and the HLC version can be interesting and useful in helping them see familiar material from a fresher angle. I suspect most longtime students of the Course could gain some new insights from the earlier versions, though I doubt there will be many who will find that these versions revolutionize their view of the Course. For the most part, they are likely to be reminded that this work was produced under circumstances that were very strange and uncomfortable for the people involved.

Some Course students prefer the earlier versions, and they are certainly entitled to their point of view. The chief danger—if I may use such a term in discussing a work that says there is no such thing as danger—lies not in choosing the wrong version or even in misunderstanding terms and concepts, but rather in falling into a trap that has caught many seekers over the centuries.

To use the language of the Course, there is a point at which the student has recognized most of the ego's more obvious tricks and is to some degree able to evade them. At this point the ego retreats to reconstitute in a subtler but far more insidious form. Suddenly it sees the imagined "enemy" as attacking, not oneself, but the ego projected onto some religious concept: God, Jesus, or even *A Course in Miracles*. One need only pick up a newspaper to find plenty of examples of religious projection, usually resulting in controversy and all too often in violence. In the Course community, such projections tend to be about the correct version of the Course, who is entitled to claim its authority, and so on.

In the end, if we are to take the central message of the Course seriously, we need to ask ourselves whether such conflicts point back to the ego and its agendas. This is one of the most powerful and insidious of all spiritual pitfalls, and, as the history of religion shows, even many so-called saints have not managed to evade it. At the dawn of the third millennium, students of *A Course in Miracles* have a chance to avoid this error.

✎ ENDNOTES ✎

1. *A Course in Miracles*, combined volume (Tiburon, CA: Foundation for Inner Peace, 1985), preface, p. 2. Quotations from the published Course in this appendix are all taken from this edition, which is more or less identical to the three-volume 1975 edition.
2. The version I have of this text is from the ACIM Files Distribution Centre and Library Project. I will use this version here in citations, including its pagination as formatted for Microsoft Word. I will refer to it as the "HLC version."

3. Urtext, 21–22. Quotations are taken from a photocopy of the transcript of the Urtext, and the pagination also refers to this version. The version I have is in five spiral-bound volumes of photocopies, consisting of three parts of the Text proper, as well as one volume of "Special Messages." Unless otherwise indicated, quotations from the Urtext are from part 1. When quoting from the Urtext, I reproduce the capitalization, spelling, and punctuation of the original typescript, except for extremely minor typographical errors.

4. The HLC version is more or less identical to the published version (HLC, 45).

5. Kenneth Wapnick et al, eds., *Concordance of A Course in Miracles* (New York: Foundation for Inner Peace/Viking, 1997).

6. The "sin of Onan" alludes to Genesis 38:3–10, wherein Onan, a son of Judah, is punished by the Lord for "spilling his seed." Onanism generally refers to masturbation, although Onan's "sin" seems to have been to practice a form of coitus interruptus.

7. The term *record* appears occasionally in the Urtext, and seems to refer to something like the "book of life" in Revelation 20:12: "And the dead were judged out of those things which were written in the books, according to their works," although the nature of the "judgment" in the Course is quite different. In another context, the Urtext speaks of the Records in connection with the idea that a miracle is never lost. "This is not your concern. . . . But it IS the concern of the Record. The Record is completely unconcerned with reliability, being perfectly valid because of the way it was set up. It ALWAYS measures what it was supposed to measure." (Urtext, 37) And later: "Sacrifice is a notion totally unknown to God. It arises solely from fear of the Records." (Urtext, 135)

8. The passages about sex have all been omitted from the HLC version, except for this one: "Psychologists are in a good position to realize that the ego is capable of making and accepting as real some very distorted associations. The confusion of sex with aggression, and the resulting behavior which is perceived as the same for both, serves as an example. This is 'understandable' to the psychologist, and does not produce surprise. The lack of surprise, however, is NOT a sign of understanding." (HLC, 42) This passage appears at the end of what is chapter 4 of the published Text, and would appear around page 60 of that version.

9. C. G. Jung, *Memories, Dreams, Reflections*, trans. Richard and Clara Winston (New York: Vintage, 1989 [1963]), 149–150.

10. By Jung's own account, it was this point of difference that was the main cause of his break with Freud in the years 1909–1912. For Jung's portrait of this break, see *Memories, Dreams, Reflections*, chapter 5.

11. For a discussion of this issue, see my book *Inner Christianity* (Boston: Shambhala, 2002), 82–84.

About Richard Smoley

Richard Smoley is one of the world's most distinguished authorities on the mystical and esoteric teachings of Western civilization. Educated at Harvard and Oxford universities, he worked at a wide range of journalistic positions before becoming editor of *Gnosis*, the award-winning journal of Western spiritual traditions, in 1990—a position he held up to 1999. He is the coauthor (with Jay Kinney) of *Hidden Wisdom: A Guide to the Western Inner Traditions* (Penguin Arkana, 1999) and author of *Inner Christianity: A Guide to the Esoteric Tradition* (Shambhala, 2002) and *The Essential Nostradamus* (Tarcher, 2006). Smoley lectures and gives workshops throughout the United States.

Index

About the Author

D. Patrick Miller has been both a seeker and researcher of spiritual wisdom for over two decades. The author of *A Little Book of Forgiveness* and *The Book of Practical Faith,* Miller has also pioneered the journalism of consciousness in over one hundred articles for such periodicals as *Yoga Journal, The Sun, Mother Jones,* and *Reader's Digest,* as well as online venues. As the founder of Fearless Books, Miller was the original publisher and editor of Gary Renard's best-selling book *The Disappearance of the Universe.* As an independent scholar he is well-versed in a number of spiritual perspectives, especially *A Course in Miracles* and the Enneagram system of personality. As an editor and literary consultant for authors, agents, and publishers, he has helped many writers develop both fiction and nonfiction manuscripts, most of them concerning spirituality from a variety of viewpoints. A native of Charlotte, North Carolina, Miller has lived in northern California for most of his adult life. Visit www.fearlessbooks.com for more information.